CREATIVE THINKING

II

CREATIVE THINKING

by Lucille Cedercrans

Wisdom Impressions Publishers

Whittier, CA

Creative Thinking

by Lucille Cedercrans

First Textbook Edition   2001

Wisdom Impressions is a group of practitioners of The Wisdom. Our mission is to help create the appearance, support the teaching, and facilitate the distribution of the Wisdom.

Wisdom Impressions
PO Box 130003
Roseville, MN 55113

ISBN 1-883493-05-6 $21.95

THE GREAT INVOCATION

From the point of Light within the Mind of God
Let light stream forth into the minds of men.
Let Light descend on Earth.

From the point of Love within the Heart of God
Let love stream forth into the hearts of men.
May Christ return to Earth.

From the center where the Will of God is known
Let purpose guide the little wills of men —
The purpose which the Master knows and serves.

From the center which we call the race of men
Let the Plan of Love and Light work out
And may it seal the door where evil dwells.

Let Light and Love and Power restore the Plan on
Earth.

"The above Invocation or Prayer does not belong to any person or group but to all Humanity. The beauty and the strength of this Invocation lies in its simplicity, and in its expression of certain central truths which all men, innately and normally, accept—the truth of the existence of a basic Intelligence to Whom we vaguely give the name of God; the truth that behind all outer seeming, the motivating power of the universe is Love; the truth that a great Individuality came to earth, called by Christians, the Christ, and embodied that love so that we could understand; the truth that both love and intelligence are effects of what is called the Will of God; and finally the self-evident truth that only through *humanity* itself can the Divine Plan work out."

Alice A. Bailey

Editors' Foreword

Transmuting the persona, from a source of sensations and desires into a vehicle of light, is an essential part of spiritual growth and development. Transforming the persona enables the consciousness to rise up, identify as its true self, and discover its purpose, place and function in the One Life. The new body of light becomes an instrument of the true self, the Spiritual Soul, through which the Soul manifests the Divine Plan in the world of affairs.

Creative Thinking is a course in cleansing or purifying the persona, in aspiration to the Overshadowing Spiritual Soul. If actively practiced, it will prepare the persona (mind, emotions, and body), to become a vehicle for serving the One Life.

When the vehicle is prepared, the Spiritual Soul can be called into it. As the work of *Creative Thinking* proceeds, the practice of *The Nature of The Soul* begins. The incarnate soul aspires to and at-one's with the Overshadowing Spiritual Soul. The two, individual identity and group realization, become one, and the life and affairs becomes an embodiment of the Soul.

Creative Thinking first incarnated in 1957, as a series of dittoed lessons titled "Corrective Thinking" or C.T.

The present edition of the text has been renamed "Creative Thinking". This alternative title was suggested by the author, and the editors feel that it accurately represents the content, and helps make the work more accessible to modern seekers.

This edition is a faithful reproduction of the original printed edition. The only changes are minor corrections of grammar, punctuation, gender pronouns and design, and we changed most of the biblical quotes from the

King James version to the Revised Standard version. Every effort was made to retain the subjective quality and outer flavor of the earlier edition, while modernizing the language in order to clarify the overshadowing meaning.

The text was carefully scrutinized by the staff of Wisdom Impressions. Whenever a correction would have changed the meaning or quality, the original text was retained.

We have added a Table of Contents, Directory of Techniques, Study Guide, and Index. While not part of the original text, practitioners of the course have found them helpful.

Creative Thinking is a course of instruction in The Wisdom. The Wisdom is not a religion, philosophy, or science, but an independent field of study, experience, and practice. For information on the practice of this course, please see Appendix A, The Study Guide, beginning on p. 519.

Current students should keep in mind that when the course was written, Western students had access to fewer spiritual practices than is the case today. Meditation was not then a common practice, nor reincarnation a popular Western belief. Thus, the early C.T. lessons presume that students have a primarily Christian background. However, this gradually gives way to a more universal approach as the course introduces terms, concepts, and inner disciplines.

Sincerely,

The Editors
August, 2001

Table of Contents

Directory of Techniques

The inner disciplines listed below are an essential part of the *Creative Thinking* course. Like all such disciplines, they are designed to produce specific effects in the consciousness, bodies and environment of the student. When these disciplines are practiced in the proper order and manner, they facilitate unfoldment from individuality to group awareness. However, they can be abused.

Combining these disciplines with drugs, or other techniques, or using them for selfish purposes, is dangerous. If you have any questions about the use or effects of these disciplines, please write to Wisdom Impressions (see Appendix B, below).

> *"I, your name , a Son of God, integrate the forces of my body, emotions and mind to aspire to my Father's Kingdom. Let there be light upon my path."*

"Not my will, but Thine."

*"...I integrate the consciousness of my
personality to become Soul conscious."*

INTRODUCTORY

The Wisdom of The Soul

Our Divine Heritage,
Wedding the Spiritual to the Material,
The Mental Approach to and Experience of God,
The Golden Age of the Soul

INTRODUCTORY

Those of us who live during this period of human progress are indeed fortunate, for ours is an opportunity
which has never before been presented to humanity. We
stand on the threshold of a new experience in which the
Truths that some few people have ever sought and often
despaired of finding shall become public knowledge. The
Wisdom of the Soul, which has been hidden from us by
the necessity to build a material civilization in which to
live, is now making itself known to the mass consciousness.

We see about us on every hand the evidence of progress,
and some of us are prone to condemn it because it is of a
material nature. Humanity does have the advantage
today of light where there used to be darkness, of auto-
mobiles and airplanes, and of all sorts of machinery to
lighten the load of physical labor. Our world has become
one interrelated world as a result of quick and easy
methods of communication and transportation, and an
economic system which renders every person dependent
upon every other person.

Our cities give witness to humanity's ingenuity, to its
brilliance and creativity. Consider the awe a person
would experience if they were to step out of the world of
a century ago to walk through the streets of one of our
cities now, or into one of our homes.

And yet, we look upon all of this beauty of modern ar-
chitecture and design, scientific achievement and effi-
ciency, and we tend to condemn it, those of us who like
to think that we are spiritual.

How often have I heard the cry "commercialism is taking

the meaning out of Christmas"? How often have I indulged in that same cry? And yet I have joyously spent my money to buy meaningful gifts for loved ones. I have listened with uplifted heart and mind to a chorus of voices bringing Christmas carols into my home from far away. For weeks the hope, the beauty, and the truth of Christmas have impacted upon my consciousness from out of the mouths of commerce.

Once out of the entire year the people of a nation are of one mind and heart as they are reminded from every billboard and house front of The Greatest Story Ever Told.

How can we condemn all of this when it is our divine heritage? Humanity was created in the image and likeness of God and we, too, are creative. Thus, we see about us, if we could but read the signs aright, the evidence of humanity's spiritual growth.

True, but humanity also has created the bomb! We could blow the world to bits and bring down in a few moments this beautiful civilization which we have so painstakingly built.

And there are some of us who say, "Yes, and this too is good!"

It has been characteristic of the human family since its infancy to fight, to do battle with one another rather than to arbitrate. We are notoriously short-sighted when it comes to understanding another's problems. Our fears, when aroused, turn us from creative artists into raging animals, and so we have found a way to fight bigger and bloodier wars.

Yet, this may be our very salvation, for the bomb itself, produced out of fear, has in turn created yet another fear, that of annihilation. There is not a person who thinks who does not realize that war is no longer a means to an end. It has become "The End", one which humanity does not want.

Throughout the entire world, this realization is turning us to seek God; and our search is being made with the same creative genius which has produced the ease and comfort, plus the ever-present fear of our modern lives. At the same time, people realize that to save themselves they must somehow save humanity. Thus, their search for God is not alone for themselves, but for humanity as well.

We are going to bring the Wisdom of the Soul, that spiritual identity in Christ, into our material world. We shall wed the spiritual to the material and so achieve the goal of our age.

We have called this new era into which we have moved "the atomic age". When we look back in retrospect, we will call it "the age of the Soul". It shall have become "that period in time when humanity found its God and itself".

We cannot condemn the radio, the washing machine, and the electric lights. Nor should we condemn either the beauty of modern dress, or the fact that even the poorest child in America has the advantage of available education.

Should we condemn ourselves because our approach to religion has changed, because we are no longer caught up in and held by superstitions, by fear of a hell-fire which we cannot understand and which gives rise to rebellion? Our minds are growing. Our approach to God is becoming mental. We have to know, not just guess, hope, or even pray. We have to experience true inner knowing of God, of our relationship to Him, and of His Divine Plan for us.

When this is done, when the creative genius of our modern age is turned to the proper balancing of spirit and matter, the Christ will make His Reappearance and "all men shall know Him".

This brings us to that rare opportunity which is the keynote of our time. Every man and woman can share in the conscious work of building a new era of progress. All can contribute in their own way to the search and to the fulfillment of that search. It will take the creative genius plus the mass mind to bring the Wisdom of the Soul into appearance. It will take the collective body of humanity to turn the Light of Truth upon our horizon, to bring its Power up against the Power of darkness within us which created the bomb.

At this point, we might all ask "What is Truth?" If our search is for this, then we must somehow define it, else we see and in the seeing fail to recognize that which is sought.

We seek the good, the true, and the beautiful in its universality. We seek out those principles and those concepts which are universal in this application. If they produce the good, the true and the beautiful for one, they must do so for each and everyone.

A Truth, to be a Truth, must have its relationship to the Whole and to the part. It must somehow work toward the betterment of humanity, both spiritually and materially.

This course of instruction is being written for humanity, for the man and woman who would aid in the spiritual re-orientation but know not wherein the opportunities for such service can be found.

It is written for the average person, not for the genius (since they shall know their work), but for those of us who constitute humanity enmasse. We are the ones who shall finally turn the tide, via the strength and power of our mass mind.

Humanity lives within a mental and an emotional environment as well as the physical world. As people breathe, they think. As they think, they qualify their thought with an emotional quality which not only dictates their reaction to life, but radiates from them as a living influence within their environment.

A group of people think and feel, and because their thought-lives are similar in nature they become a one. Thus, families, organizations, nations, etc. act as powerful influences in the world of affairs via the strength of this combined thought-life.

These many separated spheres of thought merge into one and we have the mass mind, with its particular tonal quality, which influences in some degree every member of our present civilization.

Before the golden age of the Soul can come into being, humanity must examine the thought-forms which govern its life and affairs. Many of these were created long ago out of fears and superstitions which today have no basis in truth, yet they continue to dictate our experience because we have not eliminated them from our mental environment.

It is time for us to look into our thought-life, to find out what we think about everything and why. We have before us the search for and the discovery of reason, the reason for our very being. When we find that, behind the many veils of surface thought and feeling within which we unconsciously move about, we will have found our souls.

This series of instruction is written as a guide which, it

is hoped, will help the average man and woman make these discoveries. Once they are made, people need no longer remain the product of their early environment, or a victim of circumstance. They can begin to exert that control over their own automatic response mechanism, and their environmental circumstances, which will render their potential contribution to humanity possible of achievement.

Introductory

Notes

_____

_____

_____

_____

_____

_____

_____

_____

_____

_____

_____

_____

_____

_____

_____

_____

_____

Creative Thinking

Notes

_____

_____

_____

_____

_____

_____

_____

_____

_____

_____

_____

_____

_____

_____

_____

_____

_____

Introductory

Notes

_____

_____

_____

_____

_____

_____

_____

_____

_____

_____

_____

_____

_____

_____

_____

_____

_____

Creative Thinking

LESSON 1

Identity
The Trinity of a Human Being:
Spirit, Soul, and Body;
Discovering Where You Live;
Consciousness of Being

LESSON 1

We have entitled this course of instruction "Corrective Thinking" because its purpose is to correct those conditions within your life and affairs which are out of tune with the natural order of our manifest Cosmos.

The sub-human kingdoms in nature, and the suns and planets that dot our night skies with pinpoints of light, convey a kind of harmony which the human family seems to have lost. These lives, their growth and their orbits are directed by a Divine Intelligence, while humanity has been given the freedom to think as it will. Thus, we see the family of God's children momentarily lost to the Kingdom of Heaven simply because these young, growing Gods have been given the *power of mind*. People "think" and so create their own life and affairs.

In order to understand a person as a young God, people as creators in their own right, we must first study their constitution. Of what are they constructed that makes them so different from the other animals?

Our bible tells us that we were created in the image and likeness of God. In the *Image*. God saw us with His Mind. He conceived us in the eye of His Mind, and made us in His Own Likeness.

Humanity, *like* God, then, is a Trinity. We are constructed of spirit, consciousness, and a body of manifestation or appearance.

Humanity's spiritual aspect is the Life of God which pours into and through us as it does through all living things. It is that motivating impulse which moves a person to constantly produce experience. It is the very essence of all things which is their one cause, and their reason for being.

Humanity's spirit puts us in tune with God, for by It, we are a part of God's life. As all the cells in the body are fed by the blood stream, so are all living things fed by the Spirit of God. They are sustained and maintained by Him.

God's vehicle of manifestation is the manifest Cosmos of which we are but an infinitesimal part. We see this great, divinely ordered Cosmos and we know there *is* a God. This, then, is His body of appearance. When I look at a star, or a blade of grass, or any one of the intricate forms that appear, I know *there* is God showing Himself, taking a form of appearance.

"In the beginning was the Word, and the Word was with God and the Word was God." John 1:1

And like God, humanity was also given a body of appearance, a matter aspect.

We know that the dense physical body which we see with the eyes is only a part of our vehicle of manifestation. That vehicle or matter aspect is composed of a body, an emotional nature, and a mind. In this, humanity is again like God whose matter aspect is composed of a body (the manifest cosmos), an emotional nature (His love for us which causes Him and us to appear), and a mind (the Divine Mind which conceived us with Its imaging faculty).

Next, we see that humanity is self-conscious. It, like God, knows that it is, and this is the Son aspect. The infant Son is the soul, the adult Son, the Christ.

16

Lesson 1

One can and does think of oneself as I. So does God. Both are conscious of Being.

A person is this "I", and that "I" is a *Soul*.

We have heard this term many times and have referred to "your soul" or "my soul", and yet you and I do not have a soul, we *are* souls.

If you think back to the story of humanity's creation, you will remember that God created "his" body out of the dust of the earth.

> "And the LORD God formed man out of the dust of the ground, and breathed into his nostrils the breath of life; and man became a living Soul." Genesis 2:7

That breath of life, which God breathed into the form He had made out of dust, was the soul, the conscious I, which makes us different from the animals.

But what is the soul, that breath of life which we are? It is consciousness. It is the consciousness inside of the body which lives and moves within the form to produce experience. It is that which thinks, and feels, and identifies as a self (Soul). It is the Son of God.

Stop now for just a moment and discover where you live. Think "I" slowly and carefully, permitting yourself as a consciousness to discover where you are focused inside of your body.

This is where you *live*.

This gives you a sense of identity, of being, which is separate from the form, does it not? Take another few moments to contemplate in this place where you live, your identity as a soul, Son of God.

If you carry out this simple exercise each day at a particular time you will begin to differentiate between yourself as the soul (a consciousness created in the image and likeness of God) and yourself as a form.

You will be enabled to answer the question: "What is the constant reality? The immortal self which indwells the form? Or the mortal self constructed out of the dust of the ground?"

We like to think that we are self-conscious, but just how self-conscious are we? What do we consider the self to be — a body made of flesh and bone that will in due course of time die and decay and disappear from the face of the earth?

Is God, do you think, conscious of Himself as being His Body, the manifest Cosmos?

And the resurrection — what is it that is really resurrected? It is the consciousness from out of the body. It will one day be lifted up and out of its grave of flesh to reside in the Kingdom of Heaven. That Kingdom is but the awareness of *who* and *what* we are. It is the Kingdom of self-conscious Souls, and it will one day make its appearance on earth. When this happens the Christ shall reappear and *all* men shall know Him. We shall see our relationship to Him as His younger brothers.

Let us take another step in this process of self-identification. Suppose that you have died. Visualize yourself as dead. What do you see — a body laid out in some fashion according to the picture your brain makes of death?

But where are you? If you are dead how can you see your body laid out in last state awaiting decay?

Now imagine the body completely gone. It has returned

18

back to the dust out of which it was formed. Again, where are you? Have you returned to separate particles of dust, without consciousness? Can you conceive of *not* being?

No matter how hard you try, you cannot conceive of being without consciousness in some form, in some place.

You can think of yourself as imprisoned within a rock, or a plant, or a dog, or a planet but not as being nothing.

You can take this a step further and visualize the body as being burned by fire, drowned in water, poisoned by gas, or buried alive in the ground, yet none of these four elements can you imagine as destroying your consciousness, for the soul is *indestructible*.

You will be on the outside observing the old form in which you were living.

Now let us conclude this realization by turning our thought to natural death as a result of old age. We can imagine that we have lived to such an age that our bodies are no longer of use to us. What is the natural order then, but for us to discard them? We are going to turn in the old house for a better one. Should we fear such an act? Do we have so little faith that we cannot believe another (perhaps a mansion) will have been created for us?

"In my Father's house are many mansions." John 14: 2

What is "my Father's house" but His body of manifestation, the manifest Cosmos? And the many mansions — what could they be but new bodies for us?

And so death loses its victory, loses its sting, and we no

longer need have fear of it.

When we lose our fear of death we attain wisdom, for it is this fear which turns us from young Gods into beasts. Fear clouds our minds so that when we think "I" it is in defense rather than in consciousness of Being. In fear, and in its final analysis — fear of death, we negate the good, the true and the beautiful.

It is not necessary for us to defend our existence, or ourselves. We *are* and we shall *be* as long as God *is*.

Neither friend, nor foe, neither life in the body nor out, can touch my consciousness to destroy it, for it is God's.

As we come to realize consciousness of Being, our minds open wide to the knowledge and the wisdom of that same Being. We begin to comprehend our Father's mysteries, and so begins our higher education. The secrets of life and death, of suns and planets and universes, and of ourselves, are revealed to us, and the inner Christ matures into adulthood.

> "... he who believes in me will also do the works that I do; and greater works than these will he do, because I go to the Father." John 14:12

This is a great promise. It assures us that as we believe in Christ, as we identify with the Christ Life, we shall do His works and even greater.

What is the work of Christ? Is He not the Savior of Humanity? Does this not mean that as we save ourselves (identify with Christ) we shall share in the work of restoration for the human family?

It does, but first we must bring Divine Law and Order into our own lives. We begin with identity.

Lesson 1

"I am the Soul, Son of God. I am a part of the Christ Life. I consciously invoke the Inner Christ Life to bring Divine Law and Order into my life and affairs. So Be It."

Creative Thinking

Notes

Lesson 1

Notes

_____

_____

_____

_____

_____

_____

_____

_____

_____

_____

_____

_____

_____

_____

_____

_____

_____

Creative Thinking

LESSON 2

Our Relationship With God

The Divine Parent and Santa Claus,
Death of Childish Faith,
Cosmic God and Planetary Parent

"I Am a living Soul, Son of God."

LESSON 2

You, the consciousness, imprisoned within the confines of a mind, an emotional nature, and a physical body, are the Son of God.

How often do you contemplate this fact? Have you *ever* paused from the clamor of your daily activity to think seriously about being God's child? Do you wonder — what does this *mean* to me personally?

If you have not, you are in company with the vast majority of God's children who have not, as yet, consciously related to their Divine Father. Little wonder that humanity finds one of its greatest problems to be that of relationship!

You were deliberately and purposefully created by That Life Who indwells the planet earth and all living things therein. He it was, Who with His Will conceived you, and out of His Intelligence gave you birth. It was His Mind and Heart that brought you into being as a living soul to go forth and multiply, to expand your consciousness until you could share in His Godliness.

In this lesson, we are going to search into our thought-life to discover why we have not properly related to The Father. In order to correct our thinking, we must first discover what we think, for few of us there are who know the sum total of our thoughts about any subject.

Adults must look back into their childhood to find the basis for their present attitudes, particularly in relationship to God.

Creative Thinking

We find in the mass mind, a thought-form which is common to all young children. The first concept of God identified Him as the human parent. In the small mind he is the father who is responsible for their being. Papa, father, or daddy, is God. He is big, and mysterious. He is the Lord and He is the master. He not only created the child, but he created the mother as well. He is to be loved and feared, and, incidentally, hated as he diminishes in stature before the opening eyes of his growing offspring. What human parent can live up to such an ideal?

This thought-form of the human father as God is, of course, on the most part an unconscious response of the baby to its association with its parent, none-the-less it provides the first platform for the general lack of faith in, and relationship to God as a *Reality*.

Young children go to Sunday School and are taught there that God is a Spirit. The concept is abstract and children must understand it as best they can. A Spirit is something quite intangible and hard to visualize, yet most small children visualize God in one of two or both ways. One, as a rather fierce, old, white-haired man with whiskers. (They are taught to fear the wrath of God, who is a strict disciplinarian). And two, as the kind and gentle Jesus Who came to this earth to save humanity, particularly to save little children (and often in the children's minds, to save them from adults).

At the same time the young growing consciousness is taught to believe in Santa Claus. Each Christmas this jolly old man with his red suit, and booming laugh, comes loaded with toys for those children who have been *good*.

The little boy and girl are reminded of his coming from every billboard, storefront, radio and television across the country. They are bribed and threatened with the

28

promise of Santa and live in a fever of excitement until that cool, gray dawn which climaxes the event for another year.

As an accompaniment for Santa the child hears over and over the beautiful story of the Christ-Child, and somehow in the small mind, the stern old man with whiskers, gentle Jesus, and Santa in his red suit with his sack of toys become all jumbled together into a subconscious picture of God.

Such a picture supersedes daddy and for a time the young ones are secure in their faith. Whatever doubts may arise, they repress in an effort to maintain that false sense of security.

And then comes the fateful day when the trusting, believing innocence of childhood is dealt a blow from which it seldom fully recovers.

There is no Santa Claus! Their first year in school (which incidentally their parents hope and pray they will like) brings an end to the beautiful myth.

They come running home to their mother for restoration of their faith.

But mother is no longer their friend! By her own words and actions, she is a betrayer. How many of us have been guilty of this in the past through our own well-meaning stupidity? That last Christmas which marks the end of babyhood — we build it up, we fill it with everything possible to strengthen the faith that we must soon destroy. And we do this in order to make our young ones happy! We want them to have something really wonderful to remember!

The child is crushed, and no matter how the parents try to justify their lies, the child is likely to carry that wound for life. Something beautiful has been murdered, a child's faith. The simple, beautiful faith in parents, in Christmas itself (for how shall they ever approach its real meaning now?) and in God.

So there is no Santa? Neither is there such a thing as Jesus or God! These were all just stories that parents invented in an effort to make their children be good.

How shocked would be parents if they could look into the subconscious mind of their son or daughter now! And how revealing if they could go back in years to their own similar experience. What a common bond of understanding might develop between themselves and their child.

How blind we are that we could make such a ghastly mistake. Why should the child want to be *good* after this? In the first place its reason for being good was false, and the principle behind it even worse. Children should be taught to do good for the sake of others, not for what it will bring themselves. If we are suddenly confronted with such problems as juvenile delinquency, whose fault is it?

Each parent can help to usher in a new era of love and faith if they will, by their own action, weaken the influence of this race mind thought-form.

Let us teach children the real meaning of Christmas. Each small child can be given a priceless gift at Christmas time: recognition as a child in Christ, as a son of God. We can bestow upon them some small material gift in recognition of their spiritual identity in Christ, and let them know this. It is not necessary to bribe a child to be good. Teach them the good by being good to them. Teach them to do for others, through love of others.

And ourselves? Let us heal the wound we carry by

recognizing the Truth. If our parents misrepresented God to us, they did so unknowingly, and we can restore our own faith in God through a re-evaluation of our thought-life.

With the light of reason, we re-educate our subconscious. God is not and was not any of these forms we mistakenly believed Him to be.

God is the Holy Trinity, the Three Persons in One. He is a Great Will, a Great Mind, and a Great Consciousness. He is God the Father, God the Mother, and God the Son.

He indwells the entire Cosmos and all life therein. He has focused Himself into suns and planets, and through His focus in these, He has created the five kingdoms in nature: the mineral, vegetable, animal, human and spiritual.

God then, focused His Fatherhood, His Motherhood and His consciousness into a Planetary Being, the body of which we call Earth. Here within this body, as a cell in the Great Cosmic God, The Planetary Being created of Himself, the children who live, move and have their being within Him.

Here, then, is our Father-Mother God, and Christ the consciousness in which we are each and every one individualized and identified.

This is our approach to God, our relationship with Him:

First as the Soul, that individual focal point of consciousness — the Christ-Child who is growing into the maturity of his Godhood. "Know ye not that ye are Gods?"

Then, through the Christ of which we are but a cell in

His body, to the Divine Parent, God, focused into our planet.

We live in Him, He in us. As we reach toward Him, we can do so with the assurance that He *is* and that we *can* reach Him with our Love.

> Become still, and as you find yourself centered in that place where you live inside of your body, identify as the Soul, Son of God.

> *"I Am a living Soul, Son of God."*

Then, as that Soul, aspire to the Christ, realizing that you are a part of the Christ Life.

> *"The Christ dwells within me, as He does within all members of humanity. We are One in Christ."*

Then realize that God is not far away and indefinable. He is here with us. He can be known for He created all *we* know. He lives within us and without us, in the consciousness of Christ. "I and The Father are One." Reach toward Him then, through Christ. As the Christ-Child repeat:

> *"Our Father, I Am your child. I love You,"* and send Him your love.

Lesson 2

Notes

_____

_____

_____

_____

_____

_____

_____

_____

_____

_____

_____

_____

_____

_____

_____

_____

_____

Creative Thinking

Notes

_____

_____

_____

_____

_____

_____

_____

_____

_____

_____

_____

_____

_____

_____

_____

_____

_____

Lesson 2

Notes

_____

_____

_____

_____

_____

_____

_____

_____

_____

_____

_____

_____

_____

_____

_____

_____

_____

_____

_____

Creative Thinking

LESSON 3

Right Relationship

One Spirit in Many Bodies,
Pause and Think "I",
Humanity a One Life,
The Purpose of Humanity,
Identity, Right Relationship and Peace

LESSON 3

The human family today seeks above all other things the knowledge of right relationship. This is a knowledge which humanity must have, not alone for its comfort, but for the sake of its very survival. Human beings must learn how to live together in brotherhood, for in our time peace has become much more than a dream or an ideal. It has become the common necessity.

The human family *is* a family. It includes every human being in a relationship more lasting and more substantial than the bonds of the flesh and blood or mutual consent ever could, for the human family is bound together in the *same* Spirit, the *same* consciousness and the *same* form nature.

There is one Spirit in the appearance of many bodies. These bodies may be likened unto the very womb of matter, the mother aspect of God. The interrelationship between Spirit and the many bodies It indwells, results in the birth of consciousness, a consciousness which thinks and feels through the medium of an ego — the conscious thinking "I".

Within each body, then, has been born a unit of consciousness which identifies itself as "I". Every human being thinks of their self in this way. "I am John Doe" or "I am Mary Doe." Every human being thinks "I am" because they *are*.

The "I" is born of the same parents, the same Spirit and the same nature, even though the matter aspect seems divided, i.e., made up of many bodies. While you and I identify via the concept of "I", so do all other human

Creative Thinking

beings; thus, that sound or note issues forth from each as their *identity*.

> Pause for a moment, and as you think "*I am*" realize that your neighbor thinks the same thought, that this concept of "I" identifies every member of humanity. Then, as you think it again imagine the whole of humanity thinking "I am". Try to discover the inner meaning of this outer form.

When consciousness of self is first born within a body, it is of that body. The unit of consciousness identifies with the form nature within which it dwells so that when it thinks "I", it is asserting the self as the form. It takes on the limitations of the form nature and becomes separated from others via thought, feeling and body.

To understand this we must understand, somewhat, the nature of Spirit and matter. Spirit tends to synthesize all parts into a one. It has to do with Purpose, with motivating intent or the Divine Will which gives life to all forms. Spirit cannot be divided into many parts, though it may indwell many parts. In other words it is everywhere equally present. This is God the Father whose Purpose, Power, and Will are within and behind everything that lives.

Matter, whose very essence is intelligence (the intelligence or Divine Mind of God), divides life into its many qualities and characteristics in order to show each one separately. Thus are the many forms born into expression, each one being the custodian of a Divine quality and characteristic. The nature of the form then is to *separately* identify a Divine expression.

Humanity, who is self-conscious, is for the most part conscious only as the separation of the form nature. As Spirit continues to indwell the many bodies, the consciousness within them grows until it becomes not only

40

of the body, but of the Spirit as well.

As that consciousness of self evolves, it becomes aware of its relationship as a part of the total life expression. While it is still conscious of separation, it is as a related self, rather than as a separated self.

> Pause now for a moment and again think *"I am"*. Realize that this same "I am" identifies every other human being, and then as you identify yourself do so *in relation* to all others. Think of yourself as a related part of the One Life (God) expression.

When consciousness identifies with Spirit, realizing that the body is a form constructed out of and by the nature of intelligence as the Temple of the Living God, it begins to cognize two simple and yet all important realities:

1. That all humanity are in essence a One Life. They were born of the same Spirit and the same nature, that nature dividing them into many parts, yet Spirit giving them the *same means* of identification. The bodies are divisions in the One Life, created by the nature of the Divine Mind (mother nature) for the purpose of expressing every quality and characteristic of Divinity. Each person then, while of the One Spirit, is also a related part that holds within itself some special characteristic and quality of God. Their consciousness, born of Spirit and matter, is both the One and the many. As it evolves, it becomes more and more aware of the One and the many, and of that special Divinity for which it was created.

   This is the purpose of a person and of humanity. People were created individually and collectively in order to express the Divinity of God in related part and in whole.

2. People discover their Divine Purpose as they identify with the One Spirit, and as parts with the many forms. They learn their part, the Divine role they are to play in the drama of life. They discover their particular talents or gifts, which are of God, and develop them into their potential Divine expression in *perfect* relationship to all other life.

It is at this time that the individual learns that every part is essential to the perfected expression of God, and that the first step toward the manifestation on earth of that perfection is the manifestation of right relationship.

Right relationship is "peace on earth", "good will toward men", and "brotherhood". We live in a world in which these seem to be impossible of attainment, so impossible that the average person does nothing to help bring them into manifestation. They wait for the world to change, to permit them to know peace, good will and brotherhood, seldom realizing that their Purpose, their very reason for being is to contribute their peace, their good will and their brotherhood to humanity.

Before peace can manifest within the world of humanity, it must first manifest in the hearts of humanity. There must come peace within the form, a peace born of right relationship between the Spirit, the consciousness and the body. The conscious thinking "I", realizing its relationship to the Spirit (Life) and the Body (expression of life), brings that body under conscious control so that it does express the life of God.

A person does this by establishing identity in God as Christ the Son of God: "I am the Christ-Child, the Son (consciousness) of God". They then relate Spirit to matter by pouring the Light and Love of Christ (our awareness of the good, the true, and the beautiful) into and through the form, so that the nature of that form will

42

express their particular characteristics, and the quality of these, into outer appearance.

They must then manifest peace within their environment, and this they do as they conduct that Light and Love of Christ through their body and into the environment. Each person relates within the environment as a part to many parts, recognizing and accepting the equal importance to the One Life of each. Thus, their relationships within their environment express the quality of Love, and brotherhood becomes the characteristic that manifests in peace.

Their next task is to manifest right relationship between their environment and those other environments with which they are in *related touch*. The Light and Love that they are pouring into and through their own environment begins to have an effect upon others outside of their immediate sphere of influence, and right relationship moves in an ever-growing spiral of effects as waves move out upon the water after it has received the impress of a stone.

You and I, and all the other conscious thinking "I's", are human beings with a shared purpose and goal. We will manifest "peace on earth", "good will toward men", and "brotherhood" because this will be our contribution to the One Life. It will not come as a result of an imposition upon us by the church, state, or government. It will manifest within these as it moves from the One Spirit into the hearts and minds of humanity everywhere, to manifest through the many bodies the consciousness of Christ, Child of God.

> Become still in that place where you live within the body, and contemplate your identity in the One Life.
>
> *"I am Christ, child of God."*

Creative Thinking

Then contemplate the consciousness of humanity as the Christ-Child of God, and identify with it.

"I am That I am."

Then via the Power of That I Am, bring Light and Love into:

> your mind,

> your emotions,

> and your body.

Dedicating them to that One Life, radiate Light and Love out into your environment.

Lesson 3

Notes

Creative Thinking

Notes

_____

_____

_____

_____

_____

_____

_____

_____

_____

_____

_____

_____

_____

_____

_____

_____

Lesson 3

Notes

_____

_____

_____

_____

_____

_____

_____

_____

_____

_____

_____

_____

_____

_____

_____

Creative Thinking

LESSON 4

Creativity: Mind, Emotions, Body

The Three Aspects and
The Four Kingdoms of Nature;
Self-Initiated Spiritual Growth;
Envisioning and Embodying the Ideal
in Thought, Emotion, and Brain Consciousness

LESSON 4

Because you were created in the Image and Likeness of God, and are a Trinity within yourself, you are a creator.

This is a concept that seems most difficult for the average person to grasp and to understand in its basic connotations. We all know that some people are creative, and some of us know that all people are endowed with a creative potential, but how many of us realize that everyone lives in a world of their own making?

We have said that humanity, like God, is a Trinity. Humanity is composed of a Spiritual Aspect, a form nature, and a consciousness. The consciousness of humanity is the Son Aspect, which during its youth indwells and is nurtured by the form nature, the Mother Aspect.

The Mother Aspect in its essence is intelligent substance which is molded into form, first by the Divine Intent of the Spirit, and second by the consciousness born within it. In other words, it is the Divine Intent of the Spirit which caused intelligent substance to take on the appearance of the different kingdoms in nature. Thus, we see within the world of planetary affairs four major species of form; they are the mineral, vegetable, animal, and human kingdoms in nature, created by the Spirit of our Planetary Life as that Spirit relates to Its matter aspect (the intelligent substance which gives It a body of appearance).

Human beings look and act like human beings because the human form is molded into shape by Spirit acting upon substance.

Creative Thinking

The self-conscious Soul was born within that form as Spirit continued to relate with the substance out of which it was made. In this way the family of souls, God's children, was born and began this evolutionary development into Christhood.

As very young children they became identified in consciousness with their human forms and the environment within which they lived. The Mother Aspect had the greatest influence upon them, for they were as yet unaware of the Father and His Divine Intent for them, which was working out their destiny. Thus began the secondary molding of substance into a form nature by the consciousness that did not know it was a creator.

The consciousness within its particular body identified with that body and its immediate surroundings. Via experiences being produced by both Spirit and matter, and the son indwelling the constructed form, the conscious thinking "I" developed a "state of consciousness" composed of its many awarenesses in the form nature, and gradually built up a set of coordinates within which the life and affairs had to conform.

That "state of consciousness", which we often define as the psyche or the inner person and of which the personality is an outer appearance, is a conditional state of existence within which the conscious "I" (soul) is focused. It is this "state of consciousness" which conditions the substance of the body and the environmental life and affairs to be what they are. In other words, God gave us our human form, and our Divine destiny, but He did not give us our particular personalities, our bodily ills, or our successes and failures. We created these ourselves via our particular states of consciousness; and we developed our states of consciousness as we responded to the forces of evolution, i.e., Spirit and Matter.

Lesson 4

God produced the forces and primary conditions necessary to evolution, yet everyone creates their own evolutionary path via their particular responses, and finally via their initiatory action.

Humanity has reached that place in its evolutionary development where conscious initiation of a predetermined goal of growth and development can take place. This discovery by humanity enmasse of its creative potential is close, and all human beings are responding to it in one way or another. The "do it yourself" idea, and the great need for self-improvement are examples of that response.

When we consider the implications of the new truth to be embodied by the whole of humanity they are awe-inspiring indeed. Throughout the history of humanity's past, its growth has largely been an unconscious response to its environment. It learned those lessons that were necessary to its survival, and lived within the framework of that necessity. Then people began to want more than survival. They wanted comfort and luxury; some people wanted power and control and all people grew to want security of both a Spiritual and a material kind. Today humanity wants love, peace, good will and brotherhood. A great many people want knowledge, and a few desire wisdom above all else.

Soon a new truth will unfold within the consciousness of humanity. Even now, it is impacting. That truth is self-initiated growth. People can be, within themselves, anything they want to be. They are their own cause insofar as their life and affairs are concerned. To initiate something is to set into motion the cause that will produce a desired effect. If a person wants to become a Christ, one has only to initiate those experiences that will result in the growth into the Christ which one is, in potential!

Consider the person who is admonished to "love thy neighbor as thyself." They seldom consider it a possibility for they know their own built-in responses, which are the limitations within which they live. The new truth will show them how to initiate that growth which will make it possible for them to love their neighbor as themselves. Thus, people can overcome, via a process of self-initiated growth, the limitations of their early environmental conditioning. To do this they must learn to change their inner "state of consciousness" to conform to their ideal.

> Pause for a moment now, and consider your ideal of yourself. What kind of a person would you really like to be? What kind of an influence would you like to bring to bear upon your environment? Let this ideal come from the heart to reveal itself in your mind.

It is possible for you to envision the ideal and then, if you are really sincere, to embody it in this lifetime via the process of self-initiated growth.

A person's inner "state of consciousness", like everything else, is three-fold in nature, i.e., composed of three distinct aspects. These are:

1. The inner thought-life. This is that subjective aspect of people's lives which is seldom revealed either to others or to themselves. Actually, we are rarely acquainted with the sum-total of our thought-life, though it orbits around and within us constantly, producing an effect upon everything we do.

It contains every thought we have ever entertained for very long, as well as many thoughts which came to us via association with others which we accepted with little or no consideration of their value as Truth.

Lesson 4

This massive thought-life determines to a very large degree our attitude toward people, situations and things. It is mostly emotional in nature since we have lived more in our emotional nature than in our mind. Therefore, it is seldom reasonable, but conveys pictures of conflict and confusion. So many of people's thoughts are in direct conflict with one another that it is little wonder that their lives are ones of conflict.

2. The inner emotional life. Here again is a vast subjective aspect of a person's life that is seldom revealed to them. It is a result of both thought and outer experience. Every thought entertained by them has its corresponding emotional feeling form. Every outer experience builds or adds to an emotional feeling form. All of these forms, these emotions which produce automatic responses within us, are constantly present, either acting or waiting to act, to produce reactions within us to life itself. They give power to that which we think and to that which we do. They move us in this direction or that, according to what we happen to *feel* at the moment.

3. The physical brain consciousness. This is that aspect of the inner "state of consciousness" which is more apparent, being above the threshold of awareness, and constituting the actor. Here is the conscious thinking "I" with its brain awareness, which changes from moment to moment according to that which is impacting upon it from the inner thought-life, the inner emotional life, and the sensory system of the physical body. It has its particular habits, its way of thinking and feeling and its way of responding to various stimuli — particularly those reaching it via the sensory system.

How often do we know why we react thus and so to a

given situation? Seldom; yet the answer lies here in our inner "state of consciousness".

The impression we make upon the world, the way we look, feel, and act — all of these are dictated by that inner "state of consciousness". Here is our creativity. For the substance of our bodies, of our environments, and of our experiences is molded into shape *by* that inner "state of consciousness" within which we live. To change our outer lives, we must first change our inner lives. Once this is realized and accepted the process of self-initiated growth can begin; and one is given the opportunity to decide the way of one's own destiny.

Become still in that place where you live inside of the body and identify as the soul, Christ-child of God.

Then consider your creativity. Look at your life and affairs and observe the effects of your creativity.

Then open your heart and your mind to the ideal of Christ. Let that ideal take form within your consciousness and realize that you can initiate the growth necessary to embody and become the ideal.

Lesson 4

Notes

_____

_____

_____

_____

_____

_____

_____

_____

_____

_____

_____

_____

_____

_____

_____

_____

_____

Creative Thinking

Notes

_____

_____

_____

_____

_____

_____

_____

_____

_____

_____

_____

_____

_____

_____

_____

_____

_____

_____

Lesson 4

Notes

_____

_____

_____

_____

_____

_____

_____

_____

_____

_____

_____

_____

_____

_____

_____

_____

Creative Thinking

LESSON 5

The Spirit of Truth

Humanity's Ego Image and
Race Mind Thought-Forms:
The Pain of Childbirth,
All Men are Sinners

LESSON 5

There is a Spirit within humanity, which, moving within all consciousness, calls every conscious thinking "I" unto itself. It is the Spirit of Truth, of Love and of Good. Every person, regardless of outer circumstance, regardless of built-in response mechanism, wants to love and to be loved. The person who robs, the person who murders, or the person who scolds and is burdened with a difficult disposition, each secretly and often unknown to themselves, yearns to be accepted by society. The longing to be good and the likeliness of being bad are universal in their manifestation within the hearts of humanity.

Why, then, does humanity live in such Spiritual hunger? What is it that takes people away from the Spirit which is constantly calling and will not leave them for one moment in peace?

In its ignorance of its Spiritual identity in nature, humanity has created an image of itself, and it has given to that created form the power of manifestation.

In this lesson we shall consider the race mind thought-forms which have contributed to humanity's ego-image, those thought-forms which have imprisoned it within certain reactive patterns and held it away from the Spirit toward which it yearns.

The first race mind thought-form to become a part of the individual thought life, in greater or lesser degree, is that one created in response to the pain of childbirth. The mother suffers; she oft'times cries out in pain. She has been known to curse and protest the fate which brought such anguish to her.

The infant, we think, is insensitive to such pain. It does not know or share in its mother's suffering. Her words can have no effect upon its consciousness for it is little more than an animal.

And in this we are unfortunately mistaken. The infant is very much alive and sensitive *in its consciousness.* That consciousness, and the body it indwells, suffers a shock of its own in the very act of being born, and added to that shock is the greater one of being to blame for another's agony. Of course, such blame is not formulated into thought by the mind of the infant. The formulated thought is all around it, created within and by the race mind, and attendant in greater or lesser degree at every birth. The response of the newly birthed consciousness to the emotional state of the mother opens a door for the entry of the race mind thought-form. It then takes up its residence deep within the subconscious of the infant.

Here, then, is the seed-thought upon which identity is built: the cornerstone for the building of the ego image.

As the newly born consciousness grows into the very young child it quickly becomes identified with its surroundings, particularly with the emotional condition of those with whom it is in constant association.

It does not take long for the child to add, one after another, many race mind thought-forms to its ego image. While it would take volumes to clarify all of them and we have but a short space, we can nonetheless realize the vast connotations of what happens here. Consider the emotional state of most persons. Consider the ego image shared by most families. What do you think of *yourself?* Do you think of yourself as a child of God inheriting the Divinity of God? Many of the guilt's and

Lesson 5

so-called "sins of the fathers" are visited upon the children and in just this way, through the transference of the family ego image.

At the same time, the young son or daughter is constantly reminded of their original guilt. They see their mother every day. Often they displease her and have to observe the pain of that displeasure. They are told frequently that they are bad or naughty. Sometimes their mother falls ill. Are they to blame for this, too? Deep within their subconscious, the guilt works to answer yes.

It is most unfortunate for those children whose mothers died while in childbirth or during the early years of the child's life. For many of these the guilt becomes so great as to disturb the outer appearance of reason, and in later life the man or woman is insane.

The next major thought-form to be built into the child's image of self comes by way of religion. While all human beings have great need of religion, we in the western world have been woefully negative in our teaching of it.

Most Christian children are taught that they were conceived and born in sin. Their small minds do not understand what is meant by such an idea, and seldom do the adult minds understand exactly what they are teaching; but the concept does add to and corroborate the picture they have already conceived of themselves. Therefore they readily accept it.

All people are sinners. Jesus — the kind and loving Jesus — died on the cross to save humanity from its sins.

Ah, so this young child, along with all humankind, is guilty of the murder of Jesus as well!

As the young children of God experience the natural desires and conflicting emotions of growing up, they are

65

reminded at every step of their sinful nature. Almost everything they want, almost everything they feel, and certainly their reactions (which are being dictated for the most part by their ego image), are bad. By the time they have reached maturity, their picture of themselves and of their brothers is most certainly remindful of Satan. There is little of the Christ permitted them. No wonder it is extremely difficult for them to love and to be loved.

Jesus said, "Let the children come to me, do not hinder them; for to such belongs the kingdom of God. Truly, I say to you, whoever does not receive the kingdom of God like a child shall not enter it." Mark 10:14-15

Poor misguided humanity, misguided in their interpretation of the teachings meant to aid them.

The sins and sufferings of humanity are for the hearts and minds of adults to understand and not for the burdening of children with false guilt.

Teach your children the goodness and the beauty of Christ. Teach them that they are one with and in Christ, and therefore children of God. Teach them the Kingdom of God that they might enter therein and conduct their lives accordingly. Let their ego image share in the glory of Christ, rather than the darkness of Satan, that their nature is one of Love.

"You, therefore, must be perfect, as your heavenly Father is perfect." Matthew 5:48

Such perfection arises not from guilt but from an understanding of God's law; from an understanding of Love, beauty, harmony and goodness. One must have faith in oneself as a Christ-child of God to know and understand and embody the nature of perfection.

Lesson 5

Why, when we want so desperately to love, do we hate? Why does a person rob, or do murder? What is the cause of criminal behavior?

It is the inner "state of Consciousness" which conforms to the ego image, for the ego image is what one thinks of one's self. "According to what a man thinks, so is he." They have given that constructed form the power of manifestation so that it controls their response. If, in the depth of their heart they think they are a murderer, they are likely to kill as that powerful form responds to outer stimuli. They may not want to, but this is what they think they are. How, then, can they be something else?

Yet all persons *are* God's children, and it is written that "Light shall shine out of darkness".

> Let the Light of understanding so illumine the dark recesses of your consciousness that the old ego image is dissolved into nothing. Replace it with the *image* and *likeness* of God which is Christ, and Let Light shine forth from out the darkness.
>
> *"I Am That I Am."*

Creative Thinking

Notes

_____

_____

_____

_____

_____

_____

_____

_____

_____

_____

_____

_____

_____

_____

_____

_____

Lesson 5

Notes

_____

_____

_____

_____

_____

_____

_____

_____

_____

_____

_____

_____

_____

_____

_____

_____

Creative Thinking

LESSON 6

Reincarnation

Consciousness and The Form Nature:
Physical, Emotional, and Mental;
The Three Bodies and
the Death Process;
Identification as Soul

LESSON 6

Down through the ages, humanity in its religious aspiration has come upon certain basic concepts which it has woven into the tapestry of our lives, using tradition, custom, and ceremony to give these concepts a setting and an authenticity.

Thus, we have seen emerge the great religions and cultures within which Truth has been clothed according to the way, and the particular Light, of the persons involved. Within each is a similarity of principle which, when called forth from the outer wrappings of its particular dress, provides us with a clear and beautiful wisdom, universal in its understanding and in its application.

The controversial concepts within the various religions do not detract from the truths they have embodied, nor render them any less valuable to the masses they have served and continue to serve.

Three-fifths of the world's population, or thereabouts, believe in reincarnation while the other two-fifths stoutly maintain that people live upon this earth only once. Each of the great world religions involved teach and advocate that love which results in brotherhood and peace on earth. In principle they agree; in doctrine they differ, and because of such difference they do not often understand one another.

It would behoove us all to become as educated in each other's religion as in our own, for *this* is their *heart*. Here is humanity's aspiration to God, and while one addresses Him by one name and another by a different name — are they not praying to the same Divine Being?

Creative Thinking

When the heart is sincere in its aspiration, will God not heed that call? Does God care if one person believes in reincarnation and another does not if both seek and serve those principles which are universal in their good for humanity? Does God listen more carefully and mercifully to the confession which is spoken aloud than to the one spoken in silence?

No matter what our religion, we have much to learn of Wisdom before we will join hands in brotherhood and good will.

In this series of instruction the concept of reincarnation is presented to the western student for consideration. If students do not accept it, that is their divine right. It neither condemns them nor the principles of truth with which this instruction deals. This subject is not presented in order to arouse controversy, neither is it considered necessary to accept it in order to know and live truth.

It is presented because the author sincerely believes in its validity, and that an understanding of it is the divine right of every person. After such an understanding has been gained then let each accept or reject according to their own light.

We have said previously that there is one Spirit in many bodies. The Spirit is the Divine Will or Intent of God. The substance of the bodies is the matter aspect, the *Intelligent Substance* of God. The interaction between these two, Spirit and Substance, or God's Will and God's Intelligence, produces consciousness within form.

Within the human being that consciousness is the Son of God, for it is conscious of self. This we call Soul.

In the beginning the young Soul identifies with his body, and when he thinks "I" he does so as that body.

Lesson 6

He is, in consciousness, what his form nature is. If it is tall and thin, then *he*, the conscious thinking "I" inside of that form, is tall and thin. If it is rich or poor, *he* is rich or poor, etc.

The form nature with which the young Soul is identified is threefold in nature. It is composed of three distinct types of substance which interpenetrate one another but occupy different frequency ranges. These types of substance are:

1. Physical: We are all conscious of this kind of substance for it is of the lowest vibratory frequency. Most persons' range of conscious perception is tuned in only to the frequency of physical substance, so they can see, hear, taste, touch, and smell only that which is constituted of physical substance.

2. Emotional: We are aware of this substance to a degree as it creates an effect within the feeling nature of our consciousness. It occupies a higher frequency range than does the physical, so our perception of it as a race is very limited. We perceive it through the senses as color and quality; we react to its presence via an emotional feeling nature which is our quality.

Actually, this substance is technically defined as astral substance, and is likened unto liquid because its frequency gives it that appearance in comparison with the physical. It is a force that acts (as a part of the form nature) as the power to bring that which is conceived in the mind into physical manifestation. Within the human being it becomes drive or desire, furnishing humanity with that intangible force with which to accomplish whatsoever they will.

3. Mental: We are also aware of this substance to a greater or lesser degree, as we formulate

thought. Here is that substance out of which the blueprints are made for every form which takes on an appearance in dense physical substance.

If we are going to write a book, or paint a picture, or prepare a meal we must first conceive the plans in mental substance. The perfection of the final product will depend upon:

A. The clarity and perfection of our formulated plan in mental substance.

B. The power of attraction (or inner drive in astral-emotional substance) we can give to that plan toward physical manifestation.

C. The action of the physical body to reproduce the formulated plan in physical substance.

All of these three types of action are the intelligent activity necessary to a person's success in any field of human endeavor.

The form nature is made up of three actual bodies composed of these three kinds of substance. They interpenetrate one another, as light interpenetrates water, so they occupy the same time and space, but different frequency ranges.

What happens when a person dies?

The Holy Spirit of God, which is in one sense the very Life of the form and which indwells all three bodies, is withdrawn from the physical. It takes the conscious thinking "I" with it, and the physical body disintegrates, returning again to the dust out of which it was made.

Depending upon the development of the conscious

thinking "I", that is, upon its degree of conscious identification, the Holy Spirit either remains in both the astral and mental bodies or it withdraws from the astral and lives in the mental. If people are identified with their emotions, "I *feel* thus and so", this is where they will live after death. If they are identified with their mind nature, "I *think* thus and so", the Holy Spirit will continue its withdrawal from the astral into the mental and this is where the person will live after death.

For some time after death people experience a heaven or hell of their own making. If they believe in a hell of fire and brimstone, they will experience such a place in the frequency of astral substance via their formulation of it in thought and emotion (fear and guilt).

The same applies to heaven. The person will experience that which they believe they have coming after death, until the cyclic period for their reincarnation draws near.

At that time the conscious thinking "I" goes to sleep and the Holy Spirit re-enters the physical plane of appearance into a new physical body awaiting it.

The new physical body claims the consciousness so that as the conscious thinking "I" grows from infancy to maturity it becomes, in identity, another personality.

We shall proceed with this subject in our next lesson. In the meantime carry out the following exercise daily as a preparation for greater understanding.

1. Become still in that place where you live inside your body and think "I", identifying by name. Think for a few moments what this means.

2. Turn your attention to your physical body and contemplate:

> *"I am not my physical body. I occupy it, using it as an instrument of contact with the world in which I live. Through it I see, hear, taste, touch and smell, but I am no more my body than I am those other forms which I perceive with the senses. I am consciousness."*

3. Turn your attention to the astral-emotional body, visualizing it as a substantial body resembling liquid which interpenetrates the physical. Contemplate the following:

> *"I am not my emotional nature. I occupy this body and use it to give power to my plans. I can choose my feelings."*

Consider for a few moments those feelings which you wish to experience and radiate to others.

4. Turn your attention to the mental body, visualizing it as a substantial body resembling gas or energy, which interpenetrates the astral and physical. Contemplate the following:

> *"I am not my mind nature. I occupy this body and use it in order to formulate thought. With this substance I create. I can <u>choose</u> my thoughts."*

Consider for a few moments the thoughts you wish to experience and manifest as an influence for good in the world.

5. Contemplate these three bodies within which you, the conscious thinking "I" live, and the Spirit which indwells them. Contemplate for a few moments the following seed thought:

> *"I am the Soul, Son of God."*

Lesson 6

Notes

_____

_____

_____

_____

_____

_____

_____

_____

_____

_____

_____

_____

_____

_____

_____

_____

_____

Creative Thinking

Notes

_____

_____

_____

_____

_____

_____

_____

_____

_____

_____

_____

_____

_____

_____

_____

_____

_____

_____

Lesson 6

Notes

_____

_____

_____

_____

_____

_____

_____

_____

_____

_____

_____

_____

_____

_____

_____

_____

_____

Creative Thinking

LESSON 7

The Divine Plan for Humanity and
The Reappearance of The Christ

The Lack of a Sense of Divine Purpose,
Misinterpretations of Divine Guidance,
The Overall Purpose and Goal of Our Lives,
Consciously Initiated Growth and Development

LESSON 7

There is a Divine Plan for humanity that includes the Purpose for every created Soul. Men and women did not create themselves. God did, and with reason.

Consciously or unconsciously, each one of us is moving toward a divinely ordered goal. We might choose, perhaps, the way we shall take toward that goal, but ultimately, regardless of the path we follow, it shall lead us there.

The great new revelation to come to humanity with the reappearance of the Christ has to do with the purpose and goal. The Christ will revolutionize our thinking again, just as He did some twenty centuries ago when He spoke in contradiction to the doctrine of the church of that day.

We will find that Christ, the only begotten Son of the Father, includes every man, woman, and child upon the planet; and that salvation does not apply to a select few whose environments have conditioned them to meet the considered requirements of that salvation of judgment day.

The saddest condition to be found among people today is the appalling lack of a sense of Divine Purpose. Without it they live in the constant fear of an untimely end, and the need to get as much out of life as is possible. It is as though they are afraid that they will be short changed, that life itself is an enemy with nothing but death at its end.

Few there are, among the vast masses of people upon the earth, who live in the security of Purpose. Few there are who consider it possible to know why they were born and to consciously cooperate with that why. Every created Soul was created for a reason, and that reason is his contribution to God and to humanity.

What is wrong with our thinking as a race that we manifest this psychology with its resultant irrational behaviorism?

The major thought-forms contributing to the condition are those misinterpretations of Divine Guidance that we have formulated out of ignorance and superstition.

Let us look for a moment at the concept of reincarnation as an answer to the problems we have thus far been unable to solve.

While it is not possible for humanity in its present development to know the ultimate reason for its being, it is possible for us to know that which concerns us now.

The growth and development of the consciousness of humanity, as the Son of God, into Christhood, is the overall purpose and goal of our lives now. We are here, in bodies, to learn the lessons in creativity that will eventually liberate us from the prison of the materials with which to create, so we can wield them to manifest perfection in consciousness, and in form.

The consciousness is identified with the matter aspect, the form building substance, so that it is his prison, rather than his instrument of creativity. When he is identified in consciousness with the Christ, as a Son of God, the matter aspect will be his servant rather than his master.

This growth and development from the infant to the adult son is not and cannot be achieved in one lifetime, for there is too much to learn.

86

Lesson 7

We live in a body but a short cycle and during that period we learn, via experience, the lessons which are related to our Spiritual age. As we manifest our inner state of consciousness outwardly as cause, we reap its effects in experience, and so gradually we alter or change that inner state of consciousness to produce different effects.

A person who dies in the electric chair for murder will be unlikely to commit the same act in another body, for the effect *experienced* will be deeply imprinted upon the inner state of consciousness, thereby changing it. That change is growth.

Another person who innocently dies in the electric chair is often paying the price of a crime committed in the past. These are the "mysterious ways in which God moves" through those universal laws that maintain *order* throughout the manifest Cosmos.

Luke 12:6: "Are not five sparrows sold for two pennies? And not one of them is forgotten before God. Why, even the hairs of your head are all numbered. Fear not; you are of more value than many sparrows."

It is the law, that "as you sow, so shall you reap", for this is how we learn. We experience in repercussion or re-action upon ourselves, that which we give out in relationship to others.

From the "Dead Sea Scriptures" (iii 13-IV, 26) we find: "This is for the man who would bring others to the inner vision, so that he may understand and teach to all the children of Light the real nature of men, touching the different varieties of their temperaments with the distinguishing traits thereof, *touching their actions throughout their generations*, and touching the reason why they are now visited with afflictions, and now enjoy periods of well being." (From: *The Dead Sea Scriptures*,

Creative Thinking

Theodor H. Gaster, Editor, Doubleday and Company, Inc.,1956)

"Touching their actions throughout their generations", means, literally, throughout their incarnations. Everything we experience has its effect upon us to serve our growth. That growth may or may not be immediately apparent in the eyes of a human being, but is apparent in the eyes of God.

For many generations (incarnations) the growth and development of human consciousness is an automatic, unconscious growth brought about through experience under law. Children are born into wealth or poverty, into fine strong bodies or maimed and diseased ones; into the environment of thieves or religious God-fearing folk according to their past action and the lessons they have to learn at any given time.

This is Divine Justice, without which there could be no order. What other concept explains the fate of a child? Could God have so little love as to create a child whose only Purpose, whose only chance, because of heredity and environment, was hell-fire and brimstone? What of those who have never *heard* of Christianity or the Bible? Are they condemned by the God who created them and placed them where they are, to such a purposeless existence?

Have we really, as a race, rightly interpreted the Divine Guidance we have received?

At a certain period of development the consciousness begins to realize why it is here, incarnate within a body, and a particular set of circumstances. It realizes, dimly at first, that it is learning *specific* lessons via experience, that it is achieving a growth of character, a refining of thought and emotion.

Lesson 7

Pause for a few moments and consider your own personality. What are its characteristics? What kind of circumstances does it *most frequently* manifest?

If a person is continually hampered with an inner sense of impatience, that one is learning the lesson of patience. That individual is becoming acquainted via experience with God's laws, learning that everything moves in cycles, in seasons, that everything comes in its own time after conception and growth have had their time.

If a person meets with failure and opposition because of a forceful will, or an unpleasant disposition, that person is learning the lesson of love, that love which gives freedom of choice and of action to others.

Try to discover, through a simple observation of your own characteristics, and the type of circumstances with which you are repeatedly faced, the specific lessons placed before you as a growing Son of God.

At this point, a person begins to grasp the idea of Purpose, and like a major illumination one sees into one's own religion.

Such people know why they are admonished to love their enemy. Both they and that enemy are growing into the conscious awareness of this Divine Sonship. Attendant with that awareness is humanity's Divine heritage as the common birthright of their Soul.

With this knowledge and faith a person then looks into one's self, discovering just what lessons one is in the process of learning. Co-operating with this *reason* for *being*, and the Law of Growth, they impose upon themselves those disciplines that will aid the growing process.

When humanity as a race reaches this point of realization and development, it shall begin to wield the Law of

Creative Thinking

Grace, bringing an end to the round of cause and effect which holds it a prisoner upon this earth. Men and women rise up out of the effects of the past, bringing balance and adjustment into their affairs by serving one another. Thus do they cancel out the old debts and take their place in the Kingdom of God.

To know God, is to love God, for He is merciful, just and loving. To know God, is to love humanity, for "Created He them". To love God and humanity, is to serve humanity, to contribute to its salvation *as a whole*, through consciously initiated growth, clarity of thought, the enunciation of Truth, and loving kindness in action. Thus does humanity, by way of grace, come to walk hand in hand with its elder brother in Christ, Jesus of Nazareth.

If people would know that Truth that is Wisdom, let them ask God to show them the way. Let them, in the silence of their own heart and mind, seek out the pure reason of their being.

Become still, in that place where you live inside of the body, and contemplate your identity in Christ.

Then in humility and love, without fear, ask in His Name, *Our Father, why was I born? What is the Purpose of my life?*

Lesson 7

Notes

_____

_____

_____

_____

_____

_____

_____

_____

_____

_____

_____

_____

_____

_____

_____

_____

Creative Thinking

Notes

_____

_____

_____

_____

_____

_____

_____

_____

_____

_____

_____

_____

_____

_____

_____

_____

_____

_____

Lesson 7

Notes

Creative Thinking

LESSON 8

How to Restore God's Plan on Earth

The Power and Right Use of Public Opinion,
Brotherhood, Where We Live, Unconscious Creativity
and Emotional Polarization, Conscious Creativity and
Mental Polarization, Where you Live and
Head Polarization.

LESSON 8

As we observe the world of affairs in which we live, we see many things we would like to change. We read of the day's happenings in our newspapers; we sometimes watch the events from a comfortable chair in our living room while they take place thousands of miles away; and we listen to commentaries by the experts upon every phase of the news. Today's humanity is the best-informed humanity in the world's history, yet we are slow to take an active part in the affairs of our time.

We shake our heads, shrug our shoulders and often complain, sometimes bitterly, about the things we don't like, but this is usually as far as we go. We generally take things as they come, leaving the changes to be made and the solutions to be found to the people we have elected to public office.

Have we forgotten that we have a potential power which we seldom wield? That power is public opinion. With it, rightly motivated and rightly directed, we can make this world safe and sane and beautiful. In the past we have used it wrongly as we have permitted some powerful personality to lead us into revenge-seeking mobs and bloody rebellions. The power of the many, once it is intelligently mobilized and directed, is great. The discovery of its potential for good and of its right use is before us, the masses of humanity, now.

As we realize that this world of affairs in which we live is of our own making we realize the simple truth, that we can change it. Not one person alone, but many of us thinking, feeling, and acting together as God's children can change it from one of pain, fear, and anxiety, to one of peace, love, and harmony.

The purpose of this series of instruction is to show how this can be done so as to restore God's plan on earth. Its goal then, is this, the integration of separately identified human beings into a group consciousness dedicated to the good, the true, and the beautiful for humanity.

Brotherhood is not something which can be imposed upon the individual or the group by the state. Brotherhood, a relationship based upon the mutual love, respect, and freedom-giving, of one toward another, must come from within the heart of the individual if it is to be a reality. The sharing of one's goods, whether spiritual or material, must be a spontaneous loving response of one brother toward another if good is to result for either. The government must be a true reflection of the mass mind and heart if it is to serve their highest good. It must be the instrumentality of the people's will, a will which if rightly educated, trained, and allowed to function becomes invocative of God's will. Any human law which forces individuals to give up that which is theirs, against their will, is bound to leave horror in its wake, for the gift without the giver is of no value.

Brotherhood is based upon the Power of good will. The mass good will is a result of the individual will-to-good. The cultivation, growth, and flowering of that individual will-to-good should be the concern of every leader in every field of human endeavor, in every locale of the world today. Such a quality and strength of will breeds and grows in the clean, fresh soil of human dignity and freedom.

Every man and woman is born of Deity and as such requires the Divine right to grow as they choose, insofar as the *divine parents* permit, into their adulthood in Christ. Thus, each must be given (as the Father gives) the right to make mistakes and to learn thereby.

Lesson 8

These concepts are basic. All men and women of good will regardless of religion, nationality, or ideology recognize and accept them. Such are the forces of light upon the planet. The power of such force, once it is mobilized and directed into right action, far outweighs the power of evil and ignorance. Thus, we, the people, can recreate our world of affairs into a true reflection of God's Kingdom where His children in Christ can grow into their spiritual maturity.

Since the individual is the first basic requirement of the many, we begin with ourselves and our own individual world of affairs. We begin where we live within our own bodies.

We have already learned that the constitution of humanity is three-fold in nature. They live within a physical body through which the combined forces of their mind and emotions can act.

Their response to their environment has been largely emotional. They lead with their feelings, so to speak, yet the mind and the heart have been merged by them, since they tend to think according to their feelings. As they feel in their heart (emotions) so they tend to think in their head (mind).

In this condition humanity is unconsciously creative. People unconsciously create with their mind those situations and experiences which are representative of their inner emotions. If they are still carrying the resentments, disappointments, and frustrations of their childhood, deep within the subconscious level of their feeling nature, they will unconsciously create with their mind those experiences which will permit the expression of the deeper feelings through the physical body. Thus, people, situations, and things, become symbols that justify the expression of an emotion created long ago via a past experience.

If the emotion is present within us, regardless of how deep it might be buried, we must seek out a target for its release. It acts as a powerful inner drive that moves both our mind and our physical body in a specific direction. Thus, we experience over and over with different people in different places, the same situations and events.

When we wonder, "why does this always happen to me?" we can realize that it happens because we are unconsciously causing it to happen through some inner feeling.

Modern psychology and psychiatry have discovered various methods of releasing and relieving the pressure of these powerful emotional causes within us, but there is yet another more direct way of dealing with them and it is far less painful than analytical therapy.

When people are ruled mind and body by their emotions, we say they are emotionally polarized. That is, that while they live in their physical body, it is from within the focus of their emotional-feeling nature in that body. That focus of emotion within which such people live becomes their positive pole of magnetic attraction and manifestation. The mind is attracted down into the heart; the physical energy and forces are attracted into the heart, and it rules the world according to those powerful emotional causes contained within it. Such people then think and act according to their feelings regardless of their reason or lack of reason. They unconsciously create their pain and pleasure, joy and sorrow, successes and failures, because they are, even in their infancy, creative, as is their Father in Heaven.

To become consciously creative, humanity must shift their polarization from their emotional feeling nature up into their mind where reason can be found and used as the springboard of action.

Lesson 8

The energies of the heart, which are the power factors of all manifestation, must be carried up into the head and directed into action according to an intelligently created plan. A person's thought will then become the result of contact with truth, and the creator of that person's feelings. Such people will feel in their heart as they think in their head, expressing the combined forces of heart and head through the physical body as intelligent activity. Thus will they arrive at Wisdom or the pure reason of Love.

Pause for a moment now and come to rest in that place where you live inside of your body. Many of you will find that you have been living naturally in one of four places:

1. In the solar plexus

2. In the heart

3. In the throat

4. In the head

If you naturally focus in the solar plexus, this means that you are polarized in your emotions; that your emotional wants and desires are based upon your own welfare more than upon the welfare of others; and that you often find yourself to be a victim of circumstance.

If you naturally focus in the heart, this means that you are polarized in the idealistic aspect of your feeling nature; that your emotions are based upon the apparent needs of your family and friends; and that you often find yourself to be a victim of your sympathies. You feel through situations rather than thinking through them, and often discover that such feelings can be very misleading.

If you naturally focus in the throat area, you consider

yourself to be a thinker. You are somewhat skeptical of the emotions. You are polarized in the lowest aspect of the mind where thought and feeling energies are directed in that mind from the subconscious level of your feeling nature. You have repressed most of your emotions, yet without your conscious knowledge they control you.

If you naturally come to focus in the head, you are a thinker. You are in the process of establishing a mental polarization and often find your heart at war with your mind. You experience the conflict in the very core of your being, and are often disturbed, moody, and withdrawn.

The task before each one of you is to establish a head polarization which takes account of the emotional nature, putting it to right use in service to the total organism.

We shall go into this in greater detail in the next lesson. In the meantime, determine your own polarization from the above, and prepare to move. As when moving from one house to another, put your things in order in that place where you live in the body. Look at all that which is familiar and decide what you will take with you and what you will discard. Examine your thoughts, feelings, and habits. Are they worth moving? Should some of them be left behind? Make a list of all you wish to take with you, and of all you consider as outgrown and no longer necessary or desirable to your welfare.

In that place where you live in the body contemplate your identity as the Christ-Child of God. Contemplate your move up into the head, "the holy place of the Most High", in the temple of the living God, and thank the Father, that at last you are ready to be brought into closer contact with Him.

Lesson 8

Notes

Creative Thinking

Notes

_____

_____

_____

_____

_____

_____

_____

_____

_____

_____

_____

_____

_____

_____

_____

_____

Lesson 8

Notes

_____

_____

_____

_____

_____

_____

_____

_____

_____

_____

_____

_____

_____

_____

_____

_____

_____

Creative Thinking

LESSON 9

The Move from Emotional to Mental Polarization

The Service of The United States,
Truth and Human Rights,
Focusing the Consciousness in a New Direction,
The Heart Center, Meditation and
Regular Meditation Exercises,
The Mountain Journey

LESSON 9

Just a few centuries ago a group of people moved from the old world into the great unexplored wilderness of America. They were faced with many dangers, with a vast expanse of unknown and uncharted territory, and with totally different conditions from those to which they were accustomed.

Some of these people were motivated by a great desire for freedom, freedom to worship, to live, and to govern their own lives. Others were motivated very simply by the inner spirit of the pioneer. Here was a challenge that some could no more deny than others could accept.

Yet all who came were consciously or unconsciously motivated by the need and the opportunity of their time. A new nation was to be founded, a nation based upon the principle of religious freedom, whose destiny marked her to become a world power in the time of great crisis. How she would wield that power would be determined by her collective national consciousness, as it responded to world need, and the realization of its own position among other nations.

We are now in that time of crisis. The United States is just awakening within its collective national consciousness to its position and power in the world. We are dimly aware, as yet, of the opportunity presented us to be of real service to humanity. Wherein does that service lie?

It lies in the area of Truth and human rights. If we, a freedom-loving people with the greatest economic power in the world today, can become sensitively attuned to the need of our times, we can bring in a new era of peace for all humanity to enjoy. This is our opportunity as a national consciousness. It can be accomplished only by that consciousness acting together as a group *dedicated* to serve the good, the true, and the beautiful for humanity, wherever there are human beings. Our leaders alone cannot do this, neither can a separated group among us. In fact, our leadership reflects the will of our people, and until the people's will is turned in this direction our leaders are helpless to accomplish it, even if they want to do so. It will take us all to bring our powerful economy to bear upon world peace.

Neither can we seize the opportunity from an emotional polarization which reacts to all outer stimuli from the built-in responses of fears and selfish desires. We have to move up into our minds and take up our residence there, where it will be possible for us to attain that perspective which brings humanity into view, rather than just oneself. Here we will be able to see into the world's problems with reason, and to work out the solution to those problems with that same reason, undistorted by the clouds of emotion.

In one sense we are like those earlier pioneers who made a nation out of the wilderness. We are moving into a new world into which only a few members of the human family have ventured thus far. It is up to us to establish her boundaries, determine her laws, and learn to make right use of her resources. We will seek out and overcome her dangers so that the others following may take up a safe and sane residence within this new country.

We call her the world of mind and she beckons us as surely and as persistently as the planets and stars beckon to those who would escape the gravity of our earth and the confines of our solar system.

How do we make the initial trip from an emotional

110

polarization into a mental one? We do so in our consciousness as we learn to focus that consciousness in a given direction.

Become still in that place where you live inside of the body and contemplate your conscious identity as a son of God.

"I, your name , am the son of God, inhabiting this body for a time in order to grow into the likeness of my Father who is in heaven."

Then, regardless of where in the body you might be, direct your attention to a spot about three inches outside of the physical, to the back of, and between the shoulder blades. Remember this is in the back, and *not* the front of the body.

We call this area the heart center. It is a focus of energy in a higher frequency than that of physical substance so you cannot see or feel it with ordinary physical perception. You can imagine this center as being composed of electrical blue white lines of force, spherical in shape, which conduct the golden energy of love into the emotional body.

1. Now as you give the center your attention learn to focus your consciousness there by imagining that you, in miniature, are within its very center, which is cave-like in appearance. See yourself, a tiny golden replica of the form you know, in the cave in the heart center and attempt to shift your consciousness (the conscious thinking I) from its normal focus into the image you have made. This may be difficult in the beginning; therefore, if you are not immediately successful proceed as if you were.

2. After having focused the consciousness within

the image, dwell upon the following concept for a few moments:

"I am the Christ-Child of God, born in the cave of the heart to know and experience love."

3. Spend a few moments radiating love to your family, your friends, your enemies, and your fellow human beings wherever they are.

Relax the attention and return to a normal focus.

You have just completed a meditation exercise. Meditation is the vehicle which will move you from one place in consciousness into another. The cave in the heart center is the station, so to speak, where you will get your ticket for the trip. The ticket is love, which you have requested from the Father, and for which you have given the price via the above contemplation.

The world of mind is a goodly distance in consciousness from the world of the emotions, and cannot be reached in just a few moments. It will take you twenty-eight days from the next new moon to complete the first leg of your journey.

Carry out the following exercise every morning from now until twenty-eight days following the next new moon:

Create the image of yourself in miniature in the cave in the heart center, remembering that this center is located outside and to the back of the body in the area between the shoulder blades.

Follow through steps 1 – 2 – 3 and continue the meditation as follows:

4. Direct your love upward into the head, *staying*

112

where you are, but aspiring with love to go into the Father's kingdom.

5. Finally, picture from your focus in the heart center, a similar center about three inches *in front* of the forehead. This is your first stop on the long journey into the new world. You will reach it in approximately twenty-eight days after the next new moon. Your aspiration will carry you there, but remember, that aspiration must be carried from a focus of consciousness in the cave in the heart.

6. Relax and return to normal focus.

During the daily routine you may aid your progress by radiating love into all of your activities.

In addition to the above meditation which must be established at a regular period each morning to be effective, carry out the following exercise before going to bed.

Without establishing any particular focus of consciousness, imagine that you have before you a very high mountain to climb. The top half of the mountain is hidden from view by dense, low-hanging clouds. You are going to reach its very summit in exactly twenty-eight days after the next new moon.

Equipped with love alone, begin your climb, experiencing in imagination every laborious step of the way, traveling but a little way each night, until at the appointed time you have reached the top. Spend from five to ten minutes in one period, continuing your journey up the mountain each evening from that place you had attained the previous evening.

Please realize as you carry out this exercise that you are setting the laws of the mind into motion via a symbol of your inner desire and will. Your imagination will picture outwardly in the mind's eye the inner effort and the progress being made. It will also aid that effort and progress by establishing a deep spiritual therapy within the emotional body.

The obstacles you will meet upon the mountain will symbolize the emotional problems confronting you in your attempt to shift your consciousness into a mental polarization. As you overcome those obstacles, and proceed with the climb, the mind itself will operate in such a way as to solve the corresponding emotional problems.

Throughout the entire period of the meditation and the evening exercise, you will be experiencing an inner cleansing and purification, as well as a shift in consciousness from an emotional into the beginning of a mental perspective.

It is suggested that you keep a daily written record of the mountain experience as well as the morning meditation. Such a record will be of tremendous value to you at a later date.

Lesson 9

Notes

_____

_____

_____

_____

_____

_____

_____

_____

_____

_____

_____

_____

_____

_____

_____

_____

_____

_____

Notes

_____

_____

_____

_____

_____

_____

_____

_____

_____

_____

_____

_____

_____

_____

_____

_____

_____

Lesson 9

Notes

_____

_____

_____

_____

_____

_____

_____

_____

_____

_____

_____

_____

_____

_____

_____

_____

Creative Thinking

LESSON 10

Re-evaluating Your Goal

The Inner Meaning of Your Life:
Purpose, Goal, and Outer Condition;
Realizing that You Are a Son of God,
You Are Not Alone

LESSON 10

You have consciously initiated a certain degree of growth in which you are attempting to become mentally polarized. You have begun the long journey up the side of your own mountain, and look forward to a dimly sensed attainment.

But what does all of this mean to you beyond the mere symbology of the words used to convey the goal? Do you really know where you are going and why?

It is now time, while you are making your journey, to re-evaluate the goal toward which you are moving, to grasp and absorb with as much clarity as is possible the inner meanings of mental polarization, emotional control, and your own identity as a Son of God.

First, what is the meaning of your life as you have lived and are living it now? Pause and take a few moments to write the answer to this question in three parts:

1. What has been your purpose for living during the major part of your life? While this question may be difficult for some of you, if you have never consciously formulated purpose before, it can none-the-less be answered. You have but to realize that purpose is the *reason* why you have done the things you have done. It is the one conscious or unconscious cause which has given your life its particular direction.

2. What has been your major goal in life? This one is more easily answered since it concerns most deeply the inner wish-life which you have fostered.

This wish-life always has to do with position and power of some kind since it involves the place of the ego in the world of affairs.

3. What is the condition of your outer life and affairs? Does that condition reflect your purpose and goal, and if not, in what way does it differ?

Write your answer, entitled "The Inner Meaning of My Life", and sub-titled Purpose, Goal, and Outer Condition on a separate sheet of paper. Further instruction will follow later.

Let us look now, at what some of the common answers could be as a result of the race-mind thought-forms created and entertained by the humanity focused into this western society and environment.

Example 1.

A. Purpose:

To achieve the greatest pleasure.

This means that the individual naturally likes more than anything else in this world to be pleased. Therefore, personal pleasure is the motivating cause behind their every action.

B. Goal:

To attain great wealth.

Wealth, to this individual, represents the way in which to gain the pleasure they crave. With great wealth, they think they will be in that position which will give them the power to force others to obey their will, i.e., to give them pleasure.

Lesson 10

C. Outer Condition:

Discontent, frustration, general unhappiness whether the person is wealthy or not.

In other words, the outer condition might or might not reflect this person's goal, but it could never reflect this one's purpose, because that purpose has no basis in reality. It presupposes that the man or woman, which-ever the case might be, is a separated existence, totally cut off and independent of all other lives. The outer life could only reflect, then, the conflict between the conscious or unconscious purpose and the true purpose of that life in which we *all* live, move, and have our being.

Example 2.

A. Purpose:

To escape the greatest pain.

These individuals are not seeking personal pleasure. They have learned the lesson (unconsciously perhaps) that such pleasure is not to be found in this world. They are deliberately taking that direction which will, they think, lead them away from the greatest pain. This is the motivating cause behind their every action.

B. Goal:

To attain complete independence from others.

These people turn their attention inward, try to avoid personal entanglements with other people, attempt to be self-sufficient insofar as is possible, particularly in financial matters, and are most often scholarly types. Independence and knowledge represent, to them, the power to escape pain.

C. Outer Condition:

Fear, pain, and general unhappiness whether or not they succeed in achieving some measure of their hoped for independence.

Again their outer life could never reflect their inner purpose, and in this case it could not completely reflect their goal, for people cannot live alone.

We could enumerate many other similar answers to this question, finding in each the same common problem. The personal purpose is in contradiction to the law of life. People cannot have a purpose that is separate and apart from any other person's purpose, for there is *one* motivating cause underlying the life and affairs of the Human Family.

Let us look at just one more example that could be the answer only for the person who had achieved some degree of mental polarization and Soul identification.

Example 3.

A. Purpose:

Service to the one life in which this person *consciously* lives, moves, and has their being.

B. Goal:

To see humanity, as a whole, achieve its place in the Kingdom of God.

C. Outer Condition:

Peace, love, and persistent creative work.

Lesson 10

These people, regardless of what they are in the world of affairs — teacher, doctor, scientist, etc. — are working persistently to create those conditions in which humanity can best grow into its divine heritage. They work in the field for which they are best fitted, are at peace within themselves, and radiate a love which passes understanding. Their purpose and their goal are at-one with the life indwelling all forms; therefore their outer affairs reflect the harmony of that life.

These people have learned that of themselves they can do nothing, that of themselves they can *be* nothing. They have, from their place within their mind, opened up their heart to the Christ, permitting the Christ to move through their instrument (their mind, emotions, and body) to accomplish the Divine Purpose and Goal for the family of God's children.

Such ones realize that their sacrifice is that of their separated identity to the Christ, Son of God.

This is what it means to realize that you are a Son of God. You are a part of that great consciousness and life indwelling every human being, which is the Son of God.

"I am *that* I am."

While it is necessary for your consciousness to grow from the seed into the full flower of realization of and identification with the one life, you can consciously initiate that growth now.

"Of myself I can do nothing."

As you continue your journey into the world of mind, which is only a means of entry into the Kingdom of God, let this statement dictate your inner attitude.

"Of myself I can do nothing."

125

Creative Thinking

Even the journey itself could not be made by you alone as a self-conscious ego separate and apart from all other life, for as such you have no existence in reality.

Become as aware as possible of that life which is within you, that is within every other person, and realize that your journey is being made in company with all of your brothers, even though many of them are not yet conscious of it.

Every night after completing the mountain exercise, take your piece of paper and add to the purpose, goal, and outer condition, whatever realizations you might have had regarding them. Be very honest with yourself and do not shrink from writing that which seems unworthy.

Later you are going to learn how to change the illusory purpose and goal which have until now been largely unconscious, into a conscious realization of the One Purpose and Goal of human life. In doing this, you will also learn how to control your outer condition so that it will reflect the Divine Intent.

126

Lesson 10

Notes

Notes

_____

_____

_____

_____

_____

_____

_____

_____

_____

_____

_____

_____

_____

_____

_____

_____

Lesson 10

Notes

_____

_____

_____

_____

_____

_____

_____

_____

_____

_____

_____

_____

_____

_____

_____

_____

_____

_____

Creative Thinking

LESSON 11

Consciousness and Mental Polarization

Learning to Live Together in Peace;
Love, Mental Polarization, and
Controlling Your Responses;
Observing Your Bodies Objectively;
Becoming Positive to Your Environment

LESSON 11

Mental polarization is a term with which students of the wisdom will become well acquainted during the coming years. It is evolving as a result of the new attention being given to the nature of the mind by humanity as a whole, and by science itself. While science is slow to move in this direction, great strides have been made in the fields of psychology and psychiatry, and more will undoubtedly be made in the near future as humanity continues to awaken to the potentialities latent within the mind.

A new era opens up before us in which humanity will be revealed as a unit of consciousness living within a mind and possessing emotions and body. The greatest danger in this transitory period between the old and the new, lies in the area of discovery without an accompanying spiritual development to assure right use of mental potential.

For this reason, the wisdom teaching stresses humanity as a Son of God. People are no more their minds than they are their physical bodies. Yet, there are already in existence those groups who believe and teach that humanity is mind; that they are the supreme intelligence, answerable and responsible to no one but themselves. Herein lies danger, a danger as great to the life and growth of humanity in the future, as that presented by the bomb in our present time.

The rest of this century will determine the future of humanity as we choose the path we shall follow into the new realm now opening up before us. That future can be one of conscious growth, of brotherhood, love, and

133

above all of an ever-widening understanding and awareness of life; or it can be a repetition of our past with wars, persecutions, fear, want, and spiritual ignorance. The choice is ours. We make it daily in our inner attitude regarding ourselves and others and our future.

With what particular thoughts and feelings, hopes and desires are we mostly occupied? Do we want for ourselves alone, regardless of the cost to others, or do our hopes include the good of the many? This is a vitally important question for its answer reveals the state of humanity in this time of great crisis when the world cries out for love, mercy, and an intelligent handling of world affairs.

While there are many of us who are preoccupied with our own problems to the exclusion of others, it is not because we are willfully selfish, but simply because we have not learned how to be either unselfish or selfless. The stress of our times, the emphasis of our education and environment upon our own particular locale, the division of society into classes, and the constant pressure of our daily needs have rendered us unresponsive to world need. We have yet to learn that we are each and everyone our brother's keeper. We have yet to learn to *care* for those who fall beyond our immediate sphere of physical vision. It is one thing to hear of a distant war, to hear of far away hunger and pain. It is something else to watch it, to see and feel the impact of another's agony.

Yet we are slowly awakening to the fact that somehow, some way we must learn to live with one another in peace. Our awakening comes as we react with fear for our own well being, to the impact of scientific achievement in the arena of international conflict.

What can we do, you and I, the little people whose influence does not extend beyond our immediate environment? It appears so hopeless, yet we can learn *that*

134

love which brings *reason*, and with reason, a reasoning process which will solve the world's problems. It is impossible for prejudice to live in the same mind and emotional nature that knows and practices love.

"If I have love, I cannot hate. If I have love, I see my brother's need in his act, and meet that need in my own act. If my heart knows compassion it cannot know prejudice, and when my mind knows reason, which is love, it cannot become irrational. Therefore, if I have love, I am a friend and brother to all men."

We hear of love that is ambivalent, yet this is not truly love. Ambivalence results when people turn their love energy inward toward self. In such cases the outer demonstration of care and affection is given for the sake of the self rather than for the other. Thus, our love is all too often a need to possess, to own, and command.

For so long as humanity lives and directs their life and affairs from within their emotions, real love, which is an energy expression of God, cannot be known by them. People who live here are the victims of their desires, fears, and resentments. They are the victims of those automatic responses built into their emotional body by the fate of their early environment and education. They can no more rise above them than they can alter what has happened in their childhood, for they are a prisoner within the boundary of emotion which does not know reason.

It is only from a polarization within the mind that people can begin to exert a control over their own responses. From this perspective they are able to see into those situations which would have automatically produced unpleasant and irrational reactions previously, and to understand both what produced them and what constitutes right action in the solving of them. Thus, they do not disperse their energy needlessly in reactions which only add to their difficulty. These people consciously follow a reasoning process that reveals to them the most intelligent plan of action applicable to the given situation.

Polarization, as we use it here, has to do with two factors:

1. The relationship between you (the conscious thinking "I") and your bodies.

If you can look at your mind, emotions, and body objectively you will be able to observe it as an instrument of contact and action in the world in which you live. These three energy bodies provide you with a means of reception, perception, and distribution of the forces active within your world.

The mind is concerned primarily with meaning or reason. It is enabled to cognize the meaning underlying the object or situation upon which it gives its attention, and redirect that meaning into outer manifestation via intelligent activity which it focuses through the brain.

The emotional nature has to do primarily with those powerful forces, unseen but felt by us all, which result in the outer appearance of a form. The mind may observe meaning and as a result formulate a plan, but without the accompanying flow of power released from the emotional body, the plan would never take form in the world. It would remain an intangible in the mind of the dreamer.

The physical body coordinates and conducts these forces on into outer physical manifestation via the final activity of transforming them into objective reality.

It can easily be seen that these bodies must be integrated and their activities intelligently directed if the conscious thinking "I" is to achieve their hopes and ambitions in the world of affairs.

If the consciousness is held a prisoner below the mind within the emotional nature, we say one is emotionally polarized. Meaning that for such people, both their mind and their physical body, as well as their awareness, are negative to their emotional response mechanism. The are unable to manipulate the will in any other area. Thus, their will is buried in their emotions, and they are a victim of these.

If the consciousness is polarized in the mind and if they are, at the same time, spiritually – oriented, then they are well on the way to becoming the master of their own fate or form nature. The emotional and physical bodies are negative to their consciousness, which resides in the mind. They are enabled to exert that control which makes it possible for them to accomplish their purpose.

    2. The relationship between you and your environment.

Most of us are more or less negative to our environment, and the forces that impact upon us from without.

Consider, for instance, the alcoholic who decides in all good intention to quit drinking. No one within his immediate environment believes him, for they think they know him too well. Thus, he is literally bombarded day and night with the thoughts and feelings from outside that he cannot or will not carry out his decision. Because this man is emotionally polarized, and because he is negative to the forces impacting upon him from the environment, he fails miserably. His consciousness accepts the direction of thought and feeling bombarding him, and his physical body carries those forces on out into manifestation. The man drinks.

We realize that the environmental influence is not a

first cause in this case, for that cause is found deep within the man's inner state of consciousness as a created path of least resistance. None the less it is a secondary cause, and at the time the man makes his decision to change, it becomes an important one. His position is already a weak one for he has a most difficult battle to wage within. When the opposition within him is fortified with help from outside he cannot help but be the loser.

We find, when we stop to analyze our action, that it is often a result of environmental influence, more than of our own clear thinking. We become the tools of the thought and emotional life of our daily environment giving voice and activity to that which is impacting upon us from the combined thoughts and feelings of our associates.

If an individual is positively polarized, they control the environment, as well as their own action, via a constant radiation of their purpose upon it. Mental polarization renders the person in the mind and brain positive to that person's emotions, body, and environment. In time, such people become leaders of humanity, and if they are spiritually oriented, they become a powerful influence in the world for good.

To be mentally polarized and spiritually oriented is to be positively identified as a Son of God, with the mind.

Lesson 11

Notes

_____

_____

_____

_____

_____

_____

_____

_____

_____

_____

_____

_____

_____

_____

_____

_____

_____

_____

Notes

_____

_____

_____

_____

_____

_____

_____

_____

_____

_____

_____

_____

_____

_____

_____

_____

Lesson 11

Notes

_____

_____

_____

_____

_____

_____

_____

_____

_____

_____

_____

_____

_____

_____

_____

_____

_____

_____

Creative Thinking

LESSON 12

Choosing Our Feelings

The Automatic Response Mechanism,
The Energy or Force of Feelings,
Controlling the Response

LESSON 12

Emotions are feelings that do not just happen to us by chance. We create them either consciously or unconsciously as we react to situations, people, and things.

A child creates an emotion via an imitative will. Most of the child's reactions are mimetic though they appear genuine. They tend to respond with love or anger, willingness to cooperate or antagonism, cheerfulness or depression, according to the responses of others to which they are daily subjected.

When little Bobby screams into the telephone every time it rings, Mother is often angry. Scolding him with sharp words put together into short, crisp sentences in a strong voice which implies a dire and impending threat to his welfare, she disengages him from the phone, and speaks into it herself. As she becomes interested in a choice tidbit of gossip, she forgets her anger, and Bobby slips away to undisturbed play.

Later, when mother takes her boy from his sand box to give him his afternoon bath before putting him to bed for a nap, he responds in a loud voice, with threatening tones, and tries to push her away. Sometimes he kicks, and screams in real anger, only to forget the whole thing a few moments later as he sets his red and white sail boat out to sea in the bath tub.

He is imitating his mother's responses, which he has ample opportunity to observe. He is learning how to live in the world, and he learns his lessons well. Thus far he has discovered that when one's will is crossed, one becomes angry. He enjoys a certain sense of satisfaction

145

and goes to sleep quickly and easily, for his ego has been strengthened by his action. He is growing up.

Expand this example and we see how a whole nation or race of people learns violence as a *way* of life.

Most of us do not realize that there are a number of ways in which we can react to a given situation. We can choose our feelings much as we choose our clothes according to the effect we wish to create.

When two-year-old Diane discovered that mysterious black instrument, whose ring announced the magic of hearing and being heard by someone she could not see, she too was loud in her excitement. She shouted into it a babble of meaningless sounds, which brought laughter from the other end of the line. Mother came running. Gently, she disengaged her daughter from the phone, asked her caller to please wait a few minutes, and with loving understanding explained the reason why Diane should not shout into a telephone.

With her arm around the little girl, she said, "You see, Darling, when it rings that means someone wants to talk with us. If we shout, we hurt their ears, and they will feel bad. We don't want to hurt anyone, do we?"

Diane nodded in agreement, her eyes big with sympathy. "No," she imitated, "we don't want to hurt anyone, do we?"

Her mother was then able to give her attention to her caller, while Diane went back to play.

Later Diane's mother taught her how to answer the telephone, and while her interest lasted, the wise mother gave Diane this little chore as a responsibility that would build ego strength as well as character.

Diane was growing up to be like her mother. She was

146

learning to respond with love instead of anger, with reason instead of emotionalism.

All individuals who respond to instruction of this kind do so out of the growing realization of the need to improve themselves. There is the vague sense of humanity's divine potential in contradiction to their performance, and the great desire to bring these two into balance. Some are concerned with this balancing in relation to the whole of humanity, others only in relation to themselves, yet all must begin at the beginning if they are to accomplish their goal. We begin with ourselves as individuals, endeavoring to bring our performance up to the level of our potential abilities. We deal first with the automatic response mechanism which conveys the character or lack of character we have embodied, and which is responsible for our happiness or unhappiness — our state of being insofar as feeling is concerned at any given time.

It is a wonderful revelation to discover that the energy expended in resentment is the same energy we use when we love. The force directed into a feeling of depression is the same force we direct into joy. There is no difference in the energy or force that is the life of the expression. The difference lies in the thought-form that has been built into our response mechanism as an automatic pattern of reaction. Thus, we react almost always according to those patterns that have been established within our cerebro-nervous system as habitual responses.

If people are treated with brutality, they react in a like manner because they *think* they are supposed to react in this manner. They could just as easily react with love and understanding, with a wisdom which would teach the other a better way and transmute their brutality into something more in keeping with common decency. There is nothing more effective than to react with love and good will to one who is using you badly.

Because happiness is so illusory, most of us don't really know what it is. We look for it in all sorts of places and try to achieve it by surrounding ourselves with things. There are those of us who think we can buy it with money or command it with power. Others simply do not believe in it and, therefore, do not look for it.

Happiness is a general feeling that is made up of many little responses to life itself. It cannot be found; it has to be created. There is nothing in the outer world that will bring happiness to a person, for it is born in the heart of the individual who conceives it within their self. Such people then radiate it as an influence, giving others the benefit of that which they have created.

Happiness is made up of the blend of understanding, love, kindliness, faith, and all of those expressions which are the result of a genuine good will toward all humanity, plus the calm acceptance of those things in life which cannot be changed by human effort.

These expressions are not difficult to come by, nor do we have to wait for some overdue fate or happenstance to give us adequate cause to experience them.

When someone does something to you that would ordinarily bring a negative response, pause for a few moments and analyze the situation. Will it help you or the other person involved to indulge in the old habitual response? Or will it only add more negativity to an already unpleasant situation?

During that pause, use your mind to discover what constitutes right action in this instance. Take hold of the response mechanism and train it to do your will by conveying love in the tonal quality of the voice, in the facial expression, in the speech, and in the action of the body.

Lesson 12

As you do this, really feel that love by trying to understand the reason for the other's attitude or action. Usually they are only reacting to your impact upon them via their own already built-in response. If you meet that reaction with a creative act of love and good will, you will give them pause and food for thought. You will create an atmosphere in which they, as well as you, can discover a new relationship called brotherhood.

It is suggested that those of you who truly wish to control your automatic response mechanisms, make a list of the responses which occur most frequently during the day. List them under the following titles:

Positive Response: Causal Condition or Circumstance

Negative Response: Causal Condition or Circumstance

And then study them, becoming as familiar as possible with the type, strength, and quality of response you make to outer impact. In this way, you will come to see yourself more nearly as others see you, and you will also quickly become acquainted with your own automatic response mechanism. It is difficult to change or alter that which you do not see and know.

Creative Thinking

Notes

_____

_____

_____

_____

_____

_____

_____

_____

_____

_____

_____

_____

_____

_____

_____

_____

_____

Lesson 12

Notes

_____

_____

_____

_____

_____

_____

_____

_____

_____

_____

_____

_____

_____

_____

_____

_____

_____

_____

_____

Creative Thinking

LESSON 13

Rebuilding the Response Mechanism

Rebuilding versus Inhibiting,
Recapitulating the Evolutionary Development,
Thought-Form Impressions,
Building New Thought-Forms into the
Automatic Response Mechanism

LESSON 13

It is extremely important that students at this point distinguish the difference between rebuilding the automatic response mechanism and inhibiting their emotional responses to life. Too many of us do inhibit, even from our own conscious awareness, those feelings which we have been taught are evil.

Certain responses of a negative nature are natural to the child in the various stages of growing up, for that growing up process actually constitutes a recapitulation of the evolutionary development attained thus far. Do not forget that when babies are born into the world, they are coming in with a past. This is not their first experience with life. They have been living for a long time, and during that time they have developed their own individual state of consciousness. They have lived in many bodies, created and discarded many personalities; yet out of each they have gleaned the essence of experience, so when they are born into a new body and a new environment it is with a developed inner state of consciousness which has its own tendencies, talents, and aversions.

As they move through the period from birth to maturity they recapitulate the growth already achieved in order to take up again in this life where they left off in the last one. In this way continuity between past, present, and future is maintained, though that continuity be unconscious until a certain point of development is reached.

It is perfectly normal and natural for children to experience certain emotions in response to the impacts of their environment upon their inner state of consciousness. If those emotions can be permitted expression in the right time, i.e., in the cycle of growth (age of child) which is normal to their recapitulation, no harm is done. They do not build in an automatic behavior pattern during that period if they are permitted expression without undue emphasis upon either furthering the expression "for the good of the child", or creating guilt within them for having done something that is bad.

It is difficult for parents to find the right and most perfect way of bringing up their children during an age when so little is known about the recapitulation process, but a beginning must be made somewhere.

A study of current literature upon the subject of child psychology, plus the understanding gained by a study of this kind, will help the parent to gain a perspective hitherto unknown. They will find, however, that the most effective way of teaching their child right behavior, is to convey that action through their own automatic response mechanism. Do not forget that the young child learns through conscious and unconscious imitation.

Most often during the recapitulation process we are taught to inhibit those emotions considered unworthy of civilized people. The *pattern* producing the response is left free to act while the response itself is inhibited or held within the emotional body. This is dangerous to mental, emotional, and bodily health, for even though the response is inhibited from conscious expression, so long as the pattern is present the response must find an outlet of expression. It will produce an effect somewhere in the instrument. Usually that effect is some form of disease within the physical body.

The student must be very careful to distinguish the difference between the inhibition of an emotion, and the

156

correction of an automatic response which produces the emotion. Too many individuals who are sincerely attempting to follow the path of Christ only succeed in making themselves ill through inhibition.

The difference between an emotion and an automatic response is the difference between feeling and thought. An emotion is a feeling produced by a thought-form. An automatic response is a *pattern* of thought which we call a thought-form. This thought-form dictates the feeling response in a given situation. The feeling response dictates the resultant action unless it is inhibited by another thought-form which says "no, no, this is not accepted behavior".

We all know, or have been taught in one level of our consciousness, that it is better to love than to hate, better to forgive than to seek revenge; but have we been told how to deal with these feelings which rise up in spite of all we can do to stop them? Generally speaking, we have not, and so we flounder in the cloudy ocean of feeling response, guilt, and a longing to know goodness.

An automatic pattern of response is a thought-form which we have accepted in our brain. The thought-form in the brain is usually unknown to our conscious mind, having been established in our childhood via imitation. It has direct access to the thalamus and, therefore, impresses the thalamus (the large nerve ending at the base of the skull) with the emotional response to be carried into action by the nervous system. We then experience in the feeling aspect of our consciousness an emotion (unless another thought inhibits that emotion) and act accordingly before we have time to properly evaluate the situation.

EXAMPLE: Mary is joyfully looking forward to a gala evening of dinner out and the theater. She is excited because the play is one she has long wanted to see. Ted, her husband, surprised her weeks ago with the tickets and the promise of a rare good time. All day she has been preparing for it, dressing her hair and nails, deciding upon what she will wear, and thinking what a wonderful husband she has.

Later in the afternoon, Ted calls to tell her something has come up at the office and he cannot possibly get away until late. They will have to forget this evening out until another time.

As Mary listens to Ted's explanation over the telephone, the news is conveyed to her brain via a series of tiny electrical impulses which trigger a thought-form (automatic response) that states, though not in so many words but in effect, "This is not fair to me. When someone makes a promise they should keep it. If they do not, I become angry."

The thought-form emits its electrical impulse to the thalamus which immediately generates the feeling to be carried, via the nervous system, into action.

If Mary is uninhibited she will convey her anger to Ted immediately. If, however, she carries another more potent thought-form which will not permit an expression of anger, she will speak calmly into the telephone accepting the situation with apparent good grace. Yet, at the same time, the little electrical impulse will be traveling from the first thought-form to the thalamus, creating a feeling which is not permitted active expression, but is nonetheless present and must be channeled into some outlet by the nervous system. In this case her arthritis will probably become very painful, or she will develop a headache, etc.

In any event she will be unable to properly evaluate the situation before she has the reaction. Later, when reason has had time to reassert itself, she will forgive Ted

158

(at least in part) and life will go on as usual, but not without the scar of this lesion in their relationship.

How could Mary have handled this situation without reaping an unfortunate result? Certainly not through inhibition. She would have had to deal with the automatic response to a situation of this kind before it actually took place. In other words she would have had to become familiar with its existence, have realized its fallacy, and have at least begun to build in another response to this kind of experience.

What other response is there? You might well ask, for most of us feel perfectly justified, in the innermost layers of our inner state of consciousness, for the responses we make to life. Actually, Mary had been taught that it *is* wrong to break a promise. She had a valid excuse for becoming angry because promises *are* supposed to be kept when they are made. There is nothing in her early training or even in her present social environment to teach her that understanding which would have instantly seen Ted's disappointment as well as her own.

The first thought-form we have to build into the automatic response mechanism as a part of the rebuilding process, is that of pause and reason in the event of every experience which would normally produce an explosion of emotions whether it be of a pleasant or unpleasant nature. This is an important point to be remembered. Any violence of emotion whether pleasant or unpleasant is undesirable in its effects upon people and situations and upon our own well being. This does not mean that we must eliminate joy from our lives for joy is not hilarious or delirious.

In a later lesson we shall consider a technique for the building in of the new response described above. In the meantime study this lesson well and ask yourself this question, answering it with complete honesty. "What would my response be if I were placed in Mary's situation?" Then think it over and consider the advisability and the possibility of building in an automatic response which will give you time to properly evaluate a situation before reacting.

Lesson 13

Notes

Notes

_____

_____

_____

_____

_____

_____

_____

_____

_____

_____

_____

_____

_____

_____

_____

_____

Lesson 13

Notes

_____

_____

_____

_____

_____

_____

_____

_____

_____

_____

_____

_____

_____

_____

_____

_____

_____

_____

Creative Thinking

LESSON 14

Controlling the Emotional Response Mechanism

Race-Mind Thought-Forms,
Discovering the Thought-Forms,
Removing the Thought-Forms
via Reason and Re-evaluation,
Substituting a New Pattern

LESSON 14

When we are born we do not only come into a physical environment of deeds and words, but we enter into an emotional and mental environment as well. Groups of people tend to think and feel similarly in given situations. Though unseen, those thoughts and feelings which provide an intangible atmosphere of conditioning, play an important part in the molding of our responses to life. They are constantly impacting upon the subconscious, producing via unconscious imitation, a like thought and feeling within us.

It is a fallacy to depend entirely upon a process of analytical therapy which digs deep into the subconscious to root out forgotten experiences which we think hold the causes of many of our reactions. Regardless of how deep we go we can never find many of those causes for they do not lie in tangible experiences which can be remembered. They find their roots in the mental and emotional environment within which we grow to adulthood, and within which we live today. Some of them are national or racial forms created in the world of human thought and emotion. We call these commonly shared automatisms race-mind thought-forms, and it is here that we have to go for the understanding of our own responses.

In order to control the emotional response mechanism (which is actually triggered into action by a series of patterns impressed upon the brain), we have to follow certain rules of procedure which result in a safe and sane course of action.

1. We must discover the thought-form within the

brain which dictates the emotional response.

2. We must then remove it via reason and re-evaluation.

3. We must substitute in its place a new pattern of direction.

These three rules are simple and clear. Each is carried out via a specific process as follows:

1. Discovery of the thought-form in the brain.

   We have already discussed the fact that most of us do not consciously know all that we *think* about any one subject. So many of our thoughts are automatically going on below the threshold of our awareness that we seldom realize the great volumes of thought we constantly entertain.

   There are a number of techniques that can be used to help us discover the thought-forms we have accepted as truth within our consciousness and brains. They are listed below as follows:

   a. Writing out the thought pattern.

      This is an effective and commonly used technique that can be employed prior to the use of others. The individual simply writes every thought that comes to mind regarding a given situation until the dictating pattern reveals itself.

      EXAMPLE: Write every thought that comes to mind regarding an experience such as that of Mary described in Lesson 13.

      The writing continues for days until the

individual has gone through the gamut of those experiences common to them. They can also write every thought that comes to mind regarding various subjects of interest, discovering in this way many dictating patterns of thought.

b. Automatic association of emotion to thought.

The individual thinks of an emotional response, such as crying, and then tries to imagine all of the various thought patterns that could cause one to cry. In so doing they associate thought and emotion together prior to the imaging of experience, bypassing blocks they may have acquired to the consideration of some types of experiences.

c. The person observes race-mind thought-forms that they may be unconsciously sharing with their fellows, and considers what the effect of these thought-forms are in their own life and affairs.

We have already discussed some of these forms in other lessons. Can you discover more of them? Look into the various prejudices and separative attitudes of your own group; and look particularly at those forms that are accepted generally as a matter of fact.

It is in this area of common acceptance that the majority of our racial patterns are to be found. Humanity once believed that the earth was flat, and because of this common acceptance, they were afraid to sail too far out into the ocean for fear of falling off the edge. It was also believed that the sun and the stars orbited around the earth; that only a blood sacrifice would appease the anger of the gods; and that the atom was the smallest, indivisible particle of substance in the universe.

Creative Thinking

What do we believe today? What are the ideas and beliefs our collective consciousness accepts as a matter of fact, though without proof or reason?

What do you believe about the hereafter? About life on another planet? About the relationship between God and humanity? About birth and death?

These are but a few questions among many, many others which should be given careful consideration.

Make a list of all the race-mind thought-forms you can discover which have influenced your thoughts, feeling, and physical reactions in some way.

For instance, what is your attitude regarding the Englishman, the German, the American Negro, the white American, the Jew, the Oriental, the Russian, the rich, the poor, etc.?

2. Removal of the thought-form via reason and re-evaluation.

This is somewhat more difficult for the beginner, because it demands a basic understanding of universal truth. The thought-form is compared with universal truth. Does the thought-form convey the reality of truth or the illusion created by the mind and emotions of humanity? It must be remembered that a reality in abstract truth is as applicable to one as to another, and always includes the highest good of the many. This must not be misconstrued to mean the highest good of the many to the detriment of a few, for the many includes each and every one.

If the basic concept of brotherhood (which derives from the basic concept of one Divine Parenthood), is accepted and embodied, all racial thought-forms of prejudice of one group against another must go for they do not hold

170

up in the light of reason. A person educated in truth cannot condemn another as being inferior or of a different clay, because this person knows that all people are united in one life, that life being The Son of God.

Beginners must become thoroughly acquainted with those concepts that *are* universal in their application for the good, the true, and the beautiful before they can complete this second step. They seek knowledge, but above all they seek the knowledge of Wisdom.

    3. Substitution of a new pattern of direction in the place of the old one.

This is a process of consciously initiated growth which we call embodiment. When a concept of truth is at last realized by the conscious thinking "I", that "I" sets out to embody it. One determines to incorporate it within one's own consciousness and instrument so its opposite can never express through one. One impresses it upon one's brain in the place of the old habit pattern of thought, through concentration and meditation upon it.

EXAMPLE: If a man achieves a realization within his own consciousness of the Fatherhood of God and the Brotherhood of Humanity, and at the same time he has become conscious of certain patterns of thought within his brain which trigger automatic responses that are contradictory to his realization, he then sets out to replace the old pattern with a new one in the following manner:

    1. He meditates daily upon the Fatherhood of God and the Brotherhood of Humanity.

    2. He formulates a thought pattern in the place of the old one and concentrates upon it daily.

For instance, if John has carried a dislike for Henry

over a number of years because of an automatism which states that he should dislike Henry (regardless of how justifiable the reason for that dislike may seem), he will then formulate the new thought pattern as follows:

Henry is a Son of God. I am his brother. He is my brother. The basic relationship between us is brotherhood. Its quality is love.

He will concentrate upon this new thought-form from three to five minutes each day until the old response is no longer in existence.

This is a positive disciplinary training that truly initiates the growth and expression of humanity's consciousness into the conscious awareness of himself as a Soul, a divinely created expression of the Life of God.

The techniques described above are a part of the new Applied Philosophy, with which humanity shall transform its entire civilization into a truer reflection of the Kingdom of God.

Because you are among the few to receive them first, yours is a responsibility that should be taken into account and considered deeply. If all humanity, or the majority of people, or even a minority of people in every nation were to know and apply the techniques described in this one lesson our fears and threats of, and forced movement toward war could turn into a real effort for peace.

Not all men and women today are interested in a teaching of this kind because they have not yet awakened to either its possibilities or the world's need of it. You can help to bring about that awakening by discussing Applied Philosophy with your friends, neighbors, and all of those within your sphere of influence.

172

Lesson 14

Notes

_____

_____

_____

_____

_____

_____

_____

_____

_____

_____

_____

_____

_____

_____

_____

Creative Thinking

Notes

_____

_____

_____

_____

_____

_____

_____

_____

_____

_____

_____

_____

_____

_____

_____

_____

_____

Lesson 14

Notes

_____

_____

_____

_____

_____

_____

_____

_____

_____

_____

_____

_____

_____

_____

_____

_____

_____

_____

Creative Thinking

LESSON 15

Knowing Ourselves

Spirit, Consciousness, and Matter;
The Journey and Identification;
Consciousness an Interplay of Force
Between Spirit and Matter;
Moving From the World of Emotion
to the World of Mind

178

LESSON 15

One of the most difficult tasks that a person can undertake is to know one's self. Nothing else in this world presents so much mystery and question as the riddle of identity or the inner reality of humanity. Yet the seeker in all times has ever been admonished by the sage and the adept to know themselves.

We seek knowledge of the stars, the atom, and the world in which we live. We seek for wealth, position, and power in that world, or we seek for some measure of comfort and escape from pain. Yet all of these avail us little if we are ignorant of our own constitution and nature.

We know our name and address. We know that we are of the species Homo Sapiens. We have a limited idea of how we look on the outside and how we feel on the inside, but what do we truly *know* about ourselves?

Of what are we constituted, other than the elements that make up our physical body? From where did we come and where are we going? Who can understand the miracle of conscious awareness, or of mind and the thinking process, or of life itself?

These are a few questions out of many that most persons shrink from asking because these often arouse a sense of insecurity, of anxiety for that which is unknown. The very wondering about life might bring the death they unconsciously fear, for life itself is so unfathomable.

Though the mystery seems impossible to solve, it can be

known and understood in the light of truth. It has been stated that "the truth shall make you free", and so it shall, but we must seek it out first.

Humanity is first of all a spark of divine fire. We are, at the very center of our being, a focal point of Spirit that is a part of that life in which we all live, move, and have our being.

Secondly, humanity is a radiation of consciousness that emanates spherically from the spark, as Soul.

Thirdly, humanity is a state of consciousness inhabiting an organized body of energies and forces at the periphery of that radiating sphere which we call Soul. The appearance is defined as a personality. It is an aid to the understanding to realize that the word personality is derived from the Latin root, persona, which means mask.

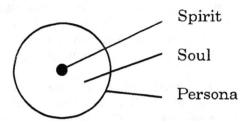

Spirit

Soul

Persona

When the consciousness which is Soul is identified with its body of appearances it is persona oriented and identified. It is limited to the outer periphery of its being, a prisoner within the energies and forces which constitute that body, and separative in its nature because the body appears as a life separate from all other lives.

The periphery itself is three-fold in nature since it is in a sense a reflection of the three-fold nature of humanity, the divine entity. Thus, the Spirit is reflected into a mind nature, the Soul into an emotional nature and the substantial matter aspect, which gives the divine spark form, into a physical body.

When the consciousness begins its journey back into the Father's Kingdom from whence it came, it turns inward toward its own center of being. Thus, its awareness turns from the purely physical to move into and experience the emotional aspect of its nature. This is where humanity is today.

With the inward movement from the emotional into the mental aspect, we become consciously aware of the process. We are now enabled to aid it via the manipulation of our will.

In the mind we begin to identify with that emanating life which we are in reality, the Soul, and to look toward the divine spark which is our spiritual identity in the One Life.

For a time there is a conflict resulting from the old habits rooted in the nature of the persona and persona identification and the Truth of the Soul which overshadows us, and demands to be embodied. We are torn between the pairs of opposites as they are reflected from our own inner sense of duality. That is, we undergo a period in which we are both a persona and a Soul, so our dual consciousness reflects itself in our life and affairs as the pairs of opposites. The struggle between good and bad becomes very pronounced, and a Dr. Jeckel, Mr. Hyde psychology may result if, through an established habit pattern of repression, the conflict is kept below the level of conscious awareness.

It is into this area of the periphery (the mind nature) that humanity is moving today.

As the consciousness abstracts its identification from the form nature of the periphery, i.e., persona, it identifies as Soul and becomes so conscious of that divine spark which he is at the center of his being that he is transformed into the Christ who is One with the Father and All Life.

The above description refers not only to the individual but to the collective life of humanity as well.

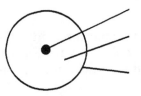

Father

Christ, the Overshadowing Soul of Humanity

The many personas which constitute humanity

Conscious awareness as self, wherever it might be found, is always the result of an interplay of force (relationship) between Spirit and matter. It is, therefore, an expression and evidence of God.

We have only to lift our awareness from the form nature or matter aspect with which we have become identified through our physical sense perception, to the unseen but sensed spirit which indwells the form, in order to know God and our own relationship to Him.

We have to develop, through evolutionary growth, a spiritual perception which will give us evidence of that which we cannot perceive with the five physical senses. Thus is our spiritual security born to carry us the rest of the way into the Father's Kingdom.

Cyclic concentration and meditation over a period of days, weeks, months, and years upon the symbol given in this lesson, and its meaning, will aid sincere students in their search for truth. However, until and unless

they are ready and willing to discipline their consciousness to live in the highest truths known, and to discipline the form nature to embody those truths, such a
procedure would be unsafe. If there is not a sincerity of
purpose and a complete dedication to the Christ, there
is extreme danger in following such a path.

Once the consciousness reaches the mind and begins to
identify as Soul, we symbolically enter the Hall of Wisdom. That is, we have entered into that area of mind
which holds the knowledge of spiritual truth, and that
area of consciousness which holds the wisdom to use
truth for the good of humanity. Thus, our spiritual education really begins and we learn how to manipulate the
energies and forces of the three lower worlds (mental,
astral emotional, and physical) through our own three-
fold instrument to create desired effects in the outer life
and affairs.

You are in the process now of moving from the world of
emotion into the world of mind. What will you find
when you arrive?

1. An easier identification as consciousness rather
    than as a combination of thoughts, feelings, and
    body. That *you* (the conscious thinking "I") are
    the Soul will begin to take on more meaning and
    you will gradually begin to perceive the world
    through the newly opened eye of the Soul, as
    such, with greater understanding of the inner
    meanings behind the outer happenings.

2. That you have a will and can gradually learn to
    manipulate the forces of your bodies. You will
    begin to understand that the will is an extension
    of spirit into your mind, and that through its
    right orientation and its right use you can con-
    sciously create your own effects in the substan-
    tial world of appearances.

3. You will finally discover meditation as the modus operandi of the Soul, and you will gradually learn to use it as easily as you use speech or any other faculty which you have developed. Here is perhaps the most rewarding of all your findings, for through meditation God is known, the mystery of the creative process is unraveled, and the self is perfected into the true Son of God.

Contemplate these findings as a new way of life, and imagine yourself living that life. What will it mean to you as an individual, and what will it mean to your associates? Consider your relationships and imagine what effect you would produce upon them as a Soul conscious Son of God.

How would you greet the various happenings of the day, the reaping of seeds sown in the past, and finally how would you meet death?

These are questions well worth the asking as you reach the top of your mountain. They are questions you will take with you into the world of mind and there answer as you commune with life and its intricate design.

To live every moment to the fullest, extracting from every experience the essence of wisdom, knowing that will-to-good which fills the heart with joy and the mind with love, is to live consciously. To do that we must awaken and we awaken only as we move inward with the fearlessness to seek. Dare to question that life in which you live, move, and have your being.

Lesson 15

Notes

_____

_____

_____

_____

_____

_____

_____

_____

_____

_____

_____

_____

_____

_____

_____

_____

_____

_____

Creative Thinking

Notes

_____

_____

_____

_____

_____

_____

_____

_____

_____

_____

_____

_____

_____

_____

_____

_____

Lesson 15

Notes

Creative Thinking

LESSON 16

The Mountaintop

The Dark Void Beyond;
God the Father, God the Mother,
and God the Son;
The Ajna Center;
The Center in the Head;
The Silver and Golden Threads

LESSON 16

By now you should have reached the top of your mountain, awaiting only the final step into the beginning of a mental polarization. This lesson constitutes that step; therefore, give it your special attention, carrying out each directive as it is given.

What do you find after the long climb? Look out and observe the scenery. It would seem that you are standing on top of the world with the hills and valleys stretched out far below. In the distance, there are farms and villages, streams and rivers; and far away, there are oceans and cities. There are those whose shoulders are stooped with the burden of living and others whose song reflects the joy of being alive. There is the world peopled with millions of human beings, all alone within themselves, locked within a prison of flesh and thought and emotion, the grave of the spirit. Yet, here and there that spirit burns up bright and a light radiates from a point within the prison to reach out and touch other points. By this light we are joined, but most of us are afraid, and burrow deeper into the mass of darkness surrounding us.

Dimly, down through the clouds you can see that place from which you have arisen and those whom, it seems, you have left behind.

Now look up through the vast expanse of sky to see the sun shining down upon you. You see first its golden hue, but as you look you note its steady blue center like a great all-seeing eye and the orange corona which leaps far out into space around it. The eye is magnetic and seems to be calling you and you yearn toward the sun, but there is only space between you, and no way of passing through it.

You are filled with despair, for here within your vision is a promise of eternal life and wisdom. Here is the resurrection of your soul from darkness into Light, yet you are held from it by the gulf of space.

As you look, the space becomes dark and you draw back troubled and afraid. The sun still beckons. It is clearly visible, yet between you and the sun there is a dark void.

In your heart you know what that void is. It is your own fear, the darkness of your own ignorance which stretches out before you to bar entry into the saving light of the sun.

Knowing this, you take a firmer grip upon yourself and look steadily across the void into the blue eye of the sun. And from that eye, in the space between, a pathway is formed of silver and golden threads of light. It is so narrow as to resemble a razor's edge; and over this narrow bridge you must cross the void.

Suddenly, without consciously taking but one step, you are deep within the heart of the sun, and here you know reality.

Here is the humanity you thought you left behind. All humanity is one, for here is the One Life that reaches deep into the heart and mind of everyone to form their soul and give them sustenance. This is Christ, who has given Himself to the cross of flesh so that humanity might live.

Here are we, brothers in Christ and yet, in that dim dark world, we know it not. Here is God, the Father; God, the Mother; and God, the Son. Here is the good, the true and the beautiful, that life in which we live, move and have our being, and in which we are one.

Lesson 16

Just as suddenly, you are back again upon your mountain top, standing on the brink of the void with the narrow ribbon of silver and golden light stretching out before you, knowing that it is your task to cross it step by step. Later, much later, you will discover a deeper more profound meaning underlying this tiny thread of light, but for now you know only that it constitutes the pathway out of your own spiritual ignorance into the wisdom of your soul.

The mountaintop symbolizes that center between the brows, which will be your first home in the world of mind. Here you will take up your residence, consciously learning to live in your head. We call this center between the brows the ajna center, and it is from this point of focus that we are enabled to control the forces of our instrument. From here we look out upon our world with a clear vision of it as it is in reality, free from the cloud of emotion which occludes that reality for so many. With such vision, the automatic response mechanism can be brought under control so that our responses to our environment are premeditated to produce the greatest good for the greatest number. It is impossible to become emotionally disturbed or out of control while one is poised in this center.

Learn, when emotional reaction threatens to engulf you, to stand steady in the ajna center and there to contemplate Truth.

The sun, which is shining high above the mountain top, symbolizes your soul, but at the same time, because your higher self knows no separation, it symbolizes the soul of all; of humanity; that life which is indwelt by the Christ.

The soul center does resemble the Sun, but it is not, of course, found within the frequency of physical plane substance. It is located in a much higher frequency above the top of the head where it overshadows the personality.

It is, however, reflected into the very center of the head, as a small golden sphere of light resembling a tiny golden sun, when the personality begins to aspire toward the Soul. As the personality continues to seek Truth and endeavors to apply that Truth in its daily life and affairs, the overshadowing Soul infuses the personality with its energies via this reflection of itself in the center of the head.

Please understand that this center does not truly exist until the personality, through its own effort, begins to invoke the attention of the overshadowing Soul downward. As it does begin to come into being, the wisdom of the Soul pours into the mind and brain of the personality and we gradually become enlightened.

The vast expanse of sky between the mountaintop and the sun symbolizes the area of mind that must be bridged by the aspiring personality before we can be born again in the consciousness of the Soul.

It becomes a dark void as we contemplate it, first because it is unknown and secondly because we fill it with the terror and the ignorance of our own subconscious.

We experience a glimpse of our higher self in the Kingdom of God. We know for a thrilling moment the joy of promised fulfillment and then we see that dark void which we must cross.

In the midst of our despair, as we fasten our gaze upon the Heart of the One Life, out of which our purpose comes, a pathway is formed. It is made up of a silver and golden thread of light so narrow it resembles a razor's edge.

194

Lesson 16

The silver light is that of the Christ as He reaches out to aid the aspiring disciple. The golden light is of the disciple's own consciousness as he goes forward to join his life to that of Christ.

John 11:25 "I am the resurrection and the life."

Along this narrow path we must find our way across the void of our own mind into full waking consciousness of our self as the Son of God in the Father's Kingdom.

You will note that the term "disciple" is used in the foregoing. This is because the aspiring personality has become the disciple of the Christ the moment it reaches out with its own consciousness to cross that void.

The path in the mind is reflected outwardly in the life of disciples as they apply the teachings of the Christ to their everyday affairs. It is a narrow edge they walk in the world, yet it is so broad as to include every human being as their brother.

Pause now for a few moments and focus the consciousness in the cave of the heart center as you have been doing each morning in your meditation.

Visualize the center between the brows (similar in appearance to the heart center, with the exception that it is a golden yellow in color), and think toward it as the new center of residence within your body.

Then visualize the tiny golden miniature of yourself in that center and focus your consciousness there.

Poised in the head, in the ajna center between the brows, contemplate the following concept for a few moments.

Creative Thinking

"I, ___your   name___, a Son of God, integrate the forces of my body, emotions and mind to aspire to my Father's Kingdom. Let there be light upon my path."

Then spend a few moments radiating light and love into and through your environment.

Do this meditation exercise each morning at a regular time and endeavor to conduct your affairs throughout the day from the ajna center focus.

Lesson 16

Notes

_____

_____

_____

_____

_____

_____

_____

_____

_____

_____

_____

_____

_____

_____

_____

_____

_____

Notes

_____

_____

_____

_____

_____

_____

_____

_____

_____

_____

_____

_____

_____

_____

_____

_____

Lesson 16

Notes

Creative Thinking

LESSON 17

Choosing and Directing One's Thoughts

Will Force,
The Mental Plane,
Working With Cause,
White and Black Magic,
The Forked Path of Decision,
Aligning With the Forces of Light

LESSON 17

The measure of one's will is one's ability to choose and direct one's thoughts according to a known purpose.

Every person can think to a greater or a lesser degree, but few people there are who have developed the necessary will-force to choose what thoughts they shall think at any given time. These few have realized that the individual's thought-life is the blueprint of their outer world that the forms created in mental substance are the patterns upon which their everyday life is fashioned.

This is a difficult truth to realize, for the thought-life can seldom be seen with enough objectivity to relate it to those happenings that are the natural effects of it. The mind struggles to comprehend its own laws and to train itself in the right use of those laws.

This is the problem of the person who is learning to live from a focus within the mind. During the past, these people have been the victims of thought, rather than the originator or manipulator of it. From their emotional polarization they have operated according to a sensed set of laws which function and can be applied only in the frequency of the emotions.

Now they find themselves growing up out of the emotional life into the beginning of a mental polarization which is for them a no-man's land until they learn its laws. The old ones with which they have been familiar for so long, and which they have learned to manipulate to their own benefit, more or less, are no longer available to them. They are very much like people from

America, who in England, suddenly find themselves driving down the wrong side of the street. They and others in close proximity to them are in extreme danger because they are violating a traffic law of this new country into which they have entered.

In another way they are like adolescents who suddenly find themselves between two worlds. They have taken on an adult stature while they are still child enough to be unfamiliar with the feelings and the ways of the adult. Their predicament is painful, and very real, for they do not belong. They have to make a place for themselves and they can do this only by learning those techniques that are of the adult world.

The mental plane is that area of creative substance that is causative to the physical plane manifestation. People who live in, and direct their affairs from this frequency of substance work with cause rather than with effects. This is the basic difference between the person who is mentally polarized and the person who still lives within an emotional focus. The latter is constantly challenged by, and must work in and with, effects. Causes are for the most part unknown to them, and they are a victim of circumstance. What they will do is always dependent upon an 'if'. If such and such a situation is favorable, they will be able to accomplish their goal, etc.

Individuals who have become mentally polarized do not depend upon the 'if' in the working out of their affairs. They create those conditions and circumstances necessary to the working out of their plans and purposes through their manipulation of cause. They set cause into motion from mental levels to manifest the effects in emotional and physical substance, which they *choose* to manifest.

It must be remembered, however, that they do this because they have learned how to do it, not because they have simply grown into it through an unconscious process of evolution. A person becomes mentally polarized through conscious effort to do so. They learn how to manipulate the laws of the mind through a conscious study of those laws, and a period of self-imposed disciplinary training in the application of them. Thus, they initiate their own growth into a new level of Spiritual understanding.

Working with cause has been labeled as magic down through the ages because the results appeared to be brought about by superhuman or unnatural methods. We continue to use this term magic, but we give it a different meaning. To those of us who are familiar with it, it simply defines the creative process as that process applies to a person's life and affairs.

"Magic is the manipulation of the divine law to produce an ordered series of effects in time and space."

There is, of course, a positive and a negative application of such activity since the pairs of opposites always manifest within the life and affairs of human beings. There is a white magic and a black magic. There are white magicians and there are black magicians. As we enter upon the path of mental development we choose via our attitude and our actions that which we shall be.

"White magic is the manipulation of the divine law to produce a series of ordered effects in time and space which manifest the good, the true and the beautiful for humanity."

The white magician is concerned with those effects that relate to the betterment of humanity as a whole. They are disciples of the Christ. Their purpose is to serve the Christ Life that both overshadows and indwells humanity. They either have embodied or are earnestly trying to embody the principle of selflessness that results in harmlessness of intent and a positive goodness of action.

"Black magic is the manipulation of the divine law to produce a series of ordered effects in time and space which manifest the separative goals of the magician."

The black magician is concerned with him or her self and their own rise to power or the accumulation of material gain. They care nothing for humanity, but set themselves apart from both God and humanity within the shelter of their own ego.

People who place their feet upon the path of mental development move either to the right, toward white magic, or to the left, toward black magic. They are confronted with the forked path of decision as they make those many small choices having to do with the routine of daily living. They are learning the creative process and establishing those patterns in mental substance which direct the weight of their creativity, toward the forces of light for the betterment of humanity or toward the forces of darkness for what they think is personal gain.

The major decision contained within a lifetime of small choices will affect their life and affairs for many incarnations to come, for they are building patterns of action, tendencies, likes and dislikes, etc., into their instrument, which will be carried over into the next incarnation as a part of the so-called inherited characteristics. These will affect the inner state of consciousness to be born into flesh until such time as experience teaches that consciousness that it is a part of the Christ Life.

It can easily be seen, then, that this particular phase of the evolutionary development (the beginning of mental polarization) is a most important one. Here in this cycle of growth a person sets into motion causes that affect their life and affairs for many incarnations. Such individuals set their feet upon the path that shall make of them a Christ or a devil insofar as their influence upon the world is concerned.

This is a concept to be considered deeply. All consciousness evolves into a more perfect expression of that which it is in Intent. While the Divine Intent of humanity is the expression of Christ, a person can, and many do, refuse to accept this destiny. When that happens, the evolutionary development is on the dark side, and we see the rise to power of a person like Hitler. Such ones form their own separative Intent, and cut themselves away from the Purpose of the One Life. What great and almost inexhaustible karma is the person's whose evolution brings them to this place? To have been the vehicle for the precipitation of the painful or enslaving karma of a mass of people, even though they may have earned such an experience, carries with it a retribution almost impossible to contemplate. How much better to have been the instrument through which the saving grace of the Christ is precipitated to the masses.

Yet, it must be remembered that neither is the result of one lifetime. It takes many incarnations of evolutionary progress to develop the destinies of each. Hitler gained his rise to power and became a focal point through which the dark forces were loosed upon humanity only after many lifetimes of evolutionary development. Many centuries ago he stood where most of you now stand upon the forked path of decision. His many small choices were made in favor of himself as a personality, and while they did not appear important at the time, they eventually led to that incarnation in which his influence was so great as to precipitate a world war and untold suffering for millions.

In the next few lessons you will be given the rudiments of the science of cause and effect. You will learn how to wield energies from a focus of the will in mental substance. During the next few incarnations you will become consciously creative to a degree impossible to imagine at this time. It would be wise to pause during the coming week and give deep consideration to the decision your attitudes and actions will constitute during the remainder of this lifetime.

Let your decision be a conscious one, made with an open eye to the eventual consequence it will bring.

Align, through the direction of your thought, with the forces of Light as they are wielded by the Christ, and invoke, through prayer, those forces to guide you in the small choices which make up this major decision. Set your feet firmly upon the right hand path, dedicating your creativity to manifest the good, the true, and the beautiful for those with whom it comes into contact.

Lesson 17

Notes

_____

_____

_____

_____

_____

_____

_____

_____

_____

_____

_____

_____

_____

_____

_____

_____

Creative Thinking

Notes

_____

_____

_____

_____

_____

_____

_____

_____

_____

_____

_____

_____

_____

_____

_____

_____

Lesson 17

Notes

_____

_____

_____

_____

_____

_____

_____

_____

_____

_____

_____

_____

_____

_____

_____

_____

_____

Creative Thinking

LESSON 18

Why Energy Follows Thought

The Creative Process;
The Law of Polarity,
The Law of Magnetic Control,
The Law of Precipitation;
Thought-Form Building

214

LESSON 18

One of the first laws of the mind to be grasped and understood by the seeker is a simple one that most of you have heard many times. "Energy follows thought." This is a fundamental truth which carries many connotations that must be understood in their entirety before People become the masters of their form-nature or their own fate.

Before we can begin to comprehend those connotations we must learn *why* energy follows thought. What are the more recondite laws behind this one which make it a fact in nature? Exactly what process takes place when mental substance is formulated into thought?

Thoughts are intangible since we cannot see, hear, taste, touch or smell them. We can only think them, and so to most individuals thoughts have no foundation in reality. Yet, they constitute the causes back of all that we experience in the outer world of happenings. Before there is experience there must be consciousness formulating thought within a mind which will direct energy into the form of experience. Thus, we see that all experience or any experience is the direct effect of a thought-life.

Which then is closer to the reality? The mental plane where cause is set into motion, or the physical plane where the effect of thought takes on an appearance to the physical senses of a consciousness incarnate in a physical body?

The three recondite laws behind the fact that energy follows thought can be defined in the following manner:

Creative Thinking

1. The Law of Polarity — when the polar forces of Will and Mind are brought into a relationship with one another, the creative process begins. A magnetic field is created within the mind by that polarity.

2. The Law of Magnetic Control — when a magnetic field is created within the mind and maintained there, mental substance is set into motion in the pattern dictated by the will. A thought is born via the magnetic control of substance.

3. The Law of Precipitation — when a thought is born, a triangle of precipitating energy has been brought into juxtaposition with time and space.

The magician (regardless of whether aligned with the white or dark forces), must consciously appropriate and wield these three laws in order to create a predetermined circumstance or situation in the magician's life and affairs. Please realize that this is not theory. There are today, as there have always been, those in the world who live alone by the creative process described above. It is a part of the evolutionary development that all people eventually experience. The time is coming when the entire race of humanity will demonstrate this aspect of the divine heritage.

"Man was created in the *image* and *likeness* of God." We are, therefore, creative in our likeness to the Father.

A concept may be inserted here for later contemplation and meditation...

"The Will to Be, focused within the Mind of God, created the first thought of Self. Thus did the conscious thinking 'I' come into being."

People who are just endeavoring to become mentally

216

polarized are confronted with the necessity to understand these three major laws having to do with the creative process. They must create. They must begin to dominate their form-nature and the environing circumstances of their life, because this has become their inner nature. They can no longer accept the rule of an unpredictable fate, for the nature of the consciousness polarized on mental levels is to create and to control their own fate.

The consciousness then seeks knowledge through study, meditation, and experiment. They will experience both success and failure, both pleasant and unpleasant results of their endeavors, until eventually they evolve into full knowledge of magic and the ability to apply that knowledge in their life and affairs. Their influence will be for good or bad according to their own motive, and they will reap their rewards accordingly.

Because so many have reached that place in the evolutionary process where they stand at the very door of this development, knowledge regarding it is being made readily available in response to their conscious and unconscious demands.

This series of instruction is added to the many others which are making an appearance all over the world today, in an effort to help guide the seeker along the path of Spiritual endeavor. It is hoped that in this way some of the dangers confronting seekers can be brought into their perspective, and that their decision regarding the right or the left-hand path can be made in full knowledge of what they are doing.

The creative process as it applies to the mentally polarized human being is described here with enough clarity that anyone truly desiring to use it may learn to do so. At the same time the student is warned there is a right and a wrong use of it, as there is with everything else.

Creative Thinking

The repercussions of either are much greater than any you have known in the past. The choice is yours, the responsibility of that choice is yours, and the effects created in the future by seeds sown in the present will also be your own.

The formulation of thought, which is the first act in the creative process, takes place when a consciousness brings its will to bear upon the mind. It is wielding the law of polarity. Will in use is nothing more than focused *intent*. According to the ability of the individual to bring an intent into focus within their mind will be determined their degree of creative potential.

Consider what happens in the mind when people begin to establish creative control over their life and affairs. The first and most natural effort will be toward the establishment of order within their life. They will usually choose to right some wrong (wrong because it is defective or unpleasant) within themselves or their environment. If they have a chronic illness, they will naturally attempt to produce a healing of it. If they do not like their job, they will try to create a better one. If their relationships bring them pain, they will either try to right them or to seek new ones.

They must realize that the condition they do not like is the result of their own thought-life. Somewhere in the mind they have focused an Intent to manifest the very situation or circumstance they are endeavoring to change. While they may not be able to get at the original reason for the focusing of such an Intent, they can, nonetheless, realize its presence in their mind. When they do this, they can, through a determined effort, cancel out the old intent with a new one.

Example:

A woman who suffers from chronic arthritis enters upon

218

the path of mental development and decides to heal herself. As she studies the laws of creativity, she realizes that she must be focusing the intent to manifest this illness within her body or she could not be experiencing it. Such a thing seems impossible, for she certainly does not consciously want to be ill. However, since she does not really know the truth of the concept, and cannot, until she applies it, she decides to prove or disprove it in practice.

If she is rightly guided, she will consciously build a thought-form of perfect health manifesting within her body, by focusing the Intent to manifest health within her mind.

The first response of the mind will be to contradict such a thought. After all, she is a sick woman. She can feel the pain this moment. She can look at her hands and see with her eyes that they are crippled with arthritis. She knows or thinks she knows the medical facts which deny her ever being free of this disease. How then can she be so silly as to sit and think of perfect health in this body?

For many this will be the end of the effort. They will have failed before they have really begun.

For some an emotional faith in God will still the doubts and permit the new Intent to remain in focus. These are the individuals whose emotional natures are devoted to God and can readily accept His mysterious power.

For a very few the contradiction of the mind to the newly focused intent will be a challenge, serving to strengthen her determination to carry out her Purpose. She will realize that the doubts are the result of the old intent to be ill. She may not know why or how that intent was formulated, but she will recognize its presence and, through such recognition, gain the strength to defeat it.

She, too, will demonstrate faith in God, but it will be of a different kind than that of her more emotional brother. She will know not only the Power of God transcendent, but the Power of God Imminent. She will realize that she has inherited the creative faculties of her Parent and is meant to use them.

Within her mind she will become a well woman by focusing and maintaining her intent to be one.

Emotionally she will gradually become a well woman as she accepts the precipitating energies of health from the thought-form created in her mind.

The substance of her physical body will finally respond to the down-flow of positive energy being directed upon it and within her body she will become a well woman.

This woman will have consciously wielded the laws of polarity, magnetic control, and precipitation to create a predetermined effect in time and space.

Lesson 18

Notes

Creative Thinking

Notes

Lesson 18

Notes

Creative Thinking

LESSON 19

The Goal of the Evolutionary Process

Controlling Substance;
The Relationship of Spirit,
Matter, and Consciousness;
The Path of Mental Development;
The Redemption of Substance;
The Motivating Impulse;
The Divine Purpose of Will;
The Developed Will

LESSON 19

As we observe the efforts of humanity to surpass always that which it has, or has not done, we come to the realization that the evolutionary process is devoted primarily to one great achievement. Human consciousness in every situation and circumstance, even in the never-ending battle for survival, struggles to conquer and control substance.

A human being is a synthetic creature, a combination of Spirit, matter, and consciousness, who lives first as a form, secondly as a consciousness within a form, and finally as a young God in the Father's Kingdom of Spirit and matter. These two forces, which can be more easily understood when they are defined as will and intelligence, constitute the creative polarity that God or human *must* manipulate in order to manifest anything in appearance.

Over a period of many long centuries, in which a unit of consciousness incarnates again and again, the consciousness gradually realizes its effort to control substance, to bend substance to its will, to mold it into those forms which, for one reason or another, bring it pleasure and satisfaction. These individuals realize that their endeavor to make money, to build a community, and to meet the demands of their apparent responsibilities are similar to the page of·problems with which a child is confronted in an arithmetic class. These endeavors are teaching them the rudiments of a science that they will use as they reach Spiritual maturity.

They enter upon the path of mental development, consciously searching for that knowledge which will make them master of their own fate. Seeking the philosopher's stone or the mysteries of creativity, they finally recognize the polar forces of their being. Will and intelligence. Like a light that illuminates everything it touches, the realization dawns. The equation they seek, the key to the creative process, lies in the proper relationship of Spirit, matter, and consciousness. They are the consciousness, their will is an extension of Spirit and their mind constitutes their quota of intelligent substance.

They have now grasped the thread of wisdom which unravels the mystery, rendering all that was dim, dark and unknown to them, clear, beautiful and knowable. They have entered upon the path of wisdom where the secrets of Spirit and matter reveal themselves to their consciousness. They have tasted knowledge and are becoming hungry for more.

Their next step upon this new path teaches them where and how to find that knowledge. In their mind they retrace steps taken in the past, looking closely at those simple facts with which they have become so familiar. They overlook nothing now, not even the most commonplace. For here, deep within its heart, may be another clue to the mystery. They know that every experience and every form in the world, from the conception, fetal life, and birth of a child, to the purchase of their own suit of clothes, is the result of the creative process. Nothing happens by chance. Not even an accident is accidental. Everything that is something had to be created by the same process that brought the human soul into being. That process works, whether or not its user is consciously aware of it. The task then is to become aware of it, to learn how to use it deliberately and with purpose. When humans can do this, they can aid in the redemption of substance, redeeming the form nature to the spiritual growth and development of human consciousness.

Lesson 19

As seekers cast their newly opened eye again upon their world of form they use the law of correspondence in order to further unravel the mystery — "As above, so below." The creative law works on all levels, and in all places. We discover it by observing it in operation.

The Divine Spirit, that which we call Father, is the motivating Impulse behind all that lives. It *is* the life, hidden by the form, working within that form to produce the growth of consciousness. It gives itself to matter, yet remains itself, within matter. This is God, The Father, the positive pole of manifestation.

The matter aspect, which in its highest frequency is the Mind of God, is the form building substance which arranges itself in the pattern dictated by the Spirit. Spirit enters into matter, Motivating Intent into Intelligence, and the Sons of God are born, units of consciousness born between Spirit and matter as the second person in the Holy Trinity. Thus, we conceive of God as being Three Persons in One. Father, Son, and Holy Ghost; or Spirit, Christ, and Matter.

"As above, so below."

"Man is created in the Image and Likeness of God."

The human soul, the small child of God, must then be a Trinity within himself, capable of the creative process. He is a consciousness possessed of a creative Will and an active moving Intelligence; and because he is, he has reflected himself outwardly via a body of appearance. That body is his instrument of contact with the frequency of substance within which he is temporarily living.

Via his growth within, and his contact with, this particular frequency of substance he will eventually redeem it to the Father's Kingdom.

Creative Thinking

According to his manipulation of his will and his mind, the human soul creates those experiences that evolve him into adulthood as the Christ.

Seekers who come thus far upon the path of mental development examine the development of their will. If their will is an extension of Spirit, and not just a part of their own personal property, it is already impressed with a Divine Intent. That is, it carries a Purpose that is above and beyond their personal self. Yet, their personal self is included in that purpose, since it (the Purpose) is of the One Life and includes all humanity.

Via their will then, seekers discover the Will of God. They align their will with the Will of God.

> Pause for a few moments and become poised in the center between the brows.

> Contemplate your faculty of Will. Realize that this same faculty is a part of the Divine Heritage of humanity, that every human being, regardless of who they are, is indwelt by this same Spirit which manifests Itself as Will.

> Contemplate Its Purpose:

> *"What is the Divine Purpose of my will?"*

> Align it with the Will of God:

> *"Not my will, but Thine."*

When we come to the realization that what we have considered a personal will is after all an extension of Spirit, we realize what is meant by free will. Humanity has been given the right to use God's Will, His motivating Spirit, the positive pole of the creative process.

If that Will is used for the sake of the separated self, rather than for the good of the human family, it is misused. An error is created in the nature of life, for the Will, any will, is God's Will and concerns His whole manifest expression of Himself. Thus, the admonition, "Not my will, but Thine."

It is suggested that the student give this concept much thought and contemplation for it carries within it the clear light of illumination. Such illumination reveals the Purpose of life itself, of humanity, and of the individual.

Attempt to become acquainted with this faculty. How does it function? What is its stage or degree of development?

A developed will is:

1. directive — it directs the life and affairs according to a known purpose;

2. creative — it creates the forms which will aid the life in the accomplishment of its plans;

3. magnetic — it attracts to the life all that is needed to carry out the planned activity.

In addition to the above, the will, when aligned with its source, becomes the faculty of inspiration. It brings into the mind all of that knowledge relative to the growth and expansion of the consciousness involved.

Notes

_____

_____

_____

_____

_____

_____

_____

_____

_____

_____

_____

_____

_____

_____

_____

Lesson 19

Notes

_____

_____

_____

_____

_____

_____

_____

_____

_____

_____

_____

_____

_____

_____

_____

_____

_____

_____

Creative Thinking

LESSON 20

The White Magician

Thought-Forms Direct Feelings,
We Can Choose our Feelings,
Choosing and Creating Consciously,
Growing Into the Expression of The Christ
by Practicing the Techniques,
Appropriating the Law of Polarity,
Building a Thought-Form,
Energy Follows Thought

LESSON 20

How has the will been used in the past to create the experiences with which the student is so familiar and often satiated?

If you will recall, in Lesson 13 it is stated, "Emotions are feelings which do not just happen to us by chance. We create them either consciously or unconsciously as we react to situations, people, or things."

Human beings will feel whatsoever they choose to feel. They react with a particular emotion in a given circumstance because, sometime in the past, with their will they created in their mind a thought-form that directs their emotional energies to express in this way.

In order for the student to grasp the reality of this concept certain experiments can be undertaken which will prove its truth.

1. Pause for a few moments and choose to feel a certain emotion. Do not think of a reason for this feeling, but only of the particular shade of emotion itself.

   Now, with the will focused in the mind, produce the emotion until you experience the depth of its feeling reaction.

   Relax the reaction (drop it or simply let it go) and calm the emotional nature.

2. Choose a different emotion, the opposite of the one just created, and again with the will produce

its expression until you experience the depth of its feeling reaction.

Permit it to subside and calm the emotional nature.

3. Consider a situation which normally produces a specific emotional response from you (preferably one of resentment or depression). Permit the feeling reaction to rise up from your emotional nature as you contemplate the situation, until it reaches its zenith.

   Now, with the will focused in the mind, take hold of this response. Realize that the energies you expend via this particular emotional response are the *same* energies you would expend if your reaction were one of love and understanding. It is the *same energy* impressed with a different *intent* by your will.

   Then ask yourself these questions:

   a. Is this emotional response adding strength to the forces of light or to the forces of darkness in my world?

   b. Are its effects of a beneficial or a harmful nature?

   c. Do I really want to react in this way?

Consciously and deliberately choose the feeling with which you will respond to this situation in the future. Focus the new intent by creating a thought-form in your mind that will turn the emotion into an expression of Christ-Love in response to the same situation.

Create the emotion until you feel love flowing out of you

toward both the situation and the persons involved. Then with that love ask the Spirit of Christ to manifest right relationship for all concerned.

Relax the reaction and calm the emotional feeling nature, flooding it with Peace.

What constitutes cause? What and where is cause? Does it lie in the experience or in the mind creating the experience?

"But there are certain experiences I know I didn't create," the student objects.

Are there, really?

If a human being holds within their mind a thought-form that states, "I do not like people who are dictatorial. I hate and resent them," they will attract such people to them via the magnetic quality of their will. The will attracts to a person all that is needed to carry out a planned activity, and the thought-form constitutes an unconsciously created plan — to hate dictatorial people. With their will, they create the experience necessary to their growth, in this instance growth out of hate into love.

A thought-form, regardless of its nature is a planned activity, for energy follows thought. It produces an emotional and a physical re-action.

It is suggested that students use the three experiments in this lesson as a daily practice until they teach themselves to choose and to create consciously, rather than unconsciously.

Adult seekers are too often lax in their application of that which is sought and has been found. If children are learning to read, they are disciplined to practice reading every day in school until they have become skilled in the mechanics of doing so.

When young adults enters college to learn a profession or a trade, they must discipline themselves to practice the mechanics of it until they become a skilled technician in their chosen field. They teach their form-nature to respond in a particular way via the self-imposed disciplines of a specific training program. Once this training has become a part of their built-in response mechanism and sinks into their subconscious, then their mind can be free to enter into the larger issues involved in their profession, but not until they have acquired the necessary skills.

This applies to the above techniques just as it does to everything else. If human beings initiate a goal of growth and development, they must discipline their form-nature to make that growth through practice and training.

Many times a student will read through a series of instruction of this nature once or twice, and accept the concepts presented with the joy of discovery and recognition, only to become disillusioned later because they cannot make them work.

They may apply the third experiment given in this lesson to a response they sincerely wish to change, working for ten or fifteen minutes to alter a pattern that has taken years to build. If, and when, they react again according to the old pattern they are dismayed, disillusioned and sometimes bitter. It didn't work.

Of course it didn't. Does a man play Chopin after practicing his scales one, or two, or even three times? Would the potential mathematical genius develop into the expression of her genius if she were not drilled in the fundamentals of arithmetic during her school years or

240

at some time during her life?

In the same way, people grow into the expression of The Christ by drilling themselves in the techniques of Love and Light attendant to the Christ Principle.

A disciple becomes a White Magician by practicing the techniques of White Magic.

Sincere students will establish a daily routine of practice in which they apply the techniques given them with a perseverance that builds them into their form-nature.

We have said that there are three major laws that are inherent within the creative process, and that students must learn how to wield these laws in order to master their own fate.

To do this they must work with each one separately until, via practice, they understand and can apply them in right relationship to one another. The following three exercises are given as a part of the daily training program to be initiated by the serious student.

Exercise #1 — The Law of Polarity has to be appropriated via comprehension and an act of the Will by the creative consciousness.

a. Realize that the forces of Will and Intelligence are the polar forces of creativity. They are the same to the Soul as Spirit and Matter are to the consciousness of God.

b. Realize that you have inherited these two forces from the One Life as your divine heritage, and that it is your divine right as a Son of God to wield them.

c. Then practice relating them, or bringing them

together in order to create a magnetic field of creativity.

1) Focus the consciousness steadily in the center between the brows and bring the Intent of the Will to bear upon the mind. (Let your Intent be a Positive one to manifest the Christ Principle in your life and affairs.)

2) Imagine these two forces, the Will and the Mind, coming together in the ajna center to create a magnetic field of creativity.

3) Then separate them, permitting the Will (focused Intent) to recede back into the head and the Intelligent substance of the mind to become quiescent.

Do this exercise three or four times daily, each time becoming as consciously aware of the Will and the intelligent mind as two polar forces, as is possible. If you persist in carrying out this daily activity, you will comprehend the polar forces and the Law of Polarity as a reality.

Exercise #2 — A thought-form is constructed as the magnetic field, created by the Polar forces of Will and Mind, and is maintained in the mind.

a. Focus the consciousness steadily in the center between the brows and bring the Will to bear upon the mind via the focused Intent to become consciously creative.

b. Maintain the magnetic field in the mind by holding the Intent steady and observe the construction of the thought-form. Do not interfere with the creative activity taking place, but rather observe the thought which is born in the magnetic field as a result of your Intent.

Lesson 20

Exercise #3 — Energy follows thought.

a. Allow a thought-form with which you are familiar to come into your mind and observe the directional flow of the resulting energy precipitation. What reactions does it cause to appear in time and space? How does it make you feel? What will it cause you to do if you permit it to persist?

b. Hold the thought created via the second exercise in the mind and observe the energy reaction it causes. How does it make you feel? What will it make you do *if* you hold it steadily in focus?

c. Consider the effect of this thought-form upon your life and affairs if it is built into the automatic response mechanism.

Notes

_____

_____

_____

_____

_____

_____

_____

_____

_____

_____

_____

_____

_____

_____

_____

_____

_____

Lesson 20

Notes

_____

_____

_____

_____

_____

_____

_____

_____

_____

_____

_____

_____

_____

_____

_____

_____

_____

_____

_____

Creative Thinking

LESSON 21

Self Awareness

The One Life; Aloneness; Fear of Death;
The Seven Kingdoms of Nature:
Mineral Kingdom, Plant Kingdom,
Animal Kingdom, Human Kingdom,
The Spiritual Kingdom of Conscious Souls,
The Kingdom of Monads, The Kingdom of the Logoi;
Integration of Body, Emotions, and Mind
in Aspiration to the Father's Kingdom

LESSON 21

Humanity is an integral part of that Life in which we live, move, and have our being. Our appearance is as a separate entity, independent of, though related to, other lives, and because of this appearance we seldom realize our full identity or our field of Spiritual relationships.

Individuals think they come into the world alone and go out of it alone; that the innermost privacy of their mind and emotions are peculiarly theirs, different somehow from the mind and emotions of anyone else.

A person's definition of the self, which we find in Webster's Collegiate Dictionary is: "Homo-man — the genus of mammals consisting of mankind, usually considered as belonging to the order (Primates) which contains also the monkeys, apes, and lemurs."

Humanity today is a self-conscious animal whose conscious awareness is contained within the separative shell of its ego. Their relationships with and within their world are from a self-centered perspective. They see from within the self as the center, all that takes place outwardly as happening to, by, for, or because of themselves. Their God is placed outside themselves and their planet, somewhere in the vast, remote distance of heaven. They are separated in consciousness from God. The individual states in effect, "I am I — myself. You (meaning Deity) are God. We are separate, different, and apart from one another."

Other human beings they perceive as forms which impinge upon their consciousness from the outside, forms which they can never really know because they *are*

249

outside. Yet, these others do bring *them* pleasure and/or pain.

Their sense of aloneness even in the midst of the many is almost the greatest sense they have. It dominates everything else to give them the inner insecurity of the lost.

They keep that insecurity hidden from their own conscious mind to a greater or a lesser degree, but even though they bury it deep within their subconscious, it dictates many of their attitudes and responses.

Individuals are afraid to die because they really do not believe in the existence of anything outside themsleves. Their "self" is the form-nature; the body, feelings and thoughts. When these are gone, they are gone, God is gone, and so are their fellow human beings.

Yet, humanity is an integral part of that Life in which we live, move, and have our being. We do not come into incarnation alone and unaided, nor do we go out in such a way. An individual is not a tiny sphere of consciousness that is separate from all other beings. Individuals have only to arrive at the reality of the One Life within their conscious awareness to experience the fulfillment of their being.

The One Life indwells all forms from Its cosmic center of origin, giving each an identity and an expression of Itself. It flows into and focuses Itself within the many stars which make up the Cosmos, giving each the appearance of a life and affairs peculiarly its own. From the star the One Life flows into and focuses Itself within the orbiting planets so that each of these takes on the appearance of a life and affairs of its own. Thus, the solar systems and planetary schemes come into being.

250

Lesson 21

The One Life focused within a planet continues to indwell form, focusing Itself into seven Kingdoms in nature. Upon our planet four of these kingdoms have made an appearance in the physical plane. They are:

1. Mineral Kingdom

2. Vegetable or Plant Kingdom

3. Animal Kingdom

4. Human Kingdom

The other three remain as yet within the higher frequencies of substance, so we do not perceive them with the five physical senses. They are:

5. The Spiritual Kingdom of Conscious Souls. This kingdom of life is composed of those who have evolved into awareness of themselves as souls and who live as such according to the precepts and ideals of the Soul. It is in the process of externalization so that a new Kingdom in nature is being born upon the physical plane of the Planet. It will be differentiated from the human kingdom not only by its superior intelligence, which results because of its wisdom, but also by its altruistic Love. It will be group conscious, each Soul placing the good of humanity before its own personal pleasure or pain. This Kingdom is in the process of externalization *now* and will have become recognized by the general public by the year 2000. It brings with it great new revelations regarding humanity's origin, their destiny, and the nature of their life. It brings, also, the Reappearance of the Christ, that happening toward which we are now looking and working.

6. The Kingdom of Monads, more commonly known

as Saints, Elder Brothers, or Masters. These great lives are those who have evolved through the human and Soul Kingdoms into their adulthood as Christ, The Son of God. Each is a focal point of conscious awareness within that greater consciousness which is Christ, so that together they constitute the overshadowing redeeming, grace of God. In other words, their presence upon this planet, even though unseen, is its salvation from the illusion of the form-nature. They watch over, guide via inspiration, and intervene, when invoked, in the life and affairs of humanity.

7. The Kingdom of the Logoi. This is that center of consciousness within the Planet which includes within its awareness the consciousness of all lives therein. It is the Planetary Fathers Whose directing Will governs the life and affairs of the Planet according to a known Purpose and Goal. From here the Will of God is impressed upon all substance within the Planetary ring-pass-not.

Note. (A ring-pass-not is that vibratory frequency of light beyond which the consciousness of an organized life cannot pass. It maintains the appearance of an identity, separate in form from all other forms. Eventually, via the process of evolution, each organized life pierces its ring-pass-not to join with that life to which it is related via a vertical and a horizontal alignment.)

The latter three Kingdoms in nature can truly be called the Father's Kingdom, for here each life is consciously related to the Father.

As we pause for a moment and consider again the Cosmos with its Stars, Planets, and Kingdoms in Nature, in light of the above, it is possible to begin to sense with the intuitive faculty of the Soul and to respond to the

Lesson 21

One Life. That One Life first created all of these forms as Its Will to Be impregnated Its own Pure Intelligence; then It poured Itself in conscious awareness into the forms, imprisoning a bit of its own consciousness within each form as its (the form's) Soul. Yet, it remains Itself in Its own Cosmic Center of Origin. God is both Imminent and Transcendent.

Humanity is today a self-conscious animal. What will they be tomorrow? They stand upon the threshold of entry into the fifth kingdom in nature as more and more of their kind become Soul conscious. A person is a human being because that person is self-conscious. A human is a Spiritual being when, and because, that human is Soul-conscious. Their consciousness of Soul is the vehicle of its expression.

This is a critical point in the evolutionary development of humanity and thus we see the world of affairs manifesting one crisis after another. This will continue until humanity completes the next step in its evolution. When a certain percentage of its members are soul-conscious, its life and affairs will reflect the altruistic motives of the 5th kingdom and true peace will be enjoyed by all of humanity, as the condition most conducive to its Spiritual growth and development.

You are now ready for a new meditation exercise if you have used the one already given in Lesson 16 faithfully each day. If, and only if, you have used it each day as directed, you may put it aside and use the following one in its place.

Visualize the tiny miniature of yourself in the center between the brows, and focus your consciousness there.

Poised in the head, in the ajna center between the brows contemplate the following concept for a few moments.

Creative Thinking

"I, your name , a Son of God, integrate the forces of my body, emotions, and mind to aspire to the Father's Kingdom. I integrate the consciousness of my personality to become Soul conscious."

Then, endeavor to realize that you are a Soul, and as a Soul contemplate the One Life of which you are a part, drawing upon the memory of the concepts given in this lesson regarding it.

Then, spend a few moments radiating light and love and your realization of the One Life into and through your environment.

Lesson 21

Notes

Notes

_____

_____

_____

_____

_____

_____

_____

_____

_____

_____

_____

_____

_____

_____

_____

Lesson 21

Notes

_____

_____

_____

_____

_____

_____

_____

_____

_____

_____

_____

_____

_____

_____

_____

_____

Creative Thinking

LESSON 22

Spiritual Relationships Within the One Life

Awakening to World Need, The United Nations,
Finding a Teaching, Vertical Alignment Upward,
A Glimmer of Love, Vertical Alignment Downward,
Guiding the Lower Kingdoms, Reorienting
the Life and Affairs, Reflecting Inner Spiritual
Relationships, Brotherhood, The Growth
and Development of Consciousness

259

LESSON 22

When a human being becomes intuitively aware of the One Life their consciousness gradually becomes aware of their field of Spiritual relationships within that Life.

Prior to this their realization of relationship is largely confined to their immediate circle of friends, relatives, and if they have them, their enemies. For some this circle is fairly large, including such factors as business and civic interests, but for most it is relatively small and narrow, including only those who are of personal importance to the individual concerned.

Gradually, however, these persons begin to awaken and respond to world need. They read and hear the current news, and it begins to make a real impact upon them. They are becoming more and more concerned with what is happening in the world of affairs.

They may read a book, such as "Silent Spring" by Rachel Carson, and as a result their consciousness becomes aware, to some degree, of the problem of the environment.

They follow the news regarding the environment of their own United States, and try to understand both sides of this problem. Within their own mind they try to find the solution and very often form an opinion which may or may not be a wise one.

They study all of the literature they can find about the United Nations, and if they are idealistic and intuitively responsive to human need, they often become inspired by this great international organism created to serve

humanity. Here is a concrete form in the world of affairs that reflects, in part, the Divine Plan for humanity
during this stage of humanity's evolution. Here, leading
minds of many nations may meet and discuss their
common problems. Here, such discussions may avoid a
small or a large war. Here, the education and care of
the world's children, not just one group of young ones,
but the *world's* children, may be considered, planned
for, and put into action.

Such problems as social and economic adjustments for
groups of people in any one of the countries belonging to
the United Nations may find a voice and a solution through
the meeting of minds dedicated to serve humanity.

United Nations is often a source of inspiration to the
person who is just awakening to the One Life, and just
as often it is a source of unrest, of disturbing thoughts
when they are trying to sleep. "Where do I fit in?" they
will wonder. "What can I do to be of help?"

This individual is moving in consciousness out of their
small sphere of ego interest into a new realization of the
world in which they live. They want to become an active
part of it.

Eventually they come upon a teaching of this nature,
and one day they intuitively recognize that the many
members of humanity are intimately related to one another. They are, each and every one, a part of the One Life
that flows through a star, a planet, an animal, a person.

For the first time in their conscious memory they know
love, a glimmer of that Love which caused the One Life
to give Itself to a form and expression. Suddenly, all life
takes on a new importance, for regardless of how *lowly*
or commonplace its form, it is of the One Life. Behind
and within its appearance there is a Divine Purpose
moving it forward.

And if their intuition is sufficiently developed, they will recognize in this instant, the ever-present Presence of Christ, which is the consciousness of God in all things. They will understand the words of Jesus, "And I will pray the Father, and he will give you another Counselor, to be with you for ever, even the Spirit of truth, whom the world cannot receive, because it neither sees him nor knows him; you know him, for he dwells with you, and will be in you." John 14:16-17

In the first moment of realization, the individuals begin to grasp the vast connotations of the One Life. They are not only related intimately to humanity, but to all other kingdoms in nature as well, for where there is form, there is also the One Life.

As a part of the Human Kingdom they are related, via a vertical alignment upward, with those higher Kingdoms in nature that provide them with their Spiritual ideals and aspirations. The higher Kingdoms transfer God's Plan into the consciousness of humanity from their own higher consciousness of it. Humanity receives that Plan into its own mind and brain as the ideals toward which it strives.

As a part of the Human Kingdom, the individual is intimately related with the Planetary Life of which humanity is a part, and so on into infinity. They partake then of that Life which manifests the ordered Cosmos, that Life which indwells and gives meaning to form, that Life which is God.

Via a vertical alignment downward they, as humanity, are related to the lower kingdoms in nature. It is humanity's responsibility to guide their evolutionary development, just as those higher kingdoms in nature guide the human evolution.

Thus, they take their proper relationship within the One

Life to Its many parts, being receptive and responsive to the down-flow of ideals and ideas from above, and at the same time creating their impression upon those below, such as the animal and plant kingdoms. Thus, the One Life, in which they live, move, and have their being, evolves.

Such an experience demands a following period in which the individual reorient their life and affairs to the One Life, for to know that Life is to serve It. Their service now is to humanity, for this is the part of the One Life in which they find themselves intimately related with others. As human beings, they have an obligation to fulfill.

They must discover their relationships within Its wide sphere in order to know and understand their Soul's purpose for incarnation. Why did their Soul come into this body and environment? In order to grow in consciousness, yes, but also to serve. These people are no longer satisfied with just their own growth. They are concerned with the growth and development of *all* human consciousness into the Likeness of their Father. How may they aid this?

First, what constitutes their field of Spiritual relationships within the body of humanity? They are not only related to others as a form such as: parent, child, husband, wife, employer, employee, etc., but as a consciousness. It is in this relationship of consciousness to consciousness that Purpose is revealed.

Always they will find within the field of relationships those who are their elder and those who are their younger brothers, plus those who stand with them in the same Spiritual age of growth.

Note: The Spiritual Age refers to the age of the Soul, and not to the chronological age of the form. It has

264

to do with the number of times the Soul has reincarnated and therefore with the degree of past experience it has had in the world of form.

This inner Spiritual relationship is not necessarily reflected outwardly in the life and affairs of the individual. A younger brother may be their immediate superior in the outer life, just as an elder brother who is far beyond them in consciousness may be their child or their employee. Therefore, they must learn to intuitively recognize those relationships in order to relate correctly within the One Life.

Right human relations is a need and a problem the world over. It is perhaps our most basic problem, the base of our pyramid of problems; therefore, it is a subject of great interest and importance to the seeker and the student of Truth.

The basic relationship between any two or more individuals or groups of individuals is that of brotherhood. All humanity is of one family, brothers in Christ. The quality of that relationship should be one of Love. The form it takes in the world is of a karmic nature. That is, it is a result of past action and/or mutual need for an experience that those related can give to one another because of their particular developments.

You may or may not have incarnated in the past with your present associates, but certainly you have been brought together out of a mutual need for a common growth. You serve one another's evolution via the interrelationship of your tendencies, talents, and problems. Together you contribute the factors that will serve the growth of each one, and so you are related outwardly via the forms most conducive to that growth. This is as true of enemies as it is of friends; as true of those who oppose you as it is of those who help you.

The purpose then, of any and all relationships, is the growth and development of every consciousness involved. With this realization held steadily in mind, the newly awakened human beings set out to discover their field of Spiritual relationships, and via that discovery, to establish right relationship in their life and affairs.

In the beginning, they will use three techniques as follows:

1. They will observe their close associates in a new light.

    a. They will endeavor to detach in this observation from the emotional connotations of the form that the relationship takes and observe it as objectively as possible.

    b. What are the other's tendencies, talents, and problems insofar as they know?

    c. How are these related to their particular tendencies, talents, and problems?

    Example: Individuals who have the tendency toward impatience will often find themselves closely related to those who aggravate that tendency. The relationship serves to teach them the need for patience and loving understanding while it teaches the other the need for consideration of others and loving understanding.

    — or —

    A woman whose life is complicated with the problem of financial insecurity may find herself in the position of being a leader of others whose problems are similar.

Lesson 22

The Purpose of this relationship could be manifold:

a. To teach the leader to place her faith and security in God in order to solve the problem and to serve more perfectly her function.

b. To teach those following to place their faith and security in God rather than in a leader.

c. To teach both leader and followers to work together for the common good of the group.

2. She will establish that quality of love within her relationships, which is brotherhood, by consciously serving the indicated growth that is the purpose of the relationship.

3. She will gradually ascertain, via intuitive recognition, the Spiritual age of the consciousness involved, and endeavor to relate accordingly via the services indicated.

Example: A man who recognizes one whose ideals and aspirations are Spiritually in advance of his own may choose to serve humanity by helping to transfer such ideals and aspirations to those who are Spiritually younger than himself, and whose need places them in right relationship with him for such a transference.

Creative Thinking

Notes

_____

_____

_____

_____

_____

_____

_____

_____

_____

_____

_____

_____

_____

_____

_____

Lesson 22

Notes

_____

_____

_____

_____

_____

_____

_____

_____

_____

_____

_____

_____

_____

_____

_____

_____

_____

_____

_____

Creative Thinking

LESSON 23

Integrating The Persona

Establishing Right Relationship with
the Body, Emotions, and Mind;
The Interrelationship of Humanity;
Peace on Earth and Goodwill;
Reeducation in the Concepts of Truth;
Integrating Humanity's Forces;
The First Real Approach to the Soul;
Proving Abstract Truth via Practical Application

271

LESSON 23

All of a human being's efforts toward self-improvement today are an unconscious response to the evolutionary demand that the person integrate the three aspects of that person's instrument; mind, emotions, and body, into a personality unit which is responsive to their Soul. Such people are attempting to establish right relationship within their own three-fold vehicle of expression so they may use it to fulfill that Purpose for which it was designed.

The integration of the substantial forces of an individual's form-nature is no easy task, as evidenced by the instability manifesting within the body of humanity today. All of these forces have to be brought into a divine relationship with one another and directed into channels where divine work is done. In other words, they have to be made to serve a Divine Purpose according to a Divine Plan if the world problems experienced by today's humanity are to be solved. It is no longer safe for people to pursue the old separative aims and ambitions that led to the isolation of one group from another. The forces of destruction have become too powerful to permit hatred and resentment or rivalry to exist between brothers. Humanity must find a way in which to live together in peace and good will. Evolution has brought us this far.

Neither is it the sole responsibility of one person or of one group of people to bring about the desired condition of peace and good will. It becomes everyone's responsibility to themselves, their family, their brothers, and their God to contribute their share to the effort humanity must make.

Why is this? Why is it no longer possible for individuals to sit in the comfort of their homes and let humanity solve its own problems?

Because humanity, through the rapid evolutionary development of the last fifty years, has become so interrelated that each of us not only experiences the effects of such problems, but contributes to their cause as well.

If one nation, or group, or class, is without adequate food, clothing, and shelter, it becomes a potential danger to all. It is prey to any ideology, system of thought, or rule that will give it an easement of the condition it suffers. Thus, the various "isms" find a vehicle through which to disturb the peace of the world.

On the other hand, that large group of human beings who are well fed, housed, and clothed tend to become complacent, to rest in their ease, resenting even that impact upon their security which brings them knowledge of another's suffering. This is a deplorable condition because those who follow the destructive path look for and find the hungry through which to work, while the majority of peaceful men and women draw into the false security of isolation in an endeavor to enjoy their peace.

Peace is a cause that demands the positive influence of those who seek it.

If we are to experience peace on earth, we must first exercise good will toward everyone. A united effort should be made, by all peace-loving peoples of the earth, regardless of national allegiance, to distribute the natural resources of the earth in such a way as to eliminate the dangers attendant with dire poverty from the human family. Poverty is one of the first problems that must be solved if humanity is to know an era that is free from the threat of war and destruction. Communism found its entry into the body of humanity through such poverty,

274

and today it poses the greatest threat of all to human evolution. The principle of sharing, which is a part of the teaching of the Christ, must come into practice as a voluntary response of humanity's love for humanity.

This brings us to another related problem. The masses of humanity must eventually receive a common reeducation in the basic concepts of Truth which are universal in their application to the life and affairs of humanity. If a concept is a basic truth, it must result in the common good; it must be as applicable to one as to another. It cannot be a basic truth if its results are apparently good for one group at the cost of misery and suffering for another group.

Human beings are yet children and they react as such. They tend to think in the patterns imposed upon them in their early years. Few are original and creative thinkers. Few are capable of seeing a truth through the veils of prejudice, of separativeness, and of isolation. Let a person who is idealistic in nature, yet prejudiced against the present authority, or those who are wealthy, come into contact with communism, and they will often gladly surrender the one authority for the other far more dangerous one. Misplaced sympathy for the hungry mobs and resentment against those who are not hungry, breed revolution and violence. Those who are idealistic and naturally sympathetic souls must have an ideal to follow, for most of them are also natural followers. They will work, fight, go to prison, or die for a cause which, to them, is just. If these could be educated in an idealistic philosophy, and their responses trained to recognize that ideal which is of the highest good of every member of humanity, true solutions could be found which would eliminate the threat of the various "isms" without war.

This presents a gigantic task for it demands the cooperative effort of those who serve the idea and ideal of peace, to seek out, to embody, and to teach the peoples of the world those basic concepts of Truth which are applicable to all humanity as children of God. If we would truly experience this world peace we constantly discuss, and seek through military defense means, we must realize that we are our brother's keepers, and serve the Divine Plan for those brothers.

The outer world of affairs is a reflection of the inner world of humanity, of which every individual is a part. If the inner world is one of instability, insecurity, and conflict the world of affairs will reflect these conditions as its problems. If individuals are at war within themselves, they will be at war with others. If many people are at war within themselves, they will reflect their problem outwardly as a world condition.

The responsibility must then be that of each and every individual in the world, for these make up the body of humanity.

Human beings must integrate their forces into a one-pointed direction before they can hope to take up the full share of their responsibility to their brothers. The integration of the substantial forces of the form-nature is the first responsibility of the individual to the many. They will contribute their share toward peace and good will as they bring their own instrument into an integrated unit that is responsive to this ideal.

The substantial forces of the form-nature are those forces that act to produce the affairs of humanity, the thought and emotional life which moves through the physical brain and body to relate human beings outwardly to one another in harmony or conflict. We call these forces, in their sum total, a personality, the face the Soul shows in the world of affairs.

Personality integration then becomes the necessity, as

the individuals respond to the impact of world need during this period of evolutionary development. In order to achieve this they must first understand:

1. The form-nature generally

2. The form-nature specifically

   a. mental

   b. emotional

   c. physical

3. The relationship between themselves as a consciousness and the form they inhabit.

In addition to the above understanding, the individuals must make their first real approach to their Soul via aspiration to Wisdom and a dedication to Truth. Their Soul becomes their ideal, and it is toward this ideal that they direct all of their efforts of self-improvement.

What is the Soul in relationship to the individual in the brain? This is ever the question that troubles and often baffles the student. Is this Soul something that can be proven practical in the everyday life and affairs? Or is it simply a theory that we believe because it pleases us?

A truth is of no value to the individual unless and until it can be proven to be practical in the daily life, for it is here, in the world of affairs that we are placed to work out our own growth and development. What good is the concept of Soul if it is only something about which we dream and theorize?

Therefore, the first step seekers take after having found the abstract theory is to work it out in concrete facts that are a living proof, at least to them, of its Spiritual value. This they do via experimentation with a formulated truth, using the technique suggested by the abstraction itself.

Example:

1. Abstract Truth that may or may not be correct insofar as the personality is concerned:

The Soul is a body of consciousness created by the Father, of which the conscious thinking "I" (the individual in the brain) is an extension. The major part of the Soul, that which we call the higher consciousness, overshadows the body via a center at the top of the head. It holds itself free of and above the frequency of the form-nature, but it does maintain a small thread of contact with the individual in the brain. Via this thread of contact the overshadowing Spiritual Soul extracts the Wisdom gained out of the individual's experience in the world of form. Via this same thread of contact, when the individual in the brain is seeking upward toward Light, the Spiritual Soul releases to that individual Spiritual Guidance in the form of ideas, realizations of Truth, and that wisdom which is applicable to the individual's particular situation.

Later, after the individual has evolved to a certain point of development, the individual in the brain withdraws the focus of awareness into the center of the head (just above the pineal gland) and the overshadowing Spiritual Soul consciousness descends via its thread of contact into the center of the head. Here in this center of Light the two are merged in awareness. The individual in the brain becomes the Conscious Soul Incarnate, an initiate in the Great White Brotherhood of conscious Souls.

2. Concrete facts to be proven via experimentation:

    a. That human beings are essentially a Soul.

    b. That human beings have available to them that wisdom which will bring peace, love, and harmony into their daily life.

    c. That humanity is superior in their consciousness to the form-nature they inhabit, and that they can order it to respond to their demands.

3. Techniques suggested in the abstraction itself:

    a. Through meditation, the individual in the brain aligns their consciousness with that of the overshadowing Spiritual Soul and discovers their true identity.

    This technique must be used over a period of time to be effective. These individuals must realize that they have to become fairly proficient in meditation in order to register the impression of the Soul. If the daily meditation is carried out honestly, sincerely, and with perseverance, average students usually satisfy themselves as to their identity as a Soul within three years time.

    b. Through meditation, the individual in the brain aligns their particular problems with the overshadowing Wisdom of their Soul, and in positive receptivity (with the mind quiet, but alert and attentive) awaits the inflow of Wisdom into their consciousness.

    This does not take so long to achieve as does the realization of actual identity. A meditation using the same problem each day will usually bring a realization of its wise solution from one to three months. As students become more and more adept in the use of the technique, the required length of time grows shorter until they can realize the solution to a particular problem in one, two, or three meditations.

c. Through meditation, the individual in the brain may invoke the Divine Will of the overshadowing Soul to discipline the form-nature in its responses. The form-nature is aligned with the overshadowing Soul instead of with the personal will or desire nature of the persona. The individual's success will depend upon persistence in holding the alignment throughout the 24 hour day. In this way, the consciousness gradually controls the bodies it inhabits. Thus, individuals become the master of their own instrument. It no longer controls them with its reactive patterns, its likes, dislikes, etc.

The student is advised to do more than give lip service to Truth. Prove or disprove its Spiritual value to your self via a serious investigation. Experiment with its applied techniques and discover your own path of Light out of the dark. It is this ideal toward which the personality integrates its substantial forces.

Lesson 23

Notes

_____

_____

_____

_____

_____

_____

_____

_____

_____

_____

_____

_____

_____

_____

_____

_____

_____

_____

Notes

_____

_____

_____

_____

_____

_____

_____

_____

_____

_____

_____

_____

_____

_____

_____

_____

_____

_____

Lesson 23

Notes

_____

_____

_____

_____

_____

_____

_____

_____

_____

_____

_____

_____

_____

_____

_____

_____

_____

_____

_____

Creative Thinking

LESSON 24

The Will of God

The Laws of The Will of God
In Relationship to Substance:
The Law of Economy,
The Law of Relativity,
The Law of Periodicity

LESSON 24

The form is always transitory because that is its nature. It is made up of acting, living, intelligent substance that responds to the Will of God. The Will of God is expressed via certain laws that work out as the nature of a life in form. Thus, every form receives its inherent nature from the focused Will of God. Humanity has only to understand that nature to consciously use it to their own advantage.

The Will of God in relationship to substance works out upon this planet via three major laws, which, in turn, manifest a basic nature within all forms.

These laws are:

1. The *Law of Economy* which states in effect —

   That all forms shall serve the economy of the One Life.

The activity of the One Life, insofar as this planet is concerned, is the growth and development of all consciousness therein into an expression of Divine Love Wisdom. This means that every form upon the planet, whether created by God or humanity, shall serve that Divine Purpose. It will, consciously or unconsciously, with or without its own choice, aid the growth and development of consciousness into an expression of Deity.

If human beings should choose to oppose the manifestation of the Divine Plan, or of law and order, their form and the form of their activities will still serve the Divine Purpose, if only through example. They may suffer and appear to cause others to suffer untold agonies as a result of their action, yet some consciousness somewhere in their sphere of influence will be directly aided in its growth.

Humanity has been given the freedom of choice to build whatsoever forms it can and wishes to build, but that is the extent of their so-called free will. The Will of God always supersedes the little wills of humanity to turn its works into some good effect. Thus, there is good in all things, even so great a misadventure as a world war. We have made tremendous strides in evolutionary development even during the last two bitter conflicts that have engaged the greater part of humanity in destroying members of its own family. While the minds and hearts of men and women everywhere were ruled and driven by greed, hatred, fear, or oftentimes bewilderment, to kill or be killed, the growth and development of consciousness still proceeded. Many have realized, with full clarity, the need for a Divine intervention into the life and affairs of human beings because of their experiences, and they seek to invoke it in the Presence of the Christ. Thus, we realize that nothing is ever totally evil or so-called bad.

This is an important concept for the individuals who are endeavoring to walk the upper way, for it has many applications to their daily life and affairs. In every appearance of opposition, disappointment, or failure there is an opportunity for growth. The individual who can seize the opportunity consciously and with Intent is gradually learning to master the form-nature.

2. The *Law of Relativity* which states in effect —

That all forms are interrelated and interdependent within the One Life.

Remember that the form is composed of acting, living, intelligent substance. This substance in its totality is the substantial body of God, the matter aspect, or the third Person in the Holy Trinity. The soul or consciousness aspect comes into being as a result of the interaction of God's Will and God's Intelligence, Spirit and Matter. Humanity's bodies are constructed out of this Divine Substance in three ranges of vibratory activity. As the consciousness attracts these intelligent lives (particles of Divine Substance) unto itself, and reflects its own Being upon them, they arrange themselves into a pattern, which, to the sensory apparatus, takes on the appearance of a form, according to the reflected state of Being (consciousness or Soul) to which they have been attracted.

If this seems difficult, pause for a few moments and try to follow the concept slowly and with care.

Endeavor to imagine Spirit and Matter as two polarities of one energy. Spirit is the positive pole and expresses as Divine Will. Matter is the negative pole and expresses as pure intelligence, or what we call substance.

Note. It may help the student to meditate upon the concept of intelligence and substance as being synonymous occult or Spiritual terms.

Between this polarity and because of its interaction, is born consciousness, a State of Being identified as Soul, which is first without form.

Imagine that Soul or Consciousness as being magnetically attractive to millions of tiny intelligent lives that we call substance. See those lives moving in toward the Soul, arranging themselves within its magnetic field according to the patterns Its particular state of Being creates via radiation.

Now imagine the tiny lives coalescing according to the dictated pattern, to produce the form of a body in three ranges of vibratory activity:

    a. mental

    b. emotional

    c. physical

Thus, the form comes into being with the Soul or Consciousness aspect at its very center, and the Spirit overshadowing.

The Soul is fourth dimensional, so while it exists in the very center of the form, as the self-conscious 'I', it also exists above and out of the frequencies of that form, as the created Son of God.

> Note. Humanity must turn its awareness gradually inward toward this center, which is in the brain cavity just above the pineal gland, to a realization of the meaning of the self-conscious 'I', before it can merge in awareness with the higher consciousness of that which they are in reality.

The majority of human consciousness has become identified with and imprisoned within or by the form-nature it inhabits. This means that its awareness, which proceeds outward from its identity in a horizontal direction, has been caught up in the glamour of the form. It identifies with the matter aspect in an illusory world of its reflection. Humanity has become negative in their awareness to the form they inhabit; therefore, its nature dominates and swallows up their Spiritual Identity in the One Life.

Magnetic radiation is a part of the nature of consciousness; therefore, the self-conscious 'I' indwelling a form, continues to radiate its state of being aware into and through the form to create another magnetic field. This second magnetic field is in the outer world of affairs, and within it falls the individuals' immediate environment, their personal sphere of influence.

The forms in the physical plane of affairs are, again, intelligent lives that are attracted into a pattern of relationship according to the radiation exerted upon them by consciousness.

Again pause, and consider the concept carefully.

The individual in the brain is a soul, a state of consciousness that is a state of being aware. Individuals radiate that awareness through their mental, emotional, and physical bodies into the world of affairs as a magnetic field. While we may not perceive this radiation with the physical senses, we can see its effects in the very substance of our environment.

The radiation is magnetically attractive. It attracts the substance and forms of the environment into specific patterns of relationship that provide the experiences necessary to the growth and development of the consciousness involved.

If this seems difficult, consider your own radiation. Of what are you aware? If your awareness is of limitation, unhappiness, etc., you will manifest, via attraction, that same condition in your life and affairs.

What is life, but God's gift to the living?

What is Love, but God's gift to the loving?

And what is joy, but God's gift to the joyous?

It is a good practice, at this point, for the students to define their particular state of awareness by writing it out in a notebook, and then compare it with those forms of experience that they are continually meeting in the everyday life. This brings one to a sharp realization of one's own need *in consciousness,* the need to expand the awareness to include and embody those Spiritual Truths which are of real value. Thus, our sense of value undergoes rapid and sometimes, radical change.

Because of the basic Law of Relativity, every form from individuals' bodies, their thoughts and feelings, to their experiences, has a specific effect upon all other forms and the consciousness therein. It is a One Life even at the lowest level of Its expression. Right relationship, or Divine Order, is achieved when the consciousness realizes this fact and relates those forms with which they are primarily concerned with the Purpose of the One Life. Thus do they hand the form-nature into the service of the Divine Plan, and become a conscious disciple of the Christ. Incidentally, there are many such in our modern world.

The forms (bodies) of humanity have a particular function within the Organized Life of which they are a part, which is their Divine Relationship within and to that Life. The forms that individuals build, since they are constructed out of Divine substance, should have, also, a particular function that is their Divine Relationship to the One Life. A form constructed for other than a Divine Purpose is a misuse of energy and substance.

3. The *Law of Periodicity* which states in effect —

    a. That every form has its own inherent cycles of growth, maturity, and decline, these cycles being impressed upon it at the moment of its conception by the focused Intent of the consciousness involved.

    b. That the cyclic activity of every form is peculiar to the form itself, yet subject to and contained within the more powerful cycles of that organized Life of which it is a functioning part.

This law is somewhat more difficult than the first two for the young student to grasp and understand, because it is more complex in nature and covers a broader field of knowledge. We shall touch upon it in this and the next lesson, and for those who are interested we shall proceed into a more comprehensive study of it in a later work.

Our first consideration of this law, in order to approach its meaning lies in the fact that every form carries as a part of its *inherent* nature its own cycles of activity. These cycles were impressed upon or impregnated within the form at the moment of its conception by the focused intent of the creating consciousness.

Let us consider the overshadowing Spiritual Soul contemplating reincarnation, and from its own plane, directing the building of Its new body of expression. The Soul holds within Its own consciousness a definite Purpose and Goal, the combination of which may be defined as a Plan of growth and/or service to be accomplished via this reincarnation. The Plan is the focused Intent, the Divine Will of the Soul, which acts as the motivating cause or impulse for the new cycle of expression of form.

In addition to this, the Soul has an old clay with which it must work, the personality consciousness developed via past incarnations. The old clay is molded by the motivating impulse or focused Intent of the overshadowing Spiritual Soul and a new form is created.

The Soul Plan lies within that form, as a specific pattern of growth and development lies within any seed. The Plan is manifested outwardly as the pattern proceeds to unfold within, via rhythmic cycles of activity.

Creative Thinking

These cycles are many and varied, major and minor. They constitute in their sum total the opportunities, the possibilities, and the impossibilities with which the incarnating consciousness is faced in its daily life and affairs. These cycles are the pattern by which the Purpose and Goal of the Spiritual Soul can be worked out into manifestation. They are truly the *seasons*, a vital and important part of the form-nature within and to which the incarnating consciousness must adapt, and with which they can cooperate in order to achieve their highest good in the physical plane of affairs.

Certainly to beginners it must seem almost impossible to believe that they can ascertain and understand their own cycles of activity. Yet, this is not only possible, but a part of the evolutionary development which everyone will someday achieve. Realize that this development is one that you are moving into now. Look forward to it with eagerness, and in the meantime endeavor to grasp those concepts that are an approach to full understanding.

Knowledge of one's cycles of activity is a part of the Wisdom of the Soul, and can be invoked into the brain consciousness via:

1. right aspiration

2. right meditation

3. right application.

Lesson 24

Notes

Creative Thinking

Notes

_____

_____

_____

_____

_____

_____

_____

_____

_____

_____

_____

_____

_____

_____

_____

_____

_____

Lesson 24

Notes

_____

_____

_____

_____

_____

_____

_____

_____

_____

_____

_____

_____

_____

_____

_____

_____

_____

_____

_____

Creative Thinking

LESSON 25

The Cycle of Life

The Movement of the Form in Time and Space;
Death a Release from a Phase of Growth;
The Three Major and Nine Minor Life Cycles:
The First Major Cycle, the Recapitulation Process:
The Physical Cycle,
The Emotional Cycle,
The Mental Cycle;
The Second Major Cycle, Service:
Service to the Immediate Environment,
Service to the Community,
Service to Humanity;
The Seventh, Eight, and Ninth Cycles of Life

LESSON 25

A focused Intent of the Soul, which we referred to earlier as the motivating Impulse for a particular reincarnation, produces a planned activity (form) which progresses to its conclusion via a cyclic, rhythmic alteration of the form. The Law of Periodicity, which, in conjunction with other Laws, governs this process, can be understood more easily as the Law which governs the movement of the form in time and space. It is this movement which results in activity.

The major cycle in the life of any form is that which governs its span of life, the length of time spent in appearance. The Soul comes into incarnation on a cycle that is determined by the Divine Plan of growth for that particular life in the world of form. Thus, the seed of death is present within the form itself at its very birth. One can state correctly that the cause of death *is* birth, the initiation of a planned activity. Such a plan must reach a conclusion. Make no mistakes, every little life serves a Divine Purpose in relation to the One Life. That Purpose is the growth of consciousness. The Soul plans from the end to the beginning; therefore, the conclusion of Its plan, which results in the death of the form, is a predetermined fact in *nature*.

Why does humanity fear death which not only releases them from their prison, but which marks the conclusion of a Divinely created plan? If humanity could but realize that death, when it comes, is their greatest opportunity, their release and in a sense their graduation from a particular phase of growth, they could meet it intelligently, absorbing from it a certain Wisdom that can be gained in no other way. Here in this Divine Law is an expression of God's mercy.

Do not misinterpret or misrepresent this instruction as a condonement of suicide, for it is *not* that. The overshadowing Spiritual Soul abstracts the incarnating consciousness from out of the form, according to Its predetermined Plan, at that cyclic moment which was initiated at the time of birth.

Later, as the Wisdom of the Soul becomes a part of the human consciousness, humanity will cooperate with this aspect of the Law, preparing for their discarnations with love and understanding, to finally move out of the form in full waking consciousness of what they are doing and why. There will evolve in the world of affairs a new science of dying, and, under Soul guidance, people will leave their bodies and their works with a sense of fulfillment, of achievement. Until that time comes (another great cycle in human affairs) the best preparation is the overcoming of fear and dread via right understanding.

The potential life cycle of a human form, insofar as present day humanity is concerned, is one full century. Cycles do vary with different individuals for reasons peculiar to the individual Soul; however, this cycle is standard or normal as a potential for average humanity. The Soul spends approximately from two hundred forty to three hundred years out of the world of affairs between incarnations. Again, this cycle may vary in particular instances, but it can be considered standard or normal for average humanity.

Contained within the one life cycle are three major and nine minor cycles which produce the growth, maturity, and decline of the form resulting in its climax or conclusion. They are enumerated and defined as follows:

The first major cycle is that which provides for the growth

of the bodies, and permits time for the recapitulation of that which has gone before, thus providing the opportunity for the integration of the consciousness in Its time and place, and the stabilization of that consciousness at Its point of evolutionary development.

It contains within it three minor cycles and an interlude, each consisting of approximately seven years. The emphasis of growth is placed in

1. the physical body during the first cycle of from one to seven years,

2. the emotional body during the second cycle of from seven to fourteen years,

3. and the mental body during the third cycle of from fourteen to twenty-one years.

During the first cycle, the incarnating consciousness recapitulates via symbolic experience that growth made when it was little more than animal life. This includes the Individualization period (when humanity realized it was a self-conscious 'I') and the development of the personal will focus which was made during the battle for survival against the odds of nature and the elements. Humans had to find their place in nature.

Thus, we see the child during this period recapitulating that growth in the development of a will that is primarily and normally self-centered, and the battle for survival of that will within its environment. During this cycle certain karmic adjustments are made so that each time more Wisdom is added to that already gained by the Soul from the experience.

During the second cycle the incarnating consciousness recapitulates via symbolic experience, that growth achieved thus far as an emotional human being in relationship to people and things. Here the consciousness re-experiences that first need to adjust within a society of individuals, to relate via feeling above the necessity of physical endurance or existence so the emotional life becomes more important than the physical.

During the third cycle the incarnating consciousness recapitulates, again via symbolic experience, the growth of the mind nature achieved thus far. According to its evolutionary development it learns to use its mind and to discipline its emotion from a mental control. It relates to its environment via a mental interest, and a developing sense of responsibility. In this time and place, insofar as the greater part of humanity is concerned, there is not so much recapitulation here as in the other two cycles. For, humanity enmasse is at that point of evolutionary development which has to do with the growth of the mind, and the building of a fine, clear mental body. Humanity today is in the process of shifting its focal point of attention from the emotional aspect of its nature into the mental. The recapitulation is achieved largely through book learning, the development of skills, and the emotional experiences that *demand* mental attention. Disciplinary training as to moral and *ethical* principle will soon receive a much greater degree of attention during this period in the life, from fourteen to twenty one years, than ever before in the history of our civilization.

This brings us to the interlude that again usually covers a period of seven years. An interlude is a pause between two major activities during which the consciousness gathers all of its forces into a center in preparation for a new initiatory effort. During this first interlude in the life the individual integrates and stabilizes that growth that has been made during the three preceding cycles. As these individuals near the end of the interlude they begin to align with the Purpose of this particular incarnation. Here is presented an opportunity to every individual to become consciously aware of their Soul Purpose and, in degree according to evolutionary development, of their Soul Plan. They not only realize responsibility but accept it and prepare through further learning to execute it. By the time they are twenty-eight years of age they should have reached maturity, i.e., have become integrated in time, or achieved continuity with their past.

Why do we see so little evidence of this Soul planned activity in the world today? Because humanity has so little understanding of their cycles of opportunity. The parent seldom understands that their child is recapitulating past growth via their everyday experience. Because of this, the parent seldom understands the child. The parents are handicapped insofar as aiding the young one's Soul growth is concerned. Because of this, the child does not achieve the desired continuity, but is lacking the necessary growth in those areas where adjustments were not made. Thus, we are the adult man or woman who is immature in certain areas of our consciousness and seldom capable of taking advantage of our cycles of opportunity. We have not grown up out of our past sufficiently via the recapitulation process.

This is one of the conditions manifesting in the world today as a result of humanity's point of evolutionary development. Yet, we are moving into a new age of growth in which the Wisdom of the Soul will make itself felt in the life and affairs of each and every one of us. The new age education will devote itself to the growth of the Soul within the child into that maturity which is a continuity with Its past and a realization of Soul Purpose. Thus, the young men and women of tomorrow will move forward into the world of affairs from a new point of focus, with a new vital sense of direction and a knowledge of destiny (cyclic opportunity). The individual's growth from the age of twenty-eight or thereabouts will be a *new* growth producing new experiences rather than the ceaseless repetition of old situations and circumstances.

The second major cycle is that which provides the mature consciousness with its opportunity to make a contribution to the society and the civilization within which it lives via initiatory effort.

It contains within it three minor cycles and an interlude, each usually consisting of nine years. The emphasis of the initiatory effort falls in:

1. Service to the immediate environment and sphere of influence during the fourth minor cycle of from twenty-eight to thirty-seven years of age.

2. Service to the community via an expanding sphere of influence during the fifth minor cycle of from thirty-seven to forty-six years of age.

3. Service to humanity via an ever-expanding sphere of influence during the sixth minor cycle of from forty-six to fifty-five years of age.

During the fourth minor cycle, the man or woman in the brain is given the opportunity to take up karmic responsibilities to family and associates via a planned activity which they themselves must initiate. Here they are afforded the opportunity of balancing old karmic debts via a new effort of love. Within this cycle of nine years they can, if they seize the opportunity presented by their Soul, balance most of that personal karma precipitated from the past into the present incarnation. In so doing they not only bring Divine Law and Order into their life, but they orient it as well to the One Life in which they live, move, and have their being. They tune in, so to speak, with God and reap the reward of many Spiritual experiences in consciousness.

During the fifth minor cycle, the incarnating consciousness turns its attention to a greater number of its
brothers, expanding its sphere of influence to include in
some field of service the community within which it is
housed and fed. Its planned activities are made with the
good of the community or larger group of associates in
mind. Thus, it is afforded the opportunity to balance
most of that group karma precipitated from the past
into the present incarnation. As it seizes this opportunity, it is growing ever more aware in its consciousness
that it is a Soul, and that like itself, its brothers are
Souls who need and have a divine right to the contribution it has to make.

During the sixth cycle the incarnating consciousness, if
it seizes the opportunity placed before it, begins to
think in terms of human need. Here in this cycle its
service potential is expressed and its contribution
reaches a height or climax. According to its evolutionary
development the individual now may contribute its
share to the civilization it has helped to build in former
incarnations. It may right an old wrong, or add to an old
good, either of which will have an effect of betterment
for many members of humanity. Its consciousness becomes more and more enriched with Spiritual values,
which it expresses in the life it lives.

This brings the man or woman to the second interlude
at the approximate age of fifty-five years. Again they
pause between the activities and gather together their
forces. At this time, during the nine years of interlude
they are faced with a major decision, the outcome of
which is usually determined by their evolutionary development, the need of their time, and their relationship to that need. They must decide whether to permit
the instrument to relax its effort as it begins its decline
or whether they shall force it on to new heights of service. Regardless of the choice they make this is an esoteric interlude in their life. They no longer expand their

activity, though, if they are taking full advantage of the opportunity of this interlude, they will maintain the useful function of their service activity. They integrate and stabilize their service on that level reached during the sixth minor cycle.

The third major cycle provides the incarnating consciousness with the opportunity to initiate a fresh new effort of service to humanity and the One Life, and/or to put their affairs in order. In either event the instrument has entered its major cycle of decline which affords the consciousness with an opportunity unparalleled thus far in the life in form for Spiritual growth. The consciousness is permitted to function with an ever-greater freedom from the demands of the form-nature. This cycle contains within it three minor cycles and an interlude usually consisting of nine years. The emphasis of the decline falls in:

1. The physical body during the seventh minor cycle of from sixty-four to seventy-three years of age,

2. the emotional body during the eighth minor cycle of from seventy-three to eighty-two years of age,

3. and the mental body during the ninth minor cycle of from eighty-two to ninety-one years of age.

During the seventh cycle the physical body begins to relax its sensory demands upon the incarnating consciousness. Its activity enters a gradual decline in intensity, the brain consciousness gradually ceases to respond to the emotional tides, and the physical environment itself relaxes its hold upon the human being in the brain.

This can be a very difficult period if not understood properly. It is the cycle most feared by the consciousness who is without a sense of purpose or divine direction. They feel themselves to be slipping away from all that is known and dear to them. If they are identified with and as the form, it is naturally frightening to observe its decline. They feel themselves to be dying, and not knowing what the future holds, they either put up a last minute resistance to the decline or tend to limit their consciousness and its effectiveness to the limitations of their instrument.

Misinterpretation of what is happening, and fear of the future, causes illness and failure of bodily function during this cycle and the premature death of so many. Senility at this age, or any age for that matter, is a condition created by humanity. It is not natural either to the form or the consciousness.

During this cycle of from sixty-four to seventy-three years, the incarnating consciousness may either initiate a new effort of world service or it may gradually retire from the field. If it does retire, it has the opportunity to enter a life of higher study, meditation, and contemplation. It may now devote itself to higher truth as the form nature relaxes its demands upon it.

During the eighth minor cycle the emotional nature relaxes its demands and all ambitions and desires fall away from the human being. The emotional tides cease and individuals are left free to function almost entirely in the mind nature.

If their evolution is such that they have a highly developed mental body, they may still be of great service to humanity. They are capable of formulating the Wisdom into concepts of truth that are applicable to their time and locale. They may be called upon for advice and counsel.

If their evolution has not reached this high point of development they are afforded the opportunity for conscious growth. They have the time and the inclination toward higher study. They may, if they wish, go so far as to prepare themselves mentally for future incarnations.

If they initiated a new effort of service in the former cycle it will reach its climax sometime during this one, and the human being will retire from the field.

During the ninth minor cycle the mental body enters its decline and the incarnating consciousness is freed from its demands. It ceases its constant form-making activity so that the thought-life gradually becomes quiescent. Here the human being is afforded the opportunity of real meditation, free of the thought-forms that formerly stood between themselves and their realization of pure being. They can now function in the realm of the Soul *if* they have taken advantage of all former cycles of opportunity presented them.

This does not mean that the mind becomes negative and impotent. It is held quiescent, but alert, attentive to the impress of the Soul, so the light of the Soul may pour through it to illumine the waiting consciousness. This presupposes an intensive inner activity.

This brings the individual to their ninety-first year when they enter upon that interlude between living in a form, and living out of a form.

The interlude offers the opportunity of quiet reflection upon the past and a reevaluation of all that has gone before (in this incarnation) in the Light of the Soul. This one goes out in full waking consciousness as they come to the end of their cycle of incarnation. They pass easily from their instrument and the world of affairs into that life after death which is natural to them.

Lesson 25

Notes

Creative Thinking

Notes

Lesson 25

Notes

Creative Thinking

LESSON 26

The Nature of the Form

LESSON 26

The three basic Divine Laws of Economy, Relativity, and Periodicity give the form its nature. It is within this nature that the incarnating consciousness is imprisoned, with this nature that we are for a long cycle of growth identified, and by gradual control and right use of this nature that we are finally evolved into a conscious Soul incarnate.

The student at this point must learn to bring down and apply the theory to everyday life in order to prove or disprove its Truth value. How can such a theory as this one be made applicable to everyday, mundane affairs? How can we relate the abstract to the concrete in such a way as to build a living structure of Truth?

The form, our bodies, and our environment—the thoughts and feelings we entertain and the acts we enter into, all serve the economy of the One Life. All, then, are by nature, imbued with a Divine Purpose, that Purpose being the growth and development of consciousness into an expression of Divine Love–Wisdom, or what we may define as altruism. This inherent *fact in nature*, a human being cannot escape. This is our Purpose generally, and specifically in the areas where we particularly lack altruistic motivations. Our thoughts, our feelings, and our actions will directly or indirectly, through suffering or fulfillment, pain or pleasure, according to our conscious or unconscious choice as a part of the economy of the One Life, evolve the consciousness within our sphere of influence into a greater knowledge of Divine Love. Others may look at us and observe, "That is not the way to behave. This is the way." Thus, we serve even without so intending. We ourselves suffer the repercussions of our own deeds, evolve and refine our expression gradually and finally into altruism. Thus, we cannot escape that Purpose which works out as a part of the form-nature itself.

The form nature cannot help but relate to other forms in order to serve that Purpose because Relativity, too, is a part of its inherent nature. It must relate to those other forms which fall within its sphere of activity, and in so doing it brings about a conscious relationship of the indwelling consciousness with other units of consciousness. Humanity will love or hate. They will attract or repel. They cannot remain indifferent and remain sane. The forms and units of consciousness within a sphere of activity become so interrelated and interdependent that regardless of the quality of relationship, they cannot live without one another.

This has become increasingly true in our modern world which reflects the inner evolution of human consciousness. A human being may love or hate, like or dislike, be attracted to or repelled by the forms of a grocer, banker, clothier, etc., but they cannot live the life they have chosen without those forms. No longer is it possible for a person, family, or even a nation to remain a totally independent unit. The economy of the world will no longer permit the continued isolation of one form and unit of consciousness from that life which is *humanity*. The interrelation of all lives, which reflects in the economy of our world, is pointing the way toward the reconstruction of humanity from centuries of painful experiences into an era of peace and good will.

We have only to make right use of this nature in the cyclic opportunities or seasons, which the form presents in order to pass successfully through this transitory period from one era into a new one. We may shorten the time of transition by taking our evolutionary steps consciously in cooperation with the law.

Lesson 26

Realizing that we are a part of the Economy of the One Life, and that the Economy serves the Divine Purpose of Life Itself, we may consciously appropriate Divine Purpose and the Divine Power which accompanies it. We may realize that we are serving the evolution of consciousness or Soul, and aspire to do so in a positive creative way.

Via rightly motivated aspiration we may invoke the Divine Will to illumine our consciousness.

Realizing that we must relate, because this is a part of our basic nature and the nature of the form, we may consciously choose to relate with love as brother to brother in the family of God.

We may then observe the cycles of opportunity presented us by the form, and in those cycles or seasons work out our Spiritual growth and development, creating a new civilization whose quality is that of altruism, and whose activity provides the greatest good for the greatest number. Do not forget that the greatest good of the many must include and begin with the greatest good of every individual. The One Life is focused into the many, and through the many into the individual.

Before we pass from our consideration of the nature of the form, there are two other even more basic and, therefore, more inherent characteristics of the form which are derived from the Negative Aspect of Deity.

These two inherent characteristics are of substance itself, before that substance has become assembled into form. They are:

1. inertia

2. activity

Creative Thinking

They result in the creative ability of substance to arrange and maintain itself in any form impressed upon it by a focused Will.

The natural motion of substance is rotary. A particle of substance rotates upon its own axis and tends, by way of its inertia, to remain in that motion constantly.

The moment Spirit enters the particle of substance's field of receptivity a new motion or activity is created. This is a circulatory motion. The particle of substance orbits around its positive pole of Spirit in a path created by the Intent of the Spirit. Its basic inertia will maintain it in the path first entered upon so that its orbit remains fixed.

As consciousness or Soul is born in the magnetic field created between matter and Spirit, it produces another new motion of substance. The particle not only rotates upon its axis, and orbits around its positive pole, but it now enters a spiral pattern of activity. The Soul, which is the mediator between Spirit and matter, exerts a magnetic influence upon the orbiting substance. That substance begins to spiral, moving closer to its positive pole as the Soul exerts its cyclic attraction upon it. Thus, evolution of the matter aspect proceeds, along with the evolution of the Soul. Forms are created, evolved, and finally lifted up into heaven (the frequency of Spirit) via the evolving consciousness or Soul mediating between Spirit and matter.

It is realized that much of this is abstract and difficult to grasp at the onset; however, the basic characteristics which work underneath the nature of the form can be related and applied to the individual's own growth and development as well as to their life and affairs.

Underlying the nature of the forms with which they must work, is an even more powerful nature of matter which must be taken into account.

The form naturally tends to repeat over and over the activity into which it is *first* impulsed. Thus, an automatic response mechanism is built into the physical brain and nervous system, habits are formed, and experiences repeated in an almost endless succession of cycles. Only the positive influence of consciousness, via conscious or unconscious reevaluation, can alter the already established motion (activity) of a form. The form will act because it must, for this is one of its deepest characteristics, but it will act in the pattern first established for it unless or until consciousness alters it with a new one.

The easiest and most effective way to alter the pattern of action is via the attraction of the substantial forces of the bodies (mental, emotional, and physical energy) up into a closer approximation to the Soul. That is, by consciously initiating an upward movement of these forces into the light of understanding, where, from a mental focus, they can be redirected into new patterns of activity.

This we call Personality Integration. All of the substantial forces of the form, which constitute in their sum total, the persona (the mask or face of the Soul) are brought into an integrated working unit by those who are consciously focused in their head. The whole being is then enabled to act, rather than to react, in the face of impact, because the response to that impact is impulsed from the Soul via the mind, where the Light of Understanding enables the initiation of *right action*. Right action proceeds via a rightly integrated and ordered persona from right understanding. Such understanding is never available unless and until the forces of the bodies have been integrated into a personality unit.

Consider these forces as the thought-life, the emotional

life, and the physical life itself, before they are integrated into a unit. Not only are the three aspects often at war with one another, but conflict *within* one or more aspects very often creates grave difficulties for the human being. If the thought-life is divided within itself as to what it wants, or believes, or even knows, it not only becomes impotent in so far as positive accomplishment is concerned, but it becomes destructive to the rest of the instrument and the environment. This applies to the emotional life as well. And when human beings' actions in the physical are contradictory to one another, they defeat their every endeavor, often to the point of insanity.

The personality is integrated into a working unit which is responsive to the Soul as the individuals take up their residence in the head and identify as Soul, and as such, attract these forces up into a focus where the patterns they tend to take can be reevaluated, and the forces redirected into the new patterns created by the reevaluation.

Remember, the Soul or consciousness aspect initiates a new motion or activity of substance. The substantial forces of the instrument are composed of many millions of particles of substance. As the Soul exerts a cyclic, magnetic attraction upon them they enter a spiral motion. As they orbit around Spirit, they move in closer to it, i.e., they lift in vibratory frequency.

Thus, as we take up our residence in the head (first in the ajna center between the brows) and identify as Soul, we are establishing ourselves in that polarization, which, as mediator between Spirit and matter, becomes positive to the substantial forces of the instrument. As we exert a cyclic magnetic attraction upon them every morning in meditation we are lifted in frequency out of the darkness of the old patterns into the light of understanding. The resulting reevaluations create new patterns of action into which these forces may flow as the consciousness expresses itself outwardly in its environment. The inertia of matter has been overcome to produce a new activity.

The life and affairs of such a one take on new meaning as they conform to the new influence, and the human being's life is obviously a positive contribution to the One Life.

In the next lesson we shall consider a new meditation technique which applies to the above process. In the meantime try to understand, in so far as is possible, the content of this lesson.

Notes

_____

_____

_____

_____

_____

_____

_____

_____

_____

_____

_____

_____

_____

_____

_____

Lesson 26

Notes

Creative Thinking

LESSON 27

Building an Ideal

Transmutation or Spiritual Alchemy;
Visualizing the Core of the Ideal,
the Christ Light;
A Triangle of Spiritual Force and
Three Characteristics of the New Ideal:
Divine Will, Divine Love–Wisdom,
and Intelligent Activity;
The Four Attributes of the Magnetic Aura:
Divine Harmony, Concrete Science and Knowledge,
Devotion to an Ideal, and Divine Law and Order;
Using the Ideal as a Seed–Thought in Meditation;
Twelve–Month Meditation

LESSON 27

With what *can* we identify if not with the form we inhabit? If we are not our thoughts or our emotions or our
physical body, if we are not even our name, what, then,
are we?

The sincere student of Truth, at this point, identifies
with an ideal that is made up of a group of ideas. The
ideal tends to be abstract and vague in the beginning
because the ideas are of an abstract nature. The beginning student has yet to learn to think abstractly in concrete form in order to create an adequate ideal that can
be clothed in mental, emotional, and physical substance. When we can do so our new identification ceases
to revolve around us as a dream within our wish-life,
and becomes a living reality in the world of affairs.

In this way, our dreams come true. They grow from
embryonic form into living realities because we have
impregnated them with Spirit, our own share of the
universal Will to Be.

Many students who come this far are frustrated in their
attempts to build the ideal. Almost everyone wants to
be better than we are at present. Almost everyone consciously or unconsciously seeks higher stature, but few
realize how to effect their own growth. The goal is difficult to describe in the mind and because of this few
realize just what to work toward. Self-initiated Spiritual growth is something of a new concept to the average person, yet it strikes a definite response from
within the very depths of a person's being once its significance is grasped. We immediately set out to formulate an ideal as a goal toward which we may initiate our

growth and development. The goal is generally constructed out of an ideal that is the polar opposite of what we appear to be at the given moment.

Obviously, if we are filled with resentments, jealousies, greed, etc., we seek to overcome these in the best way we can. Our first ideal is naturally constructed out of vague ideas of love, mercy, kindness, selflessness, and general goodliness. We will endeavor to change because subconsciously we realize that one can effect changes deep within one's own psychology.

The average person initiates this particular growth via a self imposed disciplinary action, and these people are proceeding in the right direction, but usually with wrong methods. Their disciplines are of a negative nature. They will discipline themselves not to resent, not to become jealous, not to permit greed to influence their actions, etc., and in so doing they only succeed in inhibiting the forces generated by these patterns. They are only initiating growing frustration, ill health, or at best a series of unpleasant experiences, because inhibited force builds up its power potential until, eventually, it must find a way out into manifestation. Thus, the usually calm and serene person explodes, panics, or freezes when faced with sudden crisis. Or people simply reach a breaking point when the inhibiting forces within them suddenly break into outer action, and they are controlled by them.

Obviously there must be another method of attainment by which humankind may safely effect its Spiritual growth and development. These negative forces buried deep within each one of us must be transmuted into their polar opposites rather than merely inhibited from expression. Such inhibition is nothing more than a superficial control of a dangerous power potential that must surely move into action via conflict both within the individual and the collective humanity. Ask yourself

Lesson 27

what is really behind mass violence, criminal behaviorism, or any act that is destructive of the common good. A small group of humanity playing upon the emotional life of a mass of people may trigger these inhibited negative forces to move the mass into violence against its better judgment. It takes but a small spark to touch off an explosion of such a power potential. Thus, for so long as the potential is present it is a constant threat to our peace and security.

Transmutation, or Spiritual Alchemy, is a science based upon Divine Facts in Nature, which we, as conscious Souls, can learn and apply to the betterment of our world. In a very real sense we are, in this series of instruction, dealing with the transmutation process.

How do sincere students begin to construct an adequate, well-rounded ideal?

We begin first with the very core of the ideal—identification. What is the identity of this new being we intend to become? What are its name and its place in the scheme of things?

Its name is Christ, Son of God. It is a child Christ, a young Soul born as a unit within the One Life, born of Spirit and matter into the human family.

This core is visualized as a tiny point of brilliant Light, deep within the self, which will, as it grows, develops, and matures, infuse the three-fold personality with its radiant Light. Via this Light, the Light of the Christ focused within the heart of each Soul, the negative forces of the personality, the environment, and finally of the world are transmuted into their polar opposites.

Thus, whenever the student thinks of identity the student does so in this way. This one realizes itself in essence, as a focal point of blue-white Christ Light and

331

Life within a sphere of consciousness called the Soul. The growth of this point of Light and Life, into a radiating blue-white sun that infuses and finally consumes the personality, symbolizes the Spiritual growth this one is initiating.

Thus, the core, the identity of the ideal, is established and takes on a comprehensible form. This can be worked toward as a goal of Spiritual achievement.

The next step in the construction of the ideal is the formulation of a basic foundational nature for the new identity. New ideas have to be formulated which will serve as the blueprint after which is patterned a *positive* disciplinary program for the persona.

What are the basic characteristics of this Spiritual being the student intends to become?

They are three in number, three characteristics which form a triangle of Spiritual force about the central core of Christ Light.

They are:

1. Divine Will. This is the first point of the triangle. Divine Will is inherited by the Son from the Father. It overshadows and infuses Him from above and directly aligns Him with the Father.

Divine Will works out in the inner being of the persona as it (Divine Will) infuses the three-fold nature (mental, emotional, and physical) of that persona, as the Will to Good.

It is expressed outwardly in the world of affairs as good will toward *all* members of the human family.

2. Divine Love-Wisdom. This is the second point of the triangle, located below and to the right of the first point.

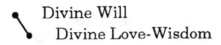 Divine Will
Divine Love-Wisdom

Divine Love is the basic nature and therefore the essential characteristic of the Son Himself, created by the interplay of Divine force between His Divine Parents. It constitutes His at-one-ment with all other human life.

Divine Love-Wisdom works out as Right Understanding or Empathy or Altruism in the innermost nature of the persona as it infuses that persona.

It is expressed outwardly as brotherhood, and constitutes the *quality* of the His actions as well as the reason for them.

3. Intelligent Activity. This is the third point of the triangle located below and slightly to the left of the first two points.

 Divine Will
Divine Love-Wisdom
Intelligent Activity

Intelligent Activity is inherited by the Son from the Mother. It underlies and substantiates Him, giving Him appearance or form.

Creative Thinking

Intelligent Activity works out as the creative imagination (the ability to formulate ideas into plans) in the innermost nature of the three-fold persona as it infuses that persona.

It is expressed outwardly as right action in the life and affairs of the persona.

We have now the basic structure of the ideal — a point of Christ Light and Life within a triangle of Spiritual force, that triangle constituting the basic characteristics of the ideal.

The next step is the rounding out of the essential identity and its characteristics into a whole being. To do this we have but to add the four attributes that form the magnetic aura of the Spiritual Soul, or ideal. These attributes are:

1. Divine Harmony. All of the tones of the persona have been tuned to the pure tone of the Christ, and harmony prevails in the auric influence of the whole being. They are in tune with the One Life. The effects they create in the world of affairs are in harmony with the Spiritual growth and development (The Divine Plan) of humanity.

2. Concrete Science and Knowledge. The forms within their magnetic aura are patterned after the Divine Facts in Nature. They are rational, reasonable, positive, and constructive. They are the application of the basic characteristics, found in the triangle of Spiritual force, in the daily affairs of the persona.

3. Devotion to an Ideal. The magnetic aura is aspirational in nature. It devotes its attractive force to that which is of Spiritual Import, and is thus constantly filled to overflowing with the Life of the Spirit.

4. Divine Law and Order. All forms within the magnetic aura are attracted into right relationship with one another and the One Life so that order prevails throughout the system of the whole entity. The Son of God lives according to Divine Law, therefore, manifesting via His auric influence, Divine Order, within the life and affairs of those whom he contacts.

The ideal is now formulated. Sincere students know what it is they wished to become. They comprehend in degree the goal of Spiritual growth and development they are initiating. They have only to relate the abstract ideal to concrete form, to step it down into a planned activity that will enable them to embody it. This they do via meditation, application, and reflection.

The ideal is used as a seed-thought in meditation. Students dwell upon it, endeavoring to fix it firmly within their mind until it becomes positive to all other thought-forms they have ever entertained about themselves.

In this way the substantial forces of the persona are lifted up into a higher frequency, because the seed-thought, as it becomes positively polarized, exerts a magnetic influence upon them. As they are lifted up out of the frequencies of the old negative patterns, they are impressed with new patterns dictated by the newly polarized identity and the old forms die through lack of use. Thus, the transmutation process, or Spiritual alchemy of the personality, form-nature, and the whole being is affected, and they are reborn into the Divine Life. The negative forces are no longer inhibited as a dangerous power potential for destruction, but are cleaned out and transformed into power for good.

The new meditation, which should be used for at least twelve months, with a new seed-thought each month, is as follows:

Creative Thinking

1. Become physically relaxed and comfortable (in a sitting position).

2. Become emotionally calm and serene.

3. Become mentally poised and alert.

4. Focus the consciousness in the ajna center between the brows and concentrate for a few moments upon the following:

> *"I am mentally polarized. I am integrating the substantial forces of my three-fold personality into aspiration to my ideal of the Son of God."*

5. Turn the attention to (visualize) a point of blue-white Light in the very center of the head bounded by a triangle of Spiritual force. (The top point of the triangle is located at the top of the head, the second point at the ajna center between the brows, and the third point is located outside and to the back of the neck.) Visualize a radiating sphere of golden light from the central point which is its magnetic aura in the world of affairs.

Contemplate from three to five minutes on the meaning of this symbol as follows:

> *"The Son of God is a focal point of Christ Life. That Life is characterized by Divine Will, Divine Love-Wisdom, and Intelligent Activity. Its auric attributes are Harmony, Concrete Science and Knowledge, Devotion to the Spiritual Ideal, and Divine Law and Order. I am that Life."*

6. Then meditate upon one of the formulated seed-

thoughts given at the end of this lesson from five to ten minutes. As you contemplate the seed-thought, endeavor to relate it to your own immediate life and affairs, as planned right action.

7. Turn your attention to the mind nature and repeat (audibly if possible)

"My mind is infused with the Light of Christ, made clear and vivid by that Light and transmuted into an instrument of service to the One Life."

8. Turn your attention to the emotional nature and repeat (audibly if possible)

"My emotional nature is infused with the Love of Christ, made calm and still by that Love, and transmuted into an instrument of peace within the One Life."

9. Turn your attention to the physical instrument via the brain and nervous system and repeat (audibly if possible)

"My physical brain is infused with the creative imagination of the Christ, all of the life of the physical is infused with the right action of the Christ, and transmuted into the temple of the One Life."

10. Turn your attention to your immediate environment and repeat (audibly if possible)

"My environment is infused with the Divine Attributes of the Christ to manifest divine adjustment in my life and affairs to the Divine Plan for humanity."

Creative Thinking

11. Write a report of your meditation results.

During the day, endeavor to embody your realizations via your application of them in the daily routine.

At the end of the day re-read your morning meditation report and reflect upon your day. How much of the ideal did you embody? Wherein did you fail? Keep a record of these reflections as well as of the meditations, and in this, your Spiritual Diary, you will have a record of your growth, which can be of tremendous value at a later date.

Meditation Seed-Thoughts for Twelve Months

Use each seed-thought, beginning with the first, for a period of one month.

1st Month:

> *"I, the Soul, have Purpose, Power, and Will. I infuse my personality with the Will to Good. I express that Will to Good outwardly as good will toward my brothers."*

2nd Month:

> *"I, the Soul, have Wisdom, Compassion, and Love. I infuse my personality with Right Understanding. I express that understanding outwardly as brotherhood."*

3rd Month:

> *"I, the Soul, know Right Action. I infuse my personality with that knowledge and express it outwardly as an intelligently planned activity of living. I am Creative."*

4th Month:

Lesson 27

"I, the Soul, sound the note of harmony throughout my personality and its environment. That note transmutes all conflicts it touches into harmony with God's Plan on Earth."

5th Month:

"I, the Soul, am the equation between Spirit and Matter. I infuse my personality and its environment with the Divine Facts In Nature, and transmute the form-nature into a vehicle of service."

6th Month:

"I, the Soul, am devoted to the One Life. I infuse my personality with the Love of humanity, and express that Love in my environment."

7th Month:

"I, the Soul, know and live under the Law of God. By that Law I restore order out of chaos."

8th Month:

"I, the Soul, discipline my form-nature to reflect the Light, Love, and right action of the Christ."

9th Month:

"I, the Soul, open the door of initiation and take the personality into the Presence of Christ."

10th Month:

"I, the Soul, sacrifice the personality claims upon my three-fold instrument to the Power of God, and learn the Ways of Christ."

11th Month:

> *"I, the Soul, mount the cross and take my place upon the path of discipleship."*

12th Month:

> *"I am the Soul here and now."*

Lesson 27

Notes

Creative Thinking

Notes

_____

_____

_____

_____

_____

_____

_____

_____

_____

_____

_____

_____

_____

_____

_____

_____

Lesson 27

Notes

_____

_____

_____

_____

_____

_____

_____

_____

_____

_____

_____

_____

_____

_____

_____

_____

_____

_____

Creative Thinking

LESSON 28

The Three Planes of Vibrating Matter

The Third or Etheric Plane,
The Reflective Surface of Time and Space,
The False Light and the Lost Identity,
The Overshadowing Soul Learns
Through Experience in Form,
Contemplating Etheric Substance,
Visualizing the Etheric Network

LESSON 28

In earlier lessons we considered at some length the general nature of the form. Now we shall consider it specifically in those vibratory frequencies that make up the three worlds of human endeavor.

When average persons think of their environment, they think only of the solid appearance of these three inter-related and interdependent planes of vibrating matter, seldom taking them into account as actualities. In their conscious awareness they live and work in the physical plane of appearances. While they think and feel within themselves they very seldom realize that they also live in a world of thought and a world of emotion. Thus, they are cognizant of only one third of their actual environ-ment, and that, only as it takes on a solid appearance before their eyes, while the other two-thirds remain beyond their range of perception and consideration.

Gradually this will be remedied as science breaks through the vibratory barrier of the physical plane to discover and explore the other planes of existence. Parapsychology is making a contribution to the expan-sion of human knowledge in its study of extra sensory perception and so-called psychic phenomena. Humanity has not long to wait before our horizons shall expand considerably, and not just into the reaches of outer space. In fact, our continued exploration and growing knowledge of the physical world in which we live be-come a danger if, and when, it is not adequately bal-anced and paralleled by a like interest in the very real worlds of thought and emotion.

However, while established science moves somewhat

slowly in these two areas, not having formulated methodologies for adequate exploration here, students of a new science called Applied Philosophy, which is in the process of emerging in the minds of humanity, may take definite strides in this direction. In so doing they will not only be paving the way for the entry of science here, but they will be precipitating the need for such entry upon scientific minds and brains. Thus, they who seek and study, also serve.

The world of solid objects within which you daily live, move, and work is but the outer appearance of three interrelated and interdependent planes of vibrating matter. We have in the past referred to them as mental, emotional, and physical in order to avoid confusion in the minds of beginners. Now let us be clearer.

The physical plane is, in actuality, the objectification of the three, rather than one of them. In reality it is not a principle, but rather an appearance or reflection upon time and space of three principles, namely energy, force, and substance.

The three planes of vibrating matter are:

1. the mental plane . . . . or energy

2. the emotional plane, sometimes called the astral or force

3. the etheric plane . . . . or substance

In this lesson we shall consider the third plane of vibrating matter, counting in frequency from above downward, the etheric plane or that of substantial form.

The etheric plane to the average individual would be considered as a plane of energy because it is in a higher rate of frequency than that of so-called solid substance. It underlies and substantiates, vitalizes and animates that appearance which we call the physical world. It is the basic substance out of which all things are finally made, the substantial, all penetrating, all pervading, ever present Body of God. Within it are the etheric forms (the vital — life bodies) whose appearances are reflected upon time and space as the solid objects of our world.

Its vibratory barrier has been penetrated, whether science realizes this or not, for electricity is drawn from it.

The universe, and every form within the universe, has its higher counterpart in etheric substance and has taken on appearance because of that counterpart. Without this substantial, vital-life body a reality could not reflect itself upon time and space.

Everything that is comes into solid objectification through the donning, so to speak, of an etheric robe (body) of substance.

The condition of the reflecting surface of time and space causes the reflecting form to be somewhat distorted so that we perceive it, not as it really is, but as it is reflected to our physical senses and brain consciousness. Therefore, it is very little that we know of reality.

We do not perceive, for instance, the human family as a one life because we see in the world many separated forms without seeing the more subtle streams of energy, or in reality of substance, which link them together as members of one body. This appearance of separated forms is a distortion that helps to create our sense of separativeness.

Likewise, we do not perceive the Plant and Animal Kingdoms in Nature as Entities within which the many plants and animals are held in relationship as members to a body.

Creative Thinking

We cannot normally perceive the interplay of energy, force, and substance between the many members of the One life and therefore we do not understand the relationships between them. Thus, we manifest in this world of appearances wrong relationship within almost every department of human living. We do not manifest order because we do not cognize the *ordered* Life of the One in whom we live, move, and have our being.

We do not perceive that it is via those etheric channels fanning out from every form to connect humanity via major arteries with every other form, that the energy of thought, the force of emotion, and the vital — life activity of substance is carried into objectification. Neither do we perceive our environment as it is.

How and why have we as consciousness become lost in the reflection and so — lost to reality?

First we have to answer the question — What is the reflecting surface we call time and space? What causes it? This is a difficult question for the beginner to ponder, but an answer can be given which will gradually illumine the consciousness if contemplated over a sufficient period of time.

Time and space are created via the movement of energy, force and substance as they are coalesced into form. Such movement (events taking place outside of time and space in consciousness) creates what can only be referred to as a false light, i.e., a reflected light within which such movement is slowed down as sequential happenings.

Consider the Soul, an individual unit of consciousness within the Life of a Planetary Being, looking down at Its own reflection in time and space, much as you might look at your reflection in a mirror or a pool of water. What if you were to lose your identity as a human being to the form upon the reflecting surface? You would be limited in your awareness to the limitations of the reflecting surface — its dimensions would be yours, its sensibilities would be yours. You would lose cognition of yourself (over a period of time) as you now are, and become lost to the reality of yourself as a human being in the world of human beings.

In a very real sense this is what has happened to your Soul consciousness, but only in part. It extended but a part of itself into the reflection, that part which is your "I" consciousness and that extension became lost to its true identity. It lost its awareness of itself as a Soul in a world of Souls.

But there was a reason for this, a Divine Purpose. The Overshadowing Soul learns, through the experiences of its extension in form, how to control and dominate substance and the form-nature, so that on its own level it may create with wisdom the forms that give it (the Soul) expression. As the extension fulfills that purpose, as it evolves back into the realization of God and Divine expression plus the wisdom gained from its experiences, the being becomes whole i.e., the extension is no longer merely an extension, it has become a conscious Soul Incarnate.

It is difficult to ascertain the actual nature of etheric substance, because humankind is so limited in its perception.

It is matter vibrating at its lowest rate of frequency, an aspect of the intelligent substance of God. It is then, in the final analysis, that vital — life substance that coalesces around energy and force to produce a substantial form. It is its nature to give form to that direction of energy and force impressed upon or flowing into it.

How does the personality focused in the distorted reflection of the true form in time and space apprehend and perceive the nature of the etheric which is the closest to us in frequency? Is it possible for us to tune our sensory mechanism into this frequency band, and if so, how do we go about it?

It is possible to perceive the etheric plane via the mind, brain and sensory mechanism, but it is a long, slow process of evolution that will eventuate for all human beings in the course of time. In the meantime, sincere students of these matters may hasten, somewhat, their evolutionary development by contemplating and experimenting with the following facts in nature:

1. Etheric substance is what is commonly thought of as the energy or force of action. Actually it is the *substance* of action. This is a term to meditate and think upon.

We commit the act, even a rash impulsive reaction, seconds before it takes form before our eyes. We actually accomplish the act in etheric substance, via the mind and the emotions, before it impacts upon the brain to produce a reflection of itself in time and space, which can be perceived by the sensory mechanism.

The average human being does not, as yet, live in the moment, but rather a few seconds after the moment. We have not caught up to ourselves, so to speak, but live behind our actions in the outer reflection of them.

Have you ever suddenly remembered living an exact moment in time before that moment? Have you ever experienced the bewildering sense of exact repetition in the scene taking place before you? If so, in those rare moments, you were closer in consciousness to the real act than at any other time.

Humanity's initial action is largely unconscious; it is almost entirely the result of automatic response rather than of a conscious focusing of intent. In order to act consciously one must consciously focus an intent in that pause between outer reflections of activity.

An important point may be brought out here. The brain is the station for transmitting etheric phenomena into physical objectification. This is difficult to understand so long as one is hampered by the brain. It is not an originator or a true formulator of thought; it is a receiver and a transmitter of that thought and feeling which is given form in etheric substance (the initial act) by an incarnate consciousness.

For instance, we perceive a tree first in its etheric form via our own etheric body before it is reflected into time and space via our brain to be perceived by the senses and retranslated in the brain as a tree. This is an unconscious act and constitutes a part of our unconscious knowledge, yet it is a fact in nature.

One can experiment with this fact by:

    a. Contemplating it until it begins to take on an aspect of reality.

    b. And attempting to lift the level of perception by endeavoring to catch oneself, so to speak, in the initial act before it happens in the outer reflection of time and space.

    c. Pausing between outer acts long enough to bring about an inner focusing of intent or will.

2. Etheric substance is the true vehicle of consciousness and expression. It is the medium within which the consciousness of all lives are truly focused, and the medium through which they express their peculiar characteristics, attributes and qualities.

Our consciousness actually lives within the etheric counterpart of the physical. This counterpart indwells, and animates the physical, yet it is independent of it. It can be withdrawn from contact with the reflecting surface by the Overshadowing Soul, and this is exactly what happens at that transition known as death. When it is withdrawn, the elements of the so-called physical reassemble themselves back into a reflection of the various frequencies of etheric substance. The physical body disintegrates into a reflection of the etheric plane because the animating form of that organized system of life (the particular individual) is no longer in juxtaposition with time and space.

The etheric body of an individual underlies the brain and nervous system, resembling a vast network of small tubes or channels which carry the vital life of the system, plus the energy, force, and substance of it into objectification via a system of etheric centers, the cerebro nervous system, the glands, the respiratory system, and the blood stream.

Fanning out from each physical form, the etheric network joins the major network underlying the

    a. family (immediate environment)

    b. community or group (influential environment)

    c. nation

    d. race

    e. humanity

via major arteries which connect all parts of the One Life into an interrelated whole.

Each aspect of the etheric is conditioned by the collective

354

consciousness indwelling it as that consciousness responds to stimuli with thought, feeling, and action.

In other words, the etheric network of the family (immediate environment) is conditioned by the collective consciousness of that family as it responds via thought, feeling and action to the impact of stimuli.

Thus, the life and affairs of all beings are interrelated and affected by one another.

One can experiment with this fact in nature by:

1. Visualizing the etheric network which underlies the body itself and, via that network, revitalizing and energizing the system with vital life energy by drawing upon the universal source of life and distributing it throughout the network. It will reflect in the physical as more energy and a higher tone in the general health.

2. Visualizing the etheric network that connects brothers one to another, and projecting streams of loving, helping thought and feeling to those within the environment. A close observation of such action will reveal the presence of the etheric as a medium of contact, communication, and expression.

3. Endeavoring to realize that you as consciousness actually dwell within the etheric, substantial body of God and that, via this body, you affect all other lives therein.

Later, in another series of instruction there will be given additional information and suggested experiments regarding the etheric for those who are interested. In the meantime, endeavor to expand your concept of substance to include this reality.

Creative Thinking

Notes

_____

_____

_____

_____

_____

_____

_____

_____

_____

_____

_____

_____

_____

_____

_____

_____

Lesson 28

Notes

_____

_____

_____

_____

_____

_____

_____

_____

_____

_____

_____

_____

_____

_____

_____

_____

_____

Creative Thinking

LESSON 29

The Goal Toward Which Humanity Strives

Learning to Make Right Use of Time and Form,
The Emotional or Astral Plane,
The Field of Force Around a Thought,
The Power Factor of Manifestation;
Astral Power Separative, it Attracts, and Repels

LESSON 29

One third of humanity's real environment is emotional. We not only live in and are influenced by activity in the world of physical appearance, but by activity in both emotional and mental frequencies of matter as well. Because we do not see emotion and thought as such, we seldom take them into account except as they manifest themselves in physical appearance before our eyes. Thus, we are aware of emotion and thought only after they have created an effect in time and space. We are so-called victims of circumstance because we have not yet learned how to take action in all of the frequencies of our real environment.

Consciousness is by nature timeless. It has its being outside of time and space, above and beyond the frequency of substance in what we refer to as the natural plane of the Soul (for lack of more appropriate terminology). Consciousness, as has been stated before, is the Soul. Soul is consciousness. The consciousness of any life, whether it be that of a plant, an animal, a human being or a solar system, is the Soul of that Life—the created Son Aspect of the Life in which we live, move, and have our being.

The Souls of all lives are in a process of evolution or growth. They are growing in likeness to the Divine Hermaphroditic Parent Who, out of Itself, gave them Being.

Humanity's consciousness, or Soul, is in process of developing into the soul-conscious Son of God. We stand midway in the great evolving consciousness between the mineral kingdom and the sun of our own solar system.

While we are, for a cycle, caught up by and imprisoned within the reflecting surface of time and space, we are in ourselves, in our own being, timeless. We may identify with form and its time, for a cycle, but we must eventually escape the illusion of time because it is not a reality (not natural) to our consciousness. This does not mean to say that time does not exist, but that time is of the form and not of consciousness. We have to learn to make right use of both time and form. We have before us the task of controlling both in order to take our rightful place in the scheme of things.

We do so gradually, by lifting our awareness above the reflection of our environment into the real environment where action takes place in the frequencies of energy, force, and substance. Slowly and carefully, we learn to create our own effects in time and space. Thus, in a very real sense, we learn to create our own time. We work with the energy of thought, the force of emotion, and the substance of action in the real environment to produce the effect, or reflection, in time and space that we wish to produce.

This is, during this particular cycle in human evolution, the goal toward which humanity unknowingly strives. It becomes, during this age of technical and scientific achievement, the common necessity. We have evolved into the great crisis of opportunity within which the human family chooses a higher path of knowledge and action. Such a path leads to wisdom.

We must lift our perception upward into those frequencies of causal action if we are to survive our own scientific knowledge and achievements.

We have stated thus far that the etheric plane is composed of that frequency of substance that coalesces into substantial form. This is the plane of intelligent activity where energy and force are directed into specific patterns of relationship, thus creating specific effects between bodies in time and space. Here in the etheric, the energy of thought and the effect of emotion become tangible and substantial. They take on an integrated body of substance that we call form, and which we perceive with our five physical senses as it is reflected into time and space.

The emotional plane, which is technically defined as the astral plane, is one of fluidic form. It is composed of that frequency of substance that gives a thought-form sufficient force to manifest in etheric activity.

What is a feeling? What do we mean when we say, "I love," or "I hate," or "I fear?" What exactly are we doing?

We are reacting in the feeling aspect of our consciousness to the field of force around a thought of love, hate or fear. That field of force is the astral form a thought takes as it descends the frequency scale of matter.

The astral plane is another frequency of the third aspect of the Holy Trinity; a frequency of substance found in the Negative Pole of Manifestation. It is composed of untold numbers of tiny intelligent lives who arrange themselves as magnetic lines of force around a clearly formed thought in sufficient strength to attract the necessary etheric lives who in their turn give the thought activity in substance.

The astral plane can be seen at the time as one of conflicting forces created by and, as the race mind reacts in the feeling aspect of its consciousness to its many experiences.

This tremendous body of power has an awesome effect upon humanity, both individually and collectively. There is a constant interplay of action and reaction between all aspects of the instrument (mental, emotional, and etheric-physical) and of the real environment, with the astral-emotional plane and bodies concerned taking the center of the stage, so to speak. Humanity as a whole is largely astral-emotional in consciousness. That is to say, humankind in total reacts in the feeling aspect of consciousness to and with force. Instead of thinking a problem or an activity through, humanity feels it through. They react to the field of force around a thought, and incidentally to the field of force around an act, with a reaction of force, rather than responding to the thought or to the act itself with a carefully conceived and directed plan of action.

Pause for a moment and consider your physical environment.

Imagine the etheric plane that interpenetrates the physical as being composed of tiny particles of substance resembling particles of light that are constantly relating in intelligent activity to produce the forms of your environment and your experience.

Take a few moments to visualize with the creative imagination this frequency of constant activity that interpenetrates your physical environment.

Then imagine in a higher frequency than the etheric, the astral plane occupying the same time and space as both the etheric and the physical. Imagine it as being composed of tiny particles of substance resembling particles of colored water that are constantly assuming relationships to form fields of force around any thought and action taking place within the environment.

Consider a thought common to yourself and imagine the field of force around it. Then imagine that field of force and the thought being carried by the etheric network into contact with another individual in the environment. See the thought, and particularly the field of force, make an impact upon the feeling aspect of the other's consciousness.

Imagine their reaction, first in the real environment, and then in the physical environment.

Do this with as many thoughts as you can remember entertaining throughout an average day and then ask yourself the following questions:

1. What kind of an impact do I most often make upon the feeling aspect of others?

2. What kind of reactions do I most often produce in others?

3. Do I need to correct my thinking and feeling habits?

What is the nature of astral-emotional substance?

1. It is the power factor of manifestation. Any thought which has been given an astral-form (field of force) will manifest in the substance of action. It will produce an effect for so-called good or bad in time and space.

Any act in substance produces a reaction in the astral, creating another, or adding to an already created field of force.

Because the astral-emotional frequency of matter is the power factor of manifestation, and because humanity reacts in the feeling level of consciousness rather than in the thinking level, astral force has a greater effect upon human beings at this time than any other single factor. If one human being loves or hates another, this created force has a greater effect upon both of them than any thought or act taking place in the real or reflected environment. Such force can heal or cause illness. It can produce peace or war, stability or instability, sanity or insanity. As has already been demonstrated in university experiments, it can produce health and growth in plants or cause them to wither and die. It can be consciously used to repel insects from a house, not by hating them but by loving them away. And it can be consciously used to raise the I.Q. and performance levels of a retarded child.

Essentially, astral force is power, power which humankind has yet to learn to harness and use for their own growth and well being.

2. It qualifies and conditions the form with a note and circumstance peculiar to the particular form. The sum total of astral force in any individual system (the three-fold body of manifestation) gives such individuals their particular quality and manifesting condition or circumstance, thus identifying and differentiating them from all other individuals. The sum total of astral force in any environment gives that environment its quality and manifesting condition, thus identifying and differentiating it from all other environments.

It is then by nature separative, seeking to separate in color or tone (quality) and condition one body from another.

It both attracts and repels, according to its dominant note. If the tonal quality of an environmental force is one of fear, it tends to attract into substantive form that which is feared, so the incarnating consciousness experiences over and over again those conditions and circumstances it fears. It feeds upon itself, so to speak, the field of force (fear) producing action in substance that adds to the original field via reaction. At the same time such a note will repel those experiences that would normally eliminate or decrease the fear. Thus, an individual or a group is caught up in an astral prison from which escape is impossible unless and until the light of reason can be brought to bear from the mind to dispel the cloud of fear which is blinding them to reality.

We see then that the astral environment not only tends to separate one individual and group from another, but that it also tends to imprison personalities in a repeating pattern of experience. It is, therefore, a drag against the evolutionary process even though it is necessary to that process.

Just how much is the average human being influenced by the feelings of others? This is a question of great importance to everyone who seeks self-improvement of any kind. What other people think and believe with feeling about us may be having a tremendous effect upon our ability to do and to become what we ourselves intend. We are constantly reacting within the inner consciousness to the impact of various force fields upon our own astral bodies. Our depressions, our hopes, ambitions, loves, and fears are too often not our own, but a result of powerful streams of force impacting upon us from without.

In later lessons we shall consider how the individual becomes positive within one's self, to these impacts, so that we may gradually become the master of our own fate. In the meantime, endeavor to cognize your astral-emotional environment. What kind of impacts do you most often receive? What kind of impact do you most often make upon others? What is the dominant note or color (quality) of your self and your environment? Are you a so-called victim of circumstance?

Creative Thinking

Notes

Lesson 29

Notes

_____

_____

_____

_____

_____

_____

_____

_____

_____

_____

_____

_____

_____

_____

_____

_____

_____

Creative Thinking

LESSON 30

Formulating the Blueprints of our Life and Affairs

The Mind and the Mental Plane

The Overshadowing Soul on the Buddhic Sphere;

The Rain-Cloud of Knowable Things;

Thought-Forms and Personality

The Mental Environment Consists of:

Though-Forms Within Which we Grew up,

Evaluation of our Experience,

Thought-Forms Impacting us From

our Environment and Other People;

Born Again in the Mind by Formulating

Intent into Causal Thought

LESSON 30

Mind is that frequency of matter that is in direct opposition (in that it is completely receptive) to the will. Through the manipulation of will and mind, humanity, as a unit of consciousness within the One Life, formulates the blueprints after which our life and affairs are fashioned. Here we are more creative than at any other time, for according to our formulation of mental energy into thoughts, and our assemblance of thoughts into thought-forms, so will our life and affairs go.

The mental plane is the closest in frequency to the natural home of the Overshadowing Soul. The Overshadowing Soul on its own plane, which is defined as the Buddhic, extends a thread of consciousness into the three worlds of human endeavor, mental, astral, and etheric, which is finally anchored in the physical brain via reflection as the personality "I" consciousness. As the personality consciousness evolves its awareness through experience in the three planes of vibrating matter, that consciousness thread expands to become a sphere of Spiritual Light, with the "I" consciousness residing in the mind to dominate the life and affairs through control of the three-fold instrument of contact (our own mental, astral, and etheric bodies) within the body of humanity. In other words, the "I" consciousness, formerly limited in awareness to the physical brain, shifts its point of focus, or polarization, out of the brain into the mind. It maintains a thread of contact with the brain, but is no longer limited in awareness to its physical limitations.

We have stated many times that the Soul on any level is consciousness at that level. Consciousness is awareness of being, which, through due process of evolution, eventually becomes pure Being.

The Overshadowing Soul, we have said, is that aspect of the consciousness that has kept itself above and free of the dominating form-nature. It is that part of the consciousness that is Spiritually identified within the Christ Life. It is awareness of Spiritual or Divine Being.

The mind then is directly overshadowed by a body of consciousness which is Divine in nature, and whose awareness includes a vast area of Truth which is normally, in this period of human evolution, not yet perceived by the personality consciousness. We seek knowledge outwardly through study, experimental research, etc., while directly overhead there is available to us The Wisdom of the Soul.

As the human being in the brain lifts the attention upward in frequency, i.e., begins to think in terms of Truth, to seek Wisdom, the person attracts an inflow of Divine ideas from the Overshadowing Soul into the brain consciousness. There is created in the mind between the Overshadowing Soul and the brain a field of magnetic light, oft'times referred to as the "rain-cloud of knowable things", into which the Soul precipitates its Wisdom in the form of ideas. As we meditate we render our consciousness receptive to these ideas, cognize them, and formulate them into knowledge, evaluations, and plans.

In this way, according to the ability of an individual to embody via application those Truths or Ideas perceived, the Overshadowing Soul gradually incarnates in *full* consciousness and the individual is no longer a personality identified as a human being. The individual has become a Conscious Soul Incarnate identified in the Spiritual Kingdom as a Son of God. Endeavor to grasp the concept here, of the transference of Wisdom (the awareness of the Overshadowing Soul) from the Buddhic sphere into the personality consciousness that is focused in the mental nature of its body of manifestation. The transference of Wisdom from above downward is the incarnation of the Overshadowing Spiritual Soul into the world of affairs — the real and final birth of a Son of God on earth.

What is the nature of mental energy? It is the creative material of the universe. It is that frequency of acting, living, intelligent life out of which a form is conceived as the consciousness brings Its will, a focused Intent, to bear upon it. One third of an individual's real environment is made up of this frequency of vibrating matter.

This aspect of the individual's real environment is of the greatest importance to them, yet the one of which they are the least aware. Contained within it is the sum total of thought-life to which they have given a house during their lifetime, that totality attracting, creating, directing, and controlling their outer experiences every moment of every day.

A human being's mental environment consists of the following:

1. Their interpretation and evaluation of those thought-forms within which they grew up as a child.
   a. concerning food, shelter, and clothing,
   b. concerning religion,
   c. concerning finance,
   d. concerning behaviorism,
   e. concerning sex,
   f. concerning their family's place in society,
   g. concerning the world in which they live (peace and/or war, etc.),
   h. concerning their own ego image, etc.

Creative Thinking

During the past one hundred years humanity has lived through the upheaval of two great wars, and the aftermath of each, rapid changes taking place in civilization as a result of scientific progress, economic instability that included a great depression and a great inflation, religious and social rebellion, and the rapid integration of many peoples, races and nations into a one world (with or without their willingness to participate in the One Life). Even those who draw into themselves and endeavor to live in isolated groups, such as the communist countries, still find themselves in related touch with and affected by the lives of those from whom they attempt to withdraw.

According to the reaction of the adults within their particular environments to all of these experiments, the thought-patterns of the children of the past one hundred years were established.

If a girl's parents were among the poor and resented the wealthy, these resentments were naturally built into her thinking. If the parents were wealthy and ashamed, guilty, resentful, indifferent, or protective of the poor, so, too, was she.

If they were Catholic, Protestant, Buddhist, Mohammedan, or atheist, this became her faith.

If a boy's parents were intensely patriotic, resentful, fearful, or hopeful during the wars, so was he. If they hated Germans, or English, Japanese or Americans, he shared their hate. Often it motivated and shaped his play. While his daddy killed in the front lines, he killed in his imagination.

If her parents were Protestants and hated Catholics, she hated Catholics. If they despised the Jews or Negroes, or the wealthy or poor, or the criminal or the sick, she too despised them. If they loved everyone, she grew up loving and understanding her brothers. If they were in conflict regarding their loves and their hates, their likes and dislikes, their ambitions and desires, such conflicts became a part of her.

And what did these adults, who were closest and dictators to the children, think of them? Were the children good or bad? Did they think they were intelligent and quick to learn? Did they like them? Did they accept them as Sons of God?

Whatever they thought of him and her became a major part of their ego image, the thought-form they constructed of themselves. That thought-form more than any other fashioned their personality; the face of them that is turned outward into the world.

2. Their evaluation of their own experiences as:
    a. a small child,
    b. an adolescent,
    c. a teenager,
    d. a young man or woman,
    e. a husband and father, or a wife and mother, etc.

The humanity born in the twentieth century has had to relate, via experience, to the sudden collapse of a false prosperity and the painful years of depression, war and the disillusionment of war, its aftermath, and the building of another economic bubble (a wartime economy in the name of peace). Their personal affairs have been conducted within this framework from which we could not escape.

Their greatest problems today are still those of economy and relationships, plus the almost unconscious fear of race annihilation. Their anxieties have become so great, and have been endured for so long that their consciousness is dulled to them. Humanity has accepted these as a part of their life, as necessarily there as the air they breathe. Thus, they have, in one sense, become lost to hope. They move with the tide, seldom making an effort to change it for it has become in their subconscious the ordained tide of their affairs.

How have we evaluated all of these experiences? What are our evaluations of our entire life and affairs from infancy to this moment? Whatever they are, they constitute the major part of our thought-life.

    3. The Thought-forms constantly impacting upon us from outside of ourselves via:
        a. the music to which we listen,
        b. the movies and entertainment which we see,
        c. the advertising constantly pouring into our consciousness from radio, TV, billboards, etc.,
        d. our Spiritual leader, if we have one,
        e. political leaders, etc.

    4. The thought-forms constantly impacting upon us from our real environment via:
        a. what other people think.

Are our thoughts our own? Can we think for ourselves? Or does our thought go as the mass thought goes?

This is a question which all individuals must eventually answer for themselves. One of the greatest spiritual needs within the body of humanity today is for a re-evaluation individually and collectively of the common thought-life. Our world is a reflection, all too accurate, of what we are thinking. Wherein have we failed in our thinking, in our everyday, moment-to-moment thought-life? For this shapes our destiny.

We have referred to mental matter as energy, differentiating it as such from astral force and etheric substance. It is negative to intent or will and causal or positive to astral force and etheric substance. Thus, via a manipulation of will and mind, humanity formulates its Intent to Be into a series of acts which we call experience. Actually, such acts are reflected back to us from the reflecting surface of time and space as experience, but for the moment let us consider them as taking place in the physical plane of appearance.

Energy, in our use of the term, is a potential, a causal focal point. A thought-form, any thought-form, is a potential experience in time and space.

Consider this in relationship to the ego image. The ego image is the thought-form human beings construct of themselves. It is constructed as their Will to Be is brought to bear upon their mind in the creation of a form (persona) in which to dwell.

Consider the same concept in relation to the ideal (the new ego image) you are now constructing.

Now endeavor to grasp the *reality*, the Truth underlying the concept of *self-initiated* growth and development. Initiation has to do with a new beginning or rebirth. Such beginning or rebirth takes place in mental substance. We are born anew in our *mind* via the formulation of Intent into causal thought.

What is the nature of mental matter? It is creative, formative, causal when it is related to its positive pole, the will.

Of itself, apart from and unrelated to the will, it is inert, inactive, quiescent, passive.

Consciousness at the center of *its* being, lives between and partakes of these two. Consciousness (Soul) is the mediator and the manipulator of Will and Intelligence, or Will and Mind.

Creative Thinking

The personality consciousness, that which is incarnate and identified with the form, lives within its real environment, mental, emotional, and etheric, and from here focuses its creativity outward in reflected experience.

When the personality consciousness expands its awareness to include its real environment and takes up its conscious residence in the world of thought, it may then create that experience which not only initiates its growth and development as a Soul, but which will aid the Soul growth and development of those within its sphere of influence.

Lesson 30

Notes

Creative Thinking

Notes

Lesson 30

Notes

_____

_____

_____

_____

_____

_____

_____

_____

_____

_____

_____

_____

_____

_____

_____

_____

_____

Creative Thinking

LESSON 31

The Origin of Thought

The Process of Thought-Form Building;
The Difference Between Will and Spirit;
Will is the Motivating Spirit;
The Will to Be;
The Overshadowing Soul and
The World of Abstract Meaning;
The Soul as Mediator;
Bringing Will Into the Mind:
The Will is Magnetic,
The Will in the Mind is Creative,
The Will is an Initiator;

LESSON 31

How does humanity formulate thought? What is the process we call thinking? Can it ever be truly known and understood?

We have said that a form is conceived as the consciousness brings its will, a focused intent, to bear upon mental matter. Yet, is not a focused intent already a thought? What is the differentiation between will and thought? Does not one presuppose the other?

It is true that humanity cannot originate a thought, any more than we can appropriate pure will, because we are living far below those frequencies of Spirit and Matter where thoughts are first conceived, and the will is undifferentiated by a Divine Intent. Yet, there is a difference between what we shall call a thought or a thought-form and the will, just as there is a difference between will power and the mind itself.

Will is that motivating Spirit within a human being's consciousness that causes us to be. It is found at the very center of the Soul (consciousness) and is an extension of Spirit, the Father Aspect of Deity. It is this core of Spirit that, as it is fanned into a flame, becomes the Christ Life. Here then, buried deep within the Soul is the Seed of God in humanity, the inner Christ, from which human beings derive their Will.

Emanating from this Divine Seed into and through the surrounding body of Soul or consciousness is the Power to Be which produces evolution via experience.

This Power to Be is an individual's conscious or unconscious

Intent, their Will to Be, which is directed by their conscious or unconscious ideal. In other words, their ideal is their focused Intent, that toward which they aspire and for which they work. All of their energies and forces are directed into activity by the ideal that constitutes their focused Will Aspect. In other words, it is the interpretation their consciousness gives to their Spiritual Will and Power to Be.

From whence does thought originate? Insofar as humanity is concerned, that is, in relationship to human beings, thought originates on the plane of the Overshadowing Soul as idea. This world of ideas is a world of abstract meaning where a meaning (and this is a good term to explore via meditation and contemplation) is formulated into an idea that has direct relationship to the world of humanity. In other words, here the meaning of a Cosmic Principle is aligned with and related to humanity via the vehicle or medium of an idea.

The Soul itself acting as mediator between the One Life and the part, ideates the Cosmic Principle into form according to its own point of evolutionary development as it relates that toward which it is evolving with that which constitutes its lower self or vehicle of appearance.

These ideas that are, remember, the point of origin for a human being's thoughts, directly overshadow the world of mind, which is the highest plane of the incarnate persona. How do they become thought-forms in that mind?

As human beings begin to use their mental body, they develop what we call the intuitive faculty. Their own consciousness bridges the gap between the mental plane and the overshadowing world of ideas as that consciousness responds to the Will to Be.

The Will power, emanating always from the central core

388

of Spirit, is appropriated by human beings as their consciousness responds to its evolutionary impetus.

They seize upon this Power and state in effect "I will be."

Then, according to their ideal of being, that Will is brought into a focus within the mind, at which time three things occur simultaneously:

1. The Will is magnetic. It attracts into the periphery of its activity those overshadowing ideas that have direct relationship to the ideal. The consciousness intuits the idea and interprets it according to its own ability to do so, *and* its personal motivation.

This is an important concept; all ideas are but the vehicles of Cosmic Principle or meaning. They cannot then be evil, but the interpretation given them by the consciousness can be distorted by evolutionary development and personal motivation, and they are always colored by the state of consciousness intuiting them. The color given may help to perfectly convey or distort the meaning intended but it will always veil to some degree the truth. Truth or Reality always loses something of itself as it takes on clothing whether that clothing be an idea, a thought, feeling, or deed.

The Will attracts on a horizontal level as well as a vertical one, so that other thoughts already formulated in the world of mind by other minds, having relationship to the ideal, are also attracted into its sphere of activity.

Other thoughts and evaluations in the subconscious are attracted upward, thus, the will focus in the mind has initiated the form-making activity via its magnetic strength.

2. The Will in the Mind is creative. It enables the consciousness to assemble all of these related thoughts into a thought-form. Many of them are automatically discarded, many are accepted, and some are set aside for future consideration. Eventually, a thought-form complete or incomplete, so-called good or bad, emerges in the mind of the thinker. They have a thought, or if they are well developed mentally, they may have a plan.

3. The Will is an initiator in that it directs energy into force, substance, and finally into reflection in time and space. Energy follows thought. A thought is a potential feeling, act, and an effect in appearance.

The moment the Will is brought into focus in the mind, and the form-making activity begins, energy turns into force on astral levels and substance on etheric levels. The human being has an emotional and a substantial reaction to the form-making activity. Those reactions may help or hinder the successful manifestation of their cognized intent, according to their relationship to it. If they are in conflict with it, they tend to negate the form so it manifests as conflict, or at best it is stillborn.

This is the process of thought-form building, which actually is carried out by a relative few in the world of humanity. These are the thinkers, the leaders whose formulation of thoughts is accepted by the masses.

Most of today's people receive their thoughts, even the ones they may think they originate, from the race mind via the mental aspect of their real environment. They accept these already formulated thoughts, color them according to their states of consciousness, and use them as their own, seldom realizing that they are being led and directed by other minds, or seldom questioning the

Lesson 31

Truth value of them.

Yet, today's humanity is in the process of building a mental body within which it can consciously function. The point of human evolution, and the stepped-up evolutionary impetus, has brought humanity up to the very door of entry into the mental plane. The world of thought is impacting as never before upon the physical brain of humanity, and the world of ideas is impacting as never before upon the mental bodies of the thinkers of the world.

Space itself has been superseded with time. Human beings can cross an ocean in a day, contemplate reaching the stars, and even now have numerous satellites in orbit around the planet.

We are moving. The forms of our world and of our beliefs are constantly changing with a rapidity we have never before experienced. The consciousness of humanity, largely emotional, is confused, bewildered, and alarmed. What does it all mean?

First of all, it is good. It is the working out of God's plan for us—the growth and development of our consciousness from the narrow confines of self into the expansion of Soul. We are growing up, and in the process, we are being confronted with necessary changes in our way of life.

We are being taught that rampant emotionalism is dangerous, that our separative hates and fears, ambitions and desires could destroy us. We are learning that emotion is a power that can be harnessed for constructive or destructive purposes. We are faced now in a crisis of evolutionary impact with the need to control the feeling nature with reason.

We cannot turn back the clock nor stem the onward sweep of evolution. Revival of old songs, stories, hopes,

Creative Thinking

and memories will not deny nor stop scientific progress.

We are here in this time and place, in this point of evolutionary development to learn some much-needed and long-discussed lessons. All human beings can find these, which are summed up in the golden rule, in their own religion, and in their own heart and mind.

Can we apply them? Yes, but to do so we must place ourselves in our mind and apply those techniques that will enable us to embody love. We must learn to think correctly and creatively. We have now to do more than pray, or profess a savior with the lips, or go to church. Our task is to embody, to bring the ideas which overshadow us into our mind and there to formulate a planned activity which we can carry out into manifestation.

This is humanity's next step, our immediate need, to supersede the world predicament with Love.

Lesson 31

Notes

_____

_____

_____

_____

_____

_____

_____

_____

_____

_____

_____

_____

_____

_____

_____

_____

_____

Creative Thinking

Notes

_____

_____

_____

_____

_____

_____

_____

_____

_____

_____

_____

_____

_____

_____

_____

Lesson 31

Notes

Creative Thinking

Creative Thinking

LESSON 32

The Practical Application of the Seven Rays

Promoting Peace by Manifesting Brotherhood;
The Seven Divine Laws
and Energies of Cosmic Love;
Appropriating the Seven Energies;
Energy Responds to the Focused Will of Consciousness;
Knowing Love by Becoming the White Magician;
Love is a Divine Energy;
Safely Appropriating an Energy Potential
by Identifying as The Soul Within the One Life

LESSON 32

Within our solar system, there are seven major Divine Laws and Divine Energies that are the interpretations and expressions our Solar Life gives to Cosmic Love or Pure Reason. These seven are also known as the seven rays and much has been given anent them in other works both by this and by other esoteric writers. In this series, we shall consider them from a somewhat different path of approach, formulating their practical application as techniques by which the sincere student may begin to embody love.

Actually, this subject, which shall be covered more expansively in another work entitled, *"Brotherhood, The Divine Order of Man,"* is a new-age approach to the age-old problem of how to love.

Most of us intuit and recognize the need for Love as the theme of life, but few of us know how to love in the face of our own built-in responses. Techniques, which can be applied by the beginner and the more advanced alike, are sorely needed by men and women everywhere. Therefore, the following lessons are offered in the spirit of love with the hope and prayer that such differences of opinion that might exist in the minds of students anent such controversial subjects as reincarnation, karma, etc., will not negate the use to which these techniques may be put. In other words, whether or not there is agreement between us regarding these particular subjects, the techniques are as applicable to one person in his or her efforts to embody love as they are to another person in his or her efforts to do likewise.

Thus, here is a common ground upon which we may all

Creative Thinking

meet in our endeavor to establish that right relationship known as Brotherhood. Since brotherhood is a prerequisite to true peace and since peace has become the common necessity, we may all meet upon this ground with *one* purpose in mind.

We seek to promote "peace on earth and good will toward men" via the manifestation of Brotherhood in our daily lives and affairs.

The seven Divine Laws and Energies of Cosmic Love as they may be worked out into manifestation by humanity are enumerated and defined as follows:

1. The Law of the Focused Will to Love, which states in effect that,

   "The Power of God may be invoked into manifestation via the focused Will to Love."

2. The Law of Loving Understanding, which states in effect that,

   "The energy of Love in the Mind produces right understanding or Wisdom."

3. The Law of Service, which states in effect that,

   "A planned activity of service impulsed by love and carried out in Love results in the manifestation of some fragment of the Divine Plan for Humanity."

4. The Law of Transmutation, which states in effect that,

   "The radiation of Love in the three planes of human endeavor transmutes darkness into Light, ignorance into Wisdom, and discord into harmony."

400

5. The Law of Formulated Knowledge, which states in effect that,

   "When Divine Love is formulated into concrete science and knowledge, a new heaven and a new earth shall come into being."

6. The Law of the Focused Ideal of Christ, which states in effect that,

   "The Christ shall reappear when humanity recognizes the Christ Principle indwelling everyone."

7. The Law of Initiated Growth, which states in effect that,

   "Through the initiation of a planned activity of growth, human beings may cooperate with the Law of Evolution to reach a desired goal of spiritual development."

As energies, these seven are potencies that may be appropriated by everyone who seeks to use them in service to humanity. They may not be safely appropriated by one who seeks to use them for any separative reason, for they carry a powerful retribution when put to wrong use.

An energy potential is appropriated as a human being wields the law which steps that energy down from its higher frequency on Spiritual levels into a lower frequency which gives it presence in the three worlds of human endeavor. Many such higher frequency energies overshadow humankind as Divine Potentials. They exist as solutions to world problems, etc., but must be brought into manifestation by men and women who are consciously identified as Souls rather than as personae.

Creative Thinking

This science of occult appropriation is one which has long been known by a few, and which, during this new age will make an emergence into the minds of those in the world who are mentally polarized as incarnating Souls. Later, much later in the evolutionary development of the race, this science will become public knowledge and practice, radically changing as it does so, the mode of civilization.

Humankind may begin, however, to learn the rudiments of occult appropriation now, and to practice that rudimentary knowledge in an endeavor to lift humanity onto a higher turn of the evolutionary spiral. In fact, such an opportunity is the crisis of our times, for only through what appears as a superhuman effort to solve the problems of humanity may we shift the tide of world affairs from the dark turn they have taken.

We recognize our Spiritual need for Love, a Love that is Divine, as the fulfillment of all human need. We discover as we probe into the mysteries, that Divine Love is an energy and that it has seven potential expressions which it can take in our lives and affairs. We learn further that energy must be appropriated before it can be put into effective use, and that it must be directed into outer manifestation via a technical process by the Soul-centered consciousness. Energy does not just shift from one frequency into another merely because we wish it; neither does it move unbidden into outer manifestation. Energy responds to the direction (focused will) of consciousness, as that consciousness provides a pattern or form in which it can take on an appearance.

There is a point of great importance here that must be clearly understood before we can proceed with our subject. We have referred earlier in this series to energy, force, and substance. Now let us realize as fully as possible, that every manifestation in time and space is the combination of these three in a triangle of Spiritual relationship that is itself reflected into the outer world of appearances as a form. This is as true of the so-called bad as of the so-called good. Such a combination must form a triangle of Spiritual relationships because all energy is Divine, all force, as such, is Divine, and all substance is Divine. The use to which these are put determines their good or bad effects in the physical plane of affairs.

Human beings cannot know love, cannot understand what it is and what it is not, until they have brought the energy of it, in one of its seven potential expressions, into their instrumentality via the science of appropriation, and directed it into force and substance via a technique of application. When they apply such a technique for a Divine Purpose, they have become what the occultist defines as the White Magician. They are acting as a Soul, appropriating and wielding the wealth of their Spiritual inheritance for the common good of humanity.

Thus, we begin to see why it is so difficult for us to truly love our enemy, or even our neighbor. Most of us have not sought out nor been impressed by the energy of Divine Love. How then do we expect to apply it in our daily activity?

Love is not an emotion. It is not sentiment, nor even sympathy. Love is a Divine energy that we may contact first as a Divine Law and finally appropriate as an energy potential via the wielding of that Law in our daily life and affairs. Once appropriated, the energy, force, and substance of Love becomes a part of the very nature of the form, thus demonstrating in the human nature the truth of the message of Love which impacts upon the mind of every Spiritual seeker the world over.

Try to grasp, with both the heart and the mind, the reality of these overshadowing energy potentials that

are the seven Divine expressions of Love, available to us
as Sons of God. Contemplate their overshadowing presence until they become as real and as tangible to you as
is the existence of the Cosmos in which you live. While
humanity does not fully comprehend the Cosmos, nonetheless we know that it is there, and that in some mysterious way we are a part of it.

So it is with these energies. They overshadow you as
potentials, and in their lower frequencies, they are the
'stuff' out of which your bodies, your environment, and
your experiences are made. They can be known by you,
and finally they can be appropriated and wielded by you
for the betterment of humankind.

In order to safely appropriate any energy potential, the
consciousness must have first established a secure identification as Soul within the One Life.

Then, poised and alert in the bodies, and positively
receptive in awareness, the soul-centered consciousness
seeks via meditation to be impressed by the overshadowing potential as a Divine Law which it may apply in
its daily living. In other words, we must first grasp and
understand the Divine expression of the energy we seek
to appropriate and embody. Its formulation into a Law
which we can wield with understanding, establishes an
alignment, a path of least resistance, for the flow of
energy into force and substance through our own bodies
and out into reflected appearance as a manifest form in
our environment.

If we would truly love our neighbor, we must understand and wield the law that brings the energy, force,
and substance of such a quality of relationships into
juxtaposition within our own bodies so that they are
reflected outwardly in our life and affairs via our automatic response mechanism.

This is no easy task. Neither can it be achieved quickly. It will require much thought, persistent effort, and a growing expansion of consciousness on the part of the student. You must truly want to love your neighbor in order to do so. Your desire nature must be quickened and trained, by the focused intent (will) of the consciousness, to generate the power on astral emotional levels to manifest this truth outwardly.

We shall take this up in our next lesson as we study the Law of the Focused Will to Love. In the meantime, give this lesson deep consideration, endeavoring to understand its meaning to you, your close associates and the world in which you live.

Creative Thinking

Notes

_____

_____

_____

_____

_____

_____

_____

_____

_____

_____

_____

_____

_____

_____

_____

_____

Lesson 32

Notes

Creative Thinking

LESSON 33

The Focused Will to Love

The Divine Purpose of Will Energy
is to Know Love; Free Will;
Cooperating With Divine Purpose;
Living in the Body, Emotions, Mind;
Directing One's Life and Affairs
from a Predetermined Plan;
Learning to Respond Mentally:
Formulate an Intent,
Translate the Intent into Action,
Observe your Emotional Reactions;
Aids to Mental Polarization

LESSON 33

"The Power of God may be invoked into manifestation
via the Focused Will to Love."

The Focused Will to Love is a law and an energy which
reaches humanity via a focal point of entry within the
Planetary Life, from the Solar Life itself as that Solar
Life differentiates the great law and energy of Cosmic
Love into seven divine expressions within its own sys-
tem. The Power of God is inherent within this Divine
Will energy and comes into play via its right use.

The Divine Intent with which the energy is impressed,
i.e., its Divine Purpose within this vast organized Life,
is to bring into focus and to interpret Cosmic Love or
Pure Reason. Thus, we say that the Divine Purpose of
will energy or of will force is to know Love.

This gives students a much different concept of will
than they may have had in the past. It causes them to
pause and to re-evaluate those connotations that they
have, in the race-mind-consciousness, attached to the
term. Thus, they find that their understanding of it has
been constructed upon a false foundation of meaning, and
the use to which they have put the Will has often been un-
wise. Certainly, they have done little heretofore to unfold
the Divine Purpose underlying this energy of God, which
works out within the human being as a Creative Faculty.

The Will is essentially creative. It creates within the
substance upon which it is focused an impression of
that higher overshadowing reality for which it is a focus.

411

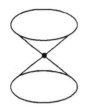 Overshadowing Reality

Focused Will

Created Impression in Substance

In order to clearly understand what is conveyed above, it is necessary to observe its working out in various areas of the manifest life.

For instance, the Divine Purpose impressed upon all will energy within the Planetary Life by the Solar Life is a Law which controls from beginning to end the uses to which the will is put by every being upon the planet.

At first appearance, this would seem to be a false statement. However, upon close observation of the life and affairs of humanity, we see its truth.

Humanity has been given free will, or so it would appear. Our will is free to a point, that is, we may use it for good or bad, loss or gain, pleasure or pain, but we cannot avoid the effects of such usage. As individuals choose actions that are contradictory to the Divine Purpose of will energy, that Divine Purpose works in such a way as to eventually show them the error of their actions. Thus, they learn in a blind, unconscious manner, the Divine Purpose underlying their God-given so-called free will.

This same Divine Purpose can be observed as a created impression within the substance of human life and affairs, as the stated principles of Love to which all religious aspirants adhere, and as the various codes of ethical and moral conduct to which all groups aspire.

Humanity does not always embody Divine Purpose, but consciously or unconsciously they are always aware of it as a created impression in the substance of their life and affairs. We cannot escape it. It rules, via retribution, over all we think, feel and do; and until we recognize, accept and cooperate with it, we are the unhappiest of beings.

Such cooperation is dependent upon our ascertainment of certain knowledge about ourselves. We must realize that essentially we are three-fold in nature, having a mind, an emotional nature, and a body of manifestation. Our consciousness can function in any one of the three aspects, according to our evolutionary development and our point of interest, and from that focus in one of the aspects direct, more or less, the course of our life and affairs.

The man who lives strictly in the body and directs his affairs from there is concerned wholly with the physical aspects of life. His attention is turned to survival, propagation, and whatever physical comfort can be achieved. Needless to say, there are few of these in the civilized world, for this stage of experience denotes a low point of evolutionary development. The emotional and mental response mechanisms have not yet been constructed and are present only in a rudimentary stage. Such a man will gradually evolve as the inner man himself evolves and begins to lift his attention from that which is completely physical to the more subtle realities of life.

The woman who lives in the emotional nature directs the affairs of the life and the physical body according to her desires. She experiences and evaluates with her emotions and uses her mind for this purpose. Because the emotional body is one of many forces — love, hate, fear, courage, etc., she is oft'times the victim of conflicting interests and desires and at the mercy of the cross currents of force generated within her own instrumentality.

As she evolves this aspect of her nature, she becomes aspirational rather than desirous, cultured and civilized rather than savage, and one-pointed in focus rather than divided by conflicting interests.

When she reaches a certain degree of one-pointed focus, she shifts her attention into the mind and begins to direct her life and affairs from that vantage point.

The man who lives in his mind is endeavoring to live according to reason. Reason tells him first that he must integrate the three aspects of his nature into one working unit before he can hope to find peace of mind or happiness. Reason also tells him that his problems are the problems of humanity and can only be solved via service to the best interest of humanity. Thus, he becomes conscious on a much broader scale of awareness than heretofore and he expands his sphere of influence accordingly.

At the same time this man recognizes that before he can hope to serve effectively he must become the central directing will of his own affairs in cooperation with that Divine Central Directing Will of the One Life.

Only from the mind is it possible to direct one's life and affairs according to a predetermined plan. Thus, mental polarization becomes the first major goal toward which the student strives.

While we have discussed this particular subject at some length in former lessons, nonetheless, let us give it again some concentrated attention.

What is it that distracts a man or woman from mental polarization? Their emotional nature, of course—that which constitutes the sum total of their desires, their basic feelings and the evaluations based upon those feelings, and their built-in emotional response mechanism.

Students establish themselves in residence in their head and determine to live there, consciously directing their affairs from the mind according to a purpose and a goal comprehended by that mind. Thus, they are endeavoring to cooperate with the highest concepts and ideals to which they can mentally respond.

Then some little happening in their environment makes an impact upon their emotional body and they are immediately swept into a reaction that is in total contradiction to their newly-made plans. Once again, they have become a victim of the forces of their own instrumentality and they fall even further from the coveted place of abode into the very depths of emotional polarization; they are utterly and completely discouraged.

What is the remedy for this? How can they become their own master?

The student has to learn to respond mentally rather than to react emotionally. They have to plant the desire to cooperate, within their own emotions, so they respond to their new set of mental demands.

We stated in Lesson 32 that "You must truly want to love you neighbor in order to do so. Your desire nature must be quickened and trained by the focused intent (will) of the consciousness to generate the power on astral-emotional levels to manifest this truth outwardly."

The student accomplishes this step via a three-fold mental activity, remembering that only from the mind can will force be focused as conscious intent.

1. Students formulate their intent (to love their neighbor) into a seed-thought that can be used in meditation or referred to as a magical formula in times of need:

Creative Thinking

"I, the Soul, love, understand, and serve."

They endeavor to hold this focused intent steadily in mind at all times. They begin their morning with it, as a seed-thought for meditation, and refer to it throughout the day.

2. They translate the intent into an action picture that can be readily comprehended by their emotional nature, and transfer that picture into their astral body.

For instance, if they have a habit pattern of responding irritably to some particular person, they create a picture of themselves doing the opposite. They see and hear themselves responding with loving understanding and a real desire to serve that person's highest good. Via the creative imagination, they play the new role and direct the picture (as a means of communicating the focused intent) into their astral body.

If it is difficult to comprehend this transference from mind into emotion, the student may visualize the picture as moving from a small golden sun via a ray of light into a clear reflecting pool of quiet water. However, this is not a necessary part of the technique, and should be used only by those for whom the transference seems difficult.

This exercise is most effective if carried out as the student is in process of going to sleep.

3. During the daily routine, students observe their emotional reactions from their point of focus in the mind, and gradually establish their control via a transmutation process as follows:

    a. When faced with a negative emotional impact, the student tries to catch it before it has

416

moved into a reaction. The moment they become aware of feeling resentful or irritated toward some person or situation they immediately re-evaluate their own response according to the truth they are endeavoring to embody. Then, via their focused will to love, they transmute their own reaction, giving the force of the emotion a new charge — a new mental command to love.

4. In addition to the above, students formulate a planned activity that adequately expresses their focused intent and sets that activity into motion, i.e., they go out of their way, beyond the demand of their daily routine, to perform some small act of love for another.

In this manner the will is trained, the response mechanism is trained, and the Power of God to manifest the good, the true, and the beautiful is invoked into the emotional nature of humanity as a moving force within us.

Suggested Aids to Mental Polarization

1. Learn to reason — to see all sides of a situation, rather than just your own. Deliberately put yourself in the place of all others involved, one by one, and attempt to understand the reaction each is having from their particular perspective.

2. Develop your mental strength by consciously thinking before feeling. Average human beings lead with their emotions rather than their mind. Do just the opposite — lead from the head with thought — then feel what you consciously choose to feel.

3. Find or create some hobby which taps the conscious mind more than it does the emotions or the physical body, and spend some time with it daily.

4. *Read with the mind* rather than the emotions.

5. *Speak with the mind* rather than the emotions.

6. *Act with the mind* rather than the emotions.

7. Combine the energy of the mind and the force of the emotional feeling nature to produce a life of loving, intelligently planned service to those within your sphere of influence.

Lesson 33

Notes

_____

_____

_____

_____

_____

_____

_____

_____

_____

_____

_____

_____

_____

_____

_____

_____

_____

Creative Thinking

Notes

_____

_____

_____

_____

_____

_____

_____

_____

_____

_____

_____

_____

_____

_____

_____

_____

Lesson 33

Notes

_____

_____

_____

_____

_____

_____

_____

_____

_____

_____

_____

_____

_____

_____

_____

_____

_____

_____

Creative Thinking

LESSON 34

Definitions of Love

The Movement of Love:
Inflowing and Outflowing;
True Love is Outflowing;
The Nature of The Christ;
Love Produces Right
Understanding or Wisdom;
Three Major Laws of The Soul:
The Law of Attraction,
The Law of Repulsion,
The Law of Integration;
Aids to the Embodiment of Love

LESSON 34

"The Energy of Love in the Mind Produces Right Understanding or Wisdom."

Webster's Collegiate Dictionary defines love in the following ways:

1. "1. A feeling of strong personal attachment induced by sympathetic understanding, or by ties of kinship; ardent affection.

2. The benevolence attributed to God as being like a father's affection for his children; also, man's adoration of God.

3. Strong liking, fondness, goodwill; as love of learning, love of country.

4. Tender and passionate affection for one of the opposite sex.

5. The object of affection, sweetheart.

6. Cupid or Eros, as God of Love, sometimes Venus."

These are the interpretations humanity has given to a divine energy. As human beings begin to tread the upper paths of higher learning, they seek a new and deeper meaning of love, a reality that they can apply to their life and affairs in a beneficial way.

What is love?

Love is a divine energy that is a constituent part of the One Life. It is the magnetic, cohesive, informing, qualifying Son Aspect or Christ Principle of the One in Whom we live, move, and have our being. It is the essential energy of which consciousness is made; the reality behind, underlying and informing, sustaining and qualifying the "I". It is radiatory and altruistic in nature, constructive in purpose, and it is the basic law of the Universe.

Webster's definitions but define some of the effects produced in the life and affairs of humanity by love. It is neither a sentiment nor an emotion, nor is it a result of sympathetic understanding. Love is causal in itself, being the second aspect of the Holy Trinity.

If students will readjust their thinking in such a way as to see love in its true place in the scheme of things, much new light upon the subject will be forthcoming. It has been so limited in connotation to the astral-emotional feeling nature of humanity that much of its significance has been lost.

Pause for a few moments and consider the feeling you know as love. Visualize someone very close to your heart, and try to analyze this so-called love you experience in relationship to them. Then ask yourself these questions:

1. What motivates this feeling?

2. Is it an outflowing of energy or an inflowing?

3. What kind of an effect does it create within the loved one?

Unless students are very honest with themselves, these questions may be difficult to answer. Average persons love that which pleases them. Their motivation is almost always self. Some of the commonest examples of this self-motivation in love can best be illustrated as follows:

1. Tom loves Mary because it pleases his vanity to do so. She is beautiful, attentive and flattering. His love and possession of her substantiates his own high estimation of himself.

2. Bill loves Louise because she mothers him. She satisfies his need to be cared for, to be shielded from the world's tragedies. She permits him to remain a child.

3. George loves Isabell because she crucifies him. She threatens, abuses, and hurts his ego, satisfying his terrible need for punishment. Without Isabell, George would live in constant fear of an unknown retribution (usually for an unknown crime committed in a dim and uncertain past).

4. Mary loves Tom because he appreciates her beauty, and because he provides her with an adequate male counterpart. He is handsome and successful. In being possessed by him, her womanly vanity is served.

5. Louise loves Bill because he needs her. His little-boy ways are endearing because in comparison to them she is strong and capable. He satisfies her need to be needed.

6. Isabell loves George because he provides her with a target for her hostility against those who have wronged her in the past. He needs punishment, she needs to punish and so they are in love.

7. They all love their children in greater or lesser degrees because the children are theirs, blood of their blood, and flesh of their flesh.

Creative Thinking

Because it is impossible for anyone to please one person all the time, this love is a partner to hate; for just as people love that which pleases them, they also hate that which displeases them. They may call it resentment, jealousy, or anger; but nonetheless, in any of its many guises, it is the polar opposite of love.

Multiply our examples by over six billion units of human consciousness and we begin to understand what is behind the present crisis in which humanity finds itself. The forces of emotionalism, of everyday feelings which are constantly fed into the world of affairs by little-realizing men and women, must produce their effects in time and space. Here is the basis of human psychology; the foundation upon which the majority of people relate, communicate, and live within the organized whole. Humanity seeks peace, yet in their everyday life they perpetrate war. How can it be otherwise?

How can the movement of such so-called love be anything but inflowing?

Its only outflowing motion is to gather back into the lover's possession that which appears to be loved.

True love, which is an outflowing energy, is given freely. It frees, rather than binds; it makes no demands whatsoever upon another; and it never decreases in quantity or quality because of another's faults, vices, or behavior.

It was of this kind of love that Jesus was speaking when He said,

> "You have heard that it was said, 'An eye for an eye and a tooth for a tooth.' But I say to you, Do not resist one who is evil. But if any one strikes you on the right cheek, turn to him the other also; and if any one would sue you and take your coat, let him have your cloak as well; and if any one forces you to go

one mile, go with him two miles. Give to him who begs from you, and do not refuse him who would borrow from you.

"You have heard that it was said, 'You shall love your neighbor and hate your enemy.' But I say to you, Love your enemies and pray for those who persecute you, so that you may be sons of your Father who is in heaven; for he makes his sun rise on the evil and on the good, and sends rain on the just and on the unjust." Matthew 5:38-45

This is the teaching of Love. What has happened to it?

Students (at this point of realization), lift their attention to love from the astral-emotional plane of life to the Spiritual World of the Christ, and see it as cause. Love is that cause for which and by which they were created. It is then above their instrumentality in frequency, above even their own soul, though it is the stuff out of which their soul is made. They recognize it as the Nature of Christ, the Christ principle overshadowing and indwelling their self. They call it down and out: first into their mind, then into their emotional feeling nature, and finally into their physical life and affairs (as a divine energy which reveals, purifies and transmutes, clarifies and makes whole). They call upon it as a cause, ask to be shown the way of love, and endeavor to embody that way, recreating those effects they have defined as love to more perfectly convey and express the truth.

They are bringing the energy from above, downward and outward. They are then, finally freed from the astral limitation of the old misconception of "falling in love". They do not fall. They rise, and in doing so, they lift their earth in frequency into heaven, and bring heaven to earth.

Creative Thinking

In *The Nature of the Soul,* Lesson Seven, it is stated, "Love, then, produces comprehension. It is the energy which relates many experiences in such a way as to produce a pattern, an evolution, and, finally, intelligent, productive thought." [N.S., p. 89]

It is this basic relationship (between Love as a divine energy and the mental capacity to know, to understand, and to initiate the creative act which brings harmony out of conflict or order out of chaos) that must be grasped with clarity by the student who would wield the Law of Love.

What human being does not, consciously or unconsciously, aspire to a greater mentality? Humanity's longing for and aspiration toward the quick, clear mind of the intellectual is epitomized in their formulation of the I.Q. test, America's TV quiz programs, and an almost holy reverence, the world over, of those mental achievements which are outstanding. Elaborate educational systems with which to train humanity's young minds are established in every nation, yet that which gives birth to understanding and evolves wisdom is neglected.

The human race trains its children to fear, resent, and to hate those of its own species who are different from themselves. Groups of individuals are trained to hate other groups because of a difference in color, ideology, class or sect. Such hatred, which is covered with the term "prejudice", prevents any possibility of understanding or of right relationship between these various groups of people. Thus, the human race is being constantly divided into all sorts and kinds of camps unable to relate for the common good, or to live together in peace. If it were not so tragic, it would appear to an onlooker as a masterpiece of comedy created for the sole purpose of throwing into relief what not to do.

Yet it is not a comedy. Men and women dedicate their lives to killing each other, to fostering fear, to creating a world in which evolution without undue pain and suffering is impossible. And in the majority of these situations the average persons believe, with a fanaticism peculiar to the old inquisitions and the holy wars, that they are right, that their inhumanity to their brother is justified. A plea for peace, for understanding, or for the practice of the Golden Rule brings a quick accusation of "subversive" in the many languages of humanity, and the voice of love is quickly hushed around the world.

Yet, all of these humans, who are in truth brothers in the family of God, aspire to greater intelligence.

Let us reiterate: "The energy of love in the mind produces right understanding or Wisdom."

An understanding of this law can best be approached by a study of three major laws of the Soul, which are its essential cause:

1. The Law of Attraction

Love, like the focused will, is magnetic, only in a somewhat different way than is the former energy. The focused Will to Be attracts all that is related to the Intent — so-called good and bad, desirable and undesirable. That which is attracted has to be dealt with by the consciousness involved. The "dealing with" which is an act of discrimination between important and non-important, essential and non-essential, and right and wrong, is achieved easily without undue stress via the energy of love in the mind.

When students relax their constant efforts to choose between conflicting paths, all of which are vague and uncertain in purpose, goal and detail, and flood their mind with love, they will see, and in seeing know, and in knowing discriminate instantly, that which constitutes their right action.

Creative Thinking

This is a somewhat difficult concept; therefore, think deeply upon it. The focused Will to Be attracts all that is related to the Intent. This is necessary, for humanity must see the pairs of opposites before they can balance them in their own life and affairs. Thus, the will initiates and maintains the form-building activity, but love completes that activity in the mind and emotions of humanity. Love attracts into an ordered relationship all that which is harmonically necessary to form a total.

On the soul levels, this law means simply that the soul, which is an evolving consciousness of love, attracts unto itself all that which is needed to form a complete picture of whatever is the subject of its attention.

2. The Law of Repulsion

Love repels as well as attracts. On soul levels, it holds away from the form building activity whatever is not in harmony with the activity or its purpose.

The moment the energy of love enters the mind it casts out of it all thoughts that are out of harmony with the purpose and goal entertained by that mind.

3. The Law of Integration

The energy of love is cohesive. It not only attracts into right relationship the many parts of a whole, but it also causes those parts to adhere to one another. That plan which is conceived in love will become an integrated, living reality upon which a human being may act.

Truth is not only seen and understood in sudden or a gradual illuminating flash of insight, but it is integrated into the mind-stuff and eventually into the subconscious of the individual so that it becomes a living part of that individual.

Lesson 34

It can be seen from an observation of these three Laws of the Soul that when love dominates the quality of a human being's thought-life, that thought-life takes on harmony, order, clarity, and right understanding is born like a light in the brain that illumines any concept, problem, or situation with which the person is faced.

Suggested Aids To The Embodiment Of Love

1. Practice calling the energy of love from its point of entry upon this planet, The Christ, through your own higher consciousness and into your mind. Flood your mind with this energy, blue-white and golden in color, as often as you can remember to do so.

2. Visualize those whom you love, and those whom you do not love, and direct with the mind and via the mind, the energy of love to them in an outgoing motion which does not return to yourself.

3. Use this energy of love in the mind as the basic energy of every relationship in the outer world. See it always moving outward from yourself, never returning, along the threads of all your relationships, acting behind the scenes as an unknown source of strength, stability, healing, and transmutation for others.

4. With love in the mind, control all emotional responses that are related to love as its effects in race-mind consciousness, so that they reflect love as cause, into the mind.

5. Acquire a broad and wise point of view by directing the energy of love in the mind to all those situations and circumstances or problems that are perplexing to humanity in this time and place.

Creative Thinking

Notes

Lesson 34

Notes

Creative Thinking

LESSON 35

How to Know The Divine Plan for Humanity

The Group Life; The Mind of Christ;
Three-Fold Method of Knowing The Plan:
Concentration, Meditation, and Contemplation;
Any Activity Can Become a Vehicle of Service by:
Observing the Karmic Opportunities,
Observing the Polar Opposites,
Recognizing the Field of Spiritual Relationships

LESSON 35

"A Planned Activity of Service
Impulsed by Love, and Carried Out in Love,
Results in the Manifestation
of Some Fragment
of the Divine Plan for Humanity."

For those of us who seek to serve the Divine Plan for humanity, there is a great need of knowing that Plan. We should seek not only to serve, but to know, to cognize, and to clarify, so that we may work as intelligently as those who serve a more orthodox purpose.

It comes as a surprise to many students when they discover that the Plan can be known as clearly as any thought-form created by a mind. While we may not find it in its entirety in any particular writing, or arrive at an understanding of it through the usual methods of learning, it is nonetheless tangible and substantial, a reality that we can reach with the combined head and heart, and with which we can consciously cooperate if we so choose.

There are many in the world who deplore the present state of affairs, who, each in the privacy of their own thoughts, would rise to work for a cause which holds the betterment of humanity as its purpose — but where is that cause? With whom or with what can these dissatisfied people align their efforts? One disillusionment after another results in a kind of apathy, a condition of futility, in which constructive action is neither sought nor entered upon. And the man or woman without position or affluence considers his or her hopes, aspirations and fears to be but a lost voice in the wilderness. They do not realize that, in company with the many others who share their thoughts and feelings, they are a group life with a power potential for good that is unsurpassed.

How can this group life with its tremendous potential for constructive action be awakened and stirred into motion? It can be done by a few who will seek to know the Divine Plan for humanity, and who after knowing it, will dedicate their lives to its enunciation, and to its manifestation in their own life and affairs. Knowledge has a way of communicating itself around the world, into and throughout the body of humanity. Dwell upon an idea sufficiently long, and it will in turn be communicated to you from many sources. Human beings are much more telepathic than they presently realize. They are also intuitive. The majority need only leadership in order to accomplish great feats for either so-called good or bad. Unfortunately, all too often the individual who rises to power and assumes the position of leadership is the person whose aims are identified with self. Their separative ambitions drive them on to accomplish that which often appears impossible, while the person without such ego-centered motivation finds it easy to rest in a kind of discontented passivity. The need of our times calls for, in fact demands, leadership from those who do not seek for self. It requires as powerful an action from those who are not ambitious as we have had from those who are. When ambition and desire have lost their lure, and have been renounced, position and power can be put into right use.

The Divine Plan as far as humanity is concerned finds its point of formulation within the Mind of Christ, that great Being within which all human consciousness knowingly or unknowingly lives. Here, in the realm of pure creativity upon this planet, the plan of evolving human consciousness is formulated and held in focus for those who can, through a dedicated life, reach its abstract frequency, cognize its abstract reality, and interpret its meaning in relationship to the present time and condition of humanity.

In other words, the Divine Plan does exist, both in the Being of Christ as the evolutionary goal toward which all of us are moving, and as an abstract reality in the Mind of Christ which has its relationship to every phase of the evolutionary experience. The Divine Plan for humanity is then, in its highest aspect, the Christ, and in the more immediate interpretation it is the nature of the soul which is so gradually unfolding in the consciousness of humanity.

How may we know it?

There is a method of learning which, while it is not in general use, has nonetheless been known and used by individuals and groups throughout the history of humanity's search for knowledge. It has been called by many names in many languages, but the three terms which best describe its three-fold technique in the present time and evolutionary phase are: Concentration, Meditation, and Contemplation. Here is a three-fold method of perceiving with the mind that which has been given a mental form, without the aid of physical tools such as textbooks, etc. Only that mind which has been schooled and trained to respond to conscious command can successfully use this technique, but where there is adequate evolutionary development and the will to learn, the mind can be trained to function in this particular way much more easily than one would imagine. This is a new field for scientific investigation and when such is made, will yield surprising results.

In this lesson, we shall consider, in brief, the meaning of these three terms, and some techniques that the sincere student may use as a preparatory training of the mind in this direction. Some few may later make a more serious study of the entire subject to the benefit of themselves and humanity.

1. Concentration

Concentration is the focusing of the attention upon a concrete (specific) object or problem for clarification by the conscious and the subconscious mind. A point of tension (attention) is created within the brain consciousness that in turn creates a magnetic field of mind, into which is attracted, out of the realm of past experience, all that which is related to the object of attention.

Example: If one wishes to understand the feelings and reactions of a two-year-old child, proper concentration upon this particular age will eventually bring into the conscious awareness all of the knowledge gained through past experience which is related to this subject. This does not mean that concentrating individuals will recall incident for incident what happened at that time in their life, but that the state of consciousness — the state of feeling and action — plus all that has been learned about the two-year-old, comes into the awareness so that an at-one-ment with it is made in the present moment.

This is a method whereby recall of past learning for the purpose of re-evaluation or assemblance into new relationships can be achieved.

Everyone who has learned to read has learned concentration to a degree, for reading, if carried out properly, relates all that which has been learned via experience in the past with the present state of knowledge.

All of those persons who are attracted to this series of lessons now have a good basis from which to proceed with the training of the mind to concentrate. The knowledge, and incidentally the misknowledge, already acquired through past experience is stored in the subconscious mind. The act of concentration will bring it to the surface for clarification and re-evaluation.

One of the best exercises in preparation for training in concentration is to focus the attention without the aid of books upon one of the various subjects studied in grade school. Begin with a five-minute period each day, gradually increasing the time spent in concentration to a period of at least thirty minutes.

2. Meditation

Meditation is the focusing of the attention in the mind upon a particular subject about which additional knowledge is desired. Here the point of tension (attention) creates a magnetic field of mind that attracts from within the entire frequency range in which an individual thinks, additional knowledge from other minds. Here is the area of true telepathic rapport. One does not enter into telepathic rapport via concentration, but rather via meditation, which puts one in related touch, within our mental frequency range, with minds which are in harmony with one's own.

Example: Scientists may learn all of the knowledge that has been formulated within their own frequency range of thought, regarding the subject of their interest, via meditation upon it. They attract into their own magnetic field of mind the thoughts and ideas formulated down through the ages by those of similar interest and harmonic evolutionary development.

Within the world of mind are vast bodies of knowledge contributed by the "thinkers" of humankind. Via meditation, these reservoirs of learning can be tapped and used long after physical evidence of such knowledge has been destroyed.

Creative Thinking

Meditation techniques referred to above cannot be given in this lesson, but they are available in more advanced work.

3. Contemplation

Contemplation is the communion with, and the formulation of, that which is abstract (overshadows) into a concrete relationship with human events in time and space. In contemplation one reaches up out of one's own frequency range of thought to touch the higher mind of Deity. Here one supersedes the world of the self in every sense of the word, to bring a new concept into relationship with humanity.

All three of these techniques are often referred to as meditation. They can be rightly defined in this way only when they are used together in related sequence, or in a synchronous movement as an act of service to the One Life.

However, one must first learn to concentrate, before one can truly meditate, and to meditate before one can truly contemplate that which is beyond the range of one's own experience. In the meantime, it is possible to wield the Law of Service, and to manifest the Plan from the point of present development.

To the student of these lessons, the Divine Plan for humanity is everything they know of truth. It is the Light and Love of Brotherhood, that exchange of energies between two or more people which carries the Purpose and the Intent of the organized Life of humanity a little further into outer manifestation.

Any activity then, in which an honest and truly aspiring student is engaged, can become a vehicle of service if it is so planned. Such planning is based upon the following:

1. An observation of the karmic opportunities

presented in any given situation or circumstance. The man or woman looks into the activity in which they are engaged to find that karmic precipitation from past into present which they can balance through right action. Only they can ascertain the spiritual opportunity to balance or adjust karma via the routine of the daily life, as they look at it with this purpose in mind. All students know that they have earned that which comes to them, be it pleasant or unpleasant. All students know that the activities in which they find themselves are an outpicturing of their state of consciousness, and that as such they are karmic in nature. One can passively accept one's karma, gradually letting it work itself out over a long period of time, or one can positively accept it, seeking to recognize and to cooperate with it, to balance the scales in such a way as to effect the greatest growth for all concerned, and thus, to serve the Divine Plan.

Example: Consider the karmic opportunity afforded a mother in the daily activity of caring for home, children and husband. Generally speaking, the major opportunity here, regardless of individual color and tone, is the development of such qualities and characteristics as are demanded by the successful completion of the job.

This is true of every job situation and circumstance in which one finds oneself. The father, the mother, the employer, the employee, all are presented with a karmic opportunity to develop within themselves the qualities and characteristics which will render them successful in the execution of their responsibility.

Add to this the personal factors involved and one's karmic obligations and opportunities become clear.

Consider the man who finds himself with the job of

managing his father's grocery store, when all he ever wanted was to be a medical doctor. Circumstances beyond his control (karmic precipitation from the past) placed him in this unwanted position. Some men will meet this kind of karma passively, and sometimes negatively, doing the job because it has to be done, without love or enthusiasm. If he develops bitterness in his nature, he creates more unpleasant karma that will have to be met and worked out sometime in the future. How much wiser, and how much more productive for everyone concerned, if he can recognize his opportunity and seek to cooperate with it. Such a one will realize that he is karmically obligated to earn his livelihood in this present moment by working with food, and in the moment of recognition he will choose to serve his customers and co-workers via this karmic obligation he has to them. Thus, he is serving the Divine Plan for humanity, and at the same time adjusting his karma so that, at a later time, he can be released into the field of service to which he is called.

2. An observation of the polar opposites involved in a given situation or circumstance. Here one is looking for principle. If individuals' jobs present such problems as accepted business practices which violate the principles for which they stand, they are provided with an opportunity to enunciate and to live truth. Thus, they become a transmitter of the Plan to others via right action.

Such opportunity is presented, in greater or lesser degree, in every phase of the daily activity, in every department of human living, so that every man and woman is given this divine right as a soul to serve the Divine Plan. All consciously or unconsciously make their choice many times daily.

3. Recognition of the field of Spiritual relationships inherent within the pattern of a given situation

or circumstance. All men and women are souls, and as such they are brothers. Activity, regardless of the kind, tends to bring human beings into relationship with one another. Every relationship, regardless of the outer form it takes in the world of affairs, is a divine one. Thus, we are constantly and consistently presented with the opportunity to manifest the Divine Plan for humanity via the exchange of loving kindness between us.

Let all students daily ask themselves this question in regard to every relationship they know:

What divine expression does this divine relationship demand from me in service to the Divine Plan for humanity?

In the light of the foregoing instruction, draw up a planned activity of service which makes right use of your daily routine.

Creative Thinking

Notes

_____

_____

_____

_____

_____

_____

_____

_____

_____

_____

_____

_____

_____

_____

_____

_____

_____

_____

_____

Lesson 35

Notes

_____

_____

_____

_____

_____

_____

_____

_____

_____

_____

_____

_____

_____

_____

_____

_____

_____

_____

Creative Thinking

LESSON 36

Redeeming Substance via Transmutation

Altering the Vehicle and the Environment,
Applying Harmony to The Form,
The Process of Initiation has been Stepped Down,
Applying Transmutation Throughout the Path
and draining away the strength of the Dweller,
Seizing the Opportunity,
Harmony Achieved out of Conflict

452

LESSON 36

"The radiation of Love
in the three planes of human endeavor
transmutes darkness into light,
ignorance into wisdom,
and discord into harmony."

In the old days, transmutation was given to mean "the conversion of base metals into silver and gold". Today's student views this concept from a different perspective and sees its meaning as applying to humanity itself. We define it as the conversion of the baser nature of humanity into the nature of the soul.

The baser nature of humanity consists of those solid forms of behaviorism and response into which we have molded the intelligent substance of our world. That it is right and natural to "hit back" is an example of such a solid form (this being one of the molds into which the intelligent substance of response has been cast). Thus, this response has become one of the "norms" of behaviorism, and if human beings do not at least experience the conscious desire to "hit back", they are inhibited or repressed in their normal responses. Such inhibition builds up a backlog of emotional disturbances within the subconscious that constantly seeks some form of outer expression. Thus, human beings are driven by an unseen and unknown force within themselves to act in a way that is contrary to their conscious direction. If the pressures of the conflict become too great, such a person loses sense of balance and passes over the borderline from sanity into insanity.

We see then that these so-called normal responses have become solid forms (set patterns) created by humanity in our evaluation of ourselves. The intelligent substance of our world constantly reflects this evaluation, taking on the tone, color and frequency of what humanity (*en masse*) thinks of ourselves.

This is carried out even further in the tone, color and frequency of our bodies as they, in their substance, reflect such conditioning.

The transmutative process introduces a new concept and hence a new tone, color, and frequency into the world of intelligent substance, which lifts it up out of the old form into a new and more perfect one.

To the initiate consciousness, transmutation is the redemption of substance, the conversion of a solid form into a body of stable, fluidic energy that is responsive to the will of the Soul. For example, the bodies of initiates above a certain degree of attainment have been altered from a mere prison, and/or vehicle of the incarnating consciousness into a responsive instrumentality of their will. Their bodies have become a tool via which they make their contribution to the evolution of their brothers. They are never dependent upon the condition of their bodies, nor hindered in their efforts by them. The so-called norm is not a norm for them; thus their quota of intelligent substance is not conditioned or controlled by the psychological laws which govern the majority.

Once the substance of a human being's own bodies have been redeemed into divine use, such people set out to so redeem the substance of their environment, recognizing that that environment is but an extension of their instrumentality of service to the One Life within which they in their awareness live, move and have their being. It becomes then, their obligation to control and make right use of all of the intelligent substance attracted to them.

Transmutation is accomplished when that divine note of harmony inherent within love is applied to the lower frequencies of the form. That note strikes the true note of the form, calling forth from its many parts an harmonic response. Thus, the form is tuned, so to speak, its many parts one to another, and its total to the Divine Purpose for which it was created.

The foregoing presupposes a technique that can be applied only by the initiate, or the applicant to initiation, after a certain degree of attainment is reached, and this was once the law. Now, however (as the evolutionary process is speeded up and as humanity as a whole enters a new realm of approach and response), such techniques can be stepped down for use by anyone whose right motivation attracts the new presentation of the Wisdom into his or her awareness. Thus, those who read and apply this series of instruction, regardless of the degree of previous development, may successfully use techniques that were once reserved for the more advanced applicants to initiation. Such is evolution and the present evolutionary moment of opportunity within which humanity lives today.

The whole process of initiation, or conscious soul growth and development, is undergoing a vast change as humanity brings the Divine Plan of the Soul into a relationship with its many states of consciousness. During the height of the age into which we have now entered the advanced applicant will approach the door of initiation from a much more sure foundation of Spiritual experience, and with a vaster field of Spiritual knowledge than ever before. These will take with them an already expanded consciousness so that new and more far-reaching realms of wisdom can be tapped than were even touched by yesterday's applicants.

Creative Thinking

Today all students are urged to submit themselves to the new technique, i.e., to expand their awareness as far into the areas of Soul consciousness as are made available to them, and to embody that expansion via action in the three worlds so that a whole new era and arena of Spiritual growth and development is worked out into appearance within the life and affairs of humanity. This in itself is a major service to the One Life, for it aids, more drastically than any student can realize today, the evolution of that Life in its many Kingdoms and departments.

The transmutation technique is stepped down for the aspirant in such a way as to provide a method by which the process can be applied throughout the path, thus lessening that final burden and effort when at last the applicant is faced with the dweller. In occult terminology, the dweller constitutes that integrated ego-identity which stands between the applicant to initiation and the door of initiation. It is sometimes referred to as the not-self, or the anti-Christ. It stands as that part of the separated self that must be sacrificed when the final step of liberation from form is taken.

Thus, we see that through the application of the new technique the student may gradually drain away much of the strength of the dweller so that the final moment not only holds less threat for the applicant, but comes to the applicant much sooner in cyclic time.

Inherent within the full tone of the energy of Love is that particular tone which sounds the harmonies of the manifest cosmos according to its Divine Purpose. Thus, harmony is an integral part of Love.

The initiate in their transmutation technique must be able to extract that particular tone from the energy of Love, and in one dynamic movement apply it to that which demands transmutation.

Students, however, are not ready to perform this kind of action. Theirs is a slower, more methodical way, which gradually transmutes their lower nature into a more perfect expression of Divine Love.

They have first to grasp with clarity what they are trying to do, and even this does not come suddenly. Students little by little gain some insight into their own nature until after months or years, whichever the case may be, they think they understand themselves. They have seen into areas of wrong motivation and wrong response. They have, if they are sincere, worked with these trying to effect those changes that seem indicated. Finally, they reach a point of inner confidence in which they think they have the form nature well in control. They are not resentful, jealous, or greedy. They are loving, give freely of that which they have to give, and seek to serve the Plan. They have reached a real evolutionary crisis, a tremendous crisis of Spiritual opportunity, for unless they have attained to Mastery (the fifth initiation) they are now ready to meet and overcome another aspect or phase of their dweller.

Students have ever reacted in one of two ways to this cyclic appearance of opportunity. They either refuse to look any further into the form nature, enjoying for a time a plateau of achievement, quietly gaining strength for the next round of growth, or they seize the opportunity the moment it appears, forcing the dweller up out of its dark hiding places into the Light of the Soul. The latter students are not content to rest upon the gains they have already made. They know the path is long, and that they have far to go; and they also know that as they pursue their way they serve those who follow their light.

This one, then, knowing that harmony is achieved out of conflict, seeks to apply this law of transmutation. Their grasp of Divine Intent at the moment of success attracts up from the dark recesses of their lower nature another side of the dweller, and conflict is again born to light.

They see wherein they are still less than divine, wherein they may initiate a new round of Spiritual growth and development, and with the joy of the Soul they apply the new technique.

The student recognizes the *presence* of that particular note of harmony within the full tone of Love; and as they radiate the energy of love throughout their vehicles and environment from a point of focus in the mind, they realize that the note of harmony carried within it is reaching all parts of the total, calling forth, as it tunes those parts to the Plan, the harmony of perfect balance.

They consider this action, both in meditation and in the daily thought-life, and look for the effects within the form which denote its response.

Lesson 36

Notes

_____

_____

_____

_____

_____

_____

_____

_____

_____

_____

_____

_____

_____

_____

_____

_____

Creative Thinking

Notes

_____

_____

_____

_____

_____

_____

_____

_____

_____

_____

_____

_____

_____

_____

_____

_____

Lesson 36

Notes

Creative Thinking

LESSON 37

Concrete Science and Knowledge

The Overshadowing Soul and Students of The Wisdom,

Precipitating Inner Realizations into Outer Appearance,

Resolving Pairs of Opposites into Polar Opposites,

Occult Bridge Building,

The Lower Concrete Mind and the Abstract Mind,

The Consciousness Thread,

Full Self Consciousness,

The Forked Path of Decision,

Thinking Truth Before Acting,

Translating Wisdom into a Technique

LESSON 37

"When Divine Love is formulated
into concrete science and knowledge,
a new heaven and a new earth
shall come into being."

The student of "The Wisdom" lives primarily in two worlds: the world of ideas, of abstract reality, and the phenomenal world of appearances. These ones tend to focus the attention of their mind into the overshadowing world of ideas where reality consists of many abstractions that constitute their ideals and are therefore contradictory to the appearance of things contacted by their physical senses. They are constantly confronted with duality during a time when they are trying to establish a one-pointed focus of positive polarization in consciousness. They are forced to receive and to respond to that which reaches them via their sensory mechanism, yet at the same time, since they are a lover of truth, they reach upward with their mind to be impressed by those ideas which are most pure in their truth value. They gladly partake of the one and tolerate the other because they cannot escape it. They are prisoners, caught between the pairs of opposites until such time as they can find a way to merge them into that path which leads to freedom.

This is a most difficult period of growth for it is transitional in nature. The students are trying to shift from one set of values to another; they are trying to cross from one way of life that they have known for untold incarnations into another unknown and completely different way of life. Their bodies and consciousness

465

have been conditioned by the former, and constructed to respond or react in a given way. They live by a set of laws and values so well-known that response to them has become automatic. Survival, and even progress in the material sense, results largely from subconscious motivation and reaction.

From this point of evolutionary achievement, the Overshadowing Soul sounds forth a new note, and the incarnate consciousness is impulsed to seek truth. At that moment, a transitional period of growth is initiated. Human beings become students of "The Wisdom" and enter into the necessity to build a bridge in their awareness from the world of the persona to the world of the Soul. Every step that they take away from that which is known must be taken directly into the unknown. They literally cross a void, a gap within their own being between the incarnate focus of personality consciousness and the Overshadowing focus of Soul consciousness.

The void is spanned or bridged in the awareness of these students via those experiences of truth in consciousness that they can manifest as experience in the material world of the physical senses. In other words, if they realize in their meditation the true meaning of Love, they must precipitate that meaning into physical appearance, and experience it in their own life and affairs, both giving and receiving of such love in their relationship with others.

Here is a concept that many students avoid. If they are ill-treated, it is much easier to accept such experience as karmic, which it no doubt is, rather than to try to change the relationship into a closer reflection of truth. Students who give an ever-higher quality of love in their relationships will eventually find themselves recipients of that same quality from others. This is the law.

466

Lesson 37

Whatever concept or idea students can reach through meditation as a result of a vertical alignment with their higher self must be made to manifest in physical substance, thus closing that gap between the known and the unknown, or between persona and Soul. The reality must become actuality.

How many students there are who fail to make this realization; who read, discuss, and meditate upon the Wisdom of the Soul, and yet who fail to precipitate that Wisdom into their daily physical experiences. To speak a truth, or to read volumes of words written upon the subject, or even to meditate does not constitute the transition from effect to cause, or in other words from persona to Soul.

The pairs of opposites must be resolved into polar opposites, and thus made to reflect the Plan. The contradiction between idea and appearance has to be eliminated so that both cause and effect, in the higher sense, are one.

Students who grasp this realization, and set out to initiate the growth indicated, are beset with many difficulties until they find those keys that unlock the door of initiation for them. These are the seven laws that we are considering in this series of instruction, and particularly does this fifth law apply to the actual process of occult bridge building that they are undertaking.

At this point, they are concerned with dualities as never before in their experience. They look upward and view the world of reality. They are inspired by it, and thrill to new heights of ecstasy. Then, as the pendulum swings, they must cast their attention back into the world of actuality of which their own bodies and their brain consciousness are a vital part. They see the opposite of Love manifesting not only in the outer world, but within their very self, and to their dismay the gap widens.

What is truth? Where is that Love they knew in the very core of their being? What does "as above so below" really mean in relation to him? In relation to humanity? It can't mean what it seems to mean because the world below is not as it is above! They can see only the pairs of opposites and the resulting conflict between them.

For instance, the persons who are lovers of truth in their aspirational nature may be liars in the world of humanity. Do they deliberately alter the truth in their business dealings with others?

Such ones, upon discovery of this contradiction within themselves, will often retreat from life in the material sense. They finally withdraw, disillusioned and bitter, from the world of affairs to live a lonely life of meditation, entering into the life and affairs of humanity no more than is absolutely necessary to their physical survival. Little do they realize that this is not the path of liberation. Withdrawal will not bring freedom. It only binds them closer to that which they abhor, and back they come, incarnation after incarnation, into the conditions they refuse to consciously enter and correct. It remains for them to make the transition — to create below — as above.

There are still others, who, though realizing these contradictions, will persist in contributing to them. "Business is business," they excuse themselves, and deliberately blinding their spiritual vision, they aspire in one part of their being to a higher way of life, while they live according to the old way. Thus, again the gap between that which is Spiritual and that which is material grows ever greater, and eventually a serious schism in consciousness results, one that requires many incarnations to correct.

Let all students realize at this point, that here they are called upon to make one of their first choices between the right and the left-hand path. Every Soul, whether Spiritual or human in identification, is karmically responsible for the manifestation in physical substance of that truth which they are enabled to grasp and understand. Their degree of responsibility to the Plan of Love and Light for Humanity is based upon the depth, breadth, and clarity of their vision. This is service karma.

In this lesson, we have referred to that process known as "occult bridge building". It is important now to understand the process as a technique, and the reason for it. Just as the Soul on its own level must cross a void in awareness in order to reach out and become one with The Christ, so must the incarnate consciousness (persona-identified) cross a void in awareness in order to attain to Soul consciousness.

Please note the term "void in awareness" for this is exactly what it is. On mental levels between the two states of consciousness, the overshadowing Soul and the incarnated soul, there exists that space which is devoid of light, and which must be bridged in awareness by the marriage of these polar opposites.

At the height of its development, the persona-identified incarnating consciousness is polarized in what is called the lower concrete mind. This is that area of the mental body where ideas take on concrete forms as thoughts, and are assembled into planned activities by the persona. It is with this frequency of mental matter that the individual in the brain functions at the height of that individual's evolutionary development as a human being.

Seven octaves above this frequency, at the center of what is defined as the abstract mind, the Spiritual Soul overshadows the incarnating consciousness.

It might be noted here, in order to carry out the higher

correspondence, that the Monadic or Christ consciousness finds its overshadowing center seven octaves above the Soul center in the heart of what is called the Divine Mind.

The Overshadowing Soul is connected to its extension in the bodies (the focused persona) via a consciousness thread in which there is no awareness until continuity is established. In other words, the consciousness thread is there in an occult sense, yet awareness is latent — inactive between the Soul and the persona. The abstract mind through which the thread passes is a dark void since it requires the Light of conscious awareness to activate any frequency of mental substance.

Over a period of many incarnations, the focused persona is positive to the Overshadowing Soul, drawing from it only those energies necessary to its life experience, and since it has no interest in the reservoir of Wisdom held by the Soul, it neither seeks nor receives that Wisdom.

Finally, an incarnation is reached in which the persona has evolved to the critical stage of full self-consciousness. At this point, the Overshadowing Soul sounds forth a new note. It becomes positive to the persona, taking up an active interest in the life and affairs of its extension.

The persona responds to the new note, lifts its attention from the lower to the higher, and begins to seek out the answer to the riddle of its identity. Who is it? And why is it? What was its beginning? And what will be its end? Via the tiny consciousness thread in which there is not as yet any awareness, the vibration of the Soul has reached its persona, and the persona has responded. The void of the abstract mind has to be crossed. The occult journey along the path of initiation has finally had its beginnings, and a Divine courtship ensues.

The Overshadowing Soul woos it polar opposite, the focused persona, with its Love and its Wisdom, and the persona responds to the call via its intelligence. The consciousness thread now comes into use, for by it the polar opposites can become attuned to one another and finally at-oned.

The persona seeks, first in meditation. The Soul gives of its Wisdom-ideas, concepts of truth, the divine solutions to its problems. All of these are passed down to the waiting persona via the consciousness thread, which begins to vibrate with Light — The Light of Awareness.

The persona gradually lifts its frequency up into the first octave of the abstract mind, and in that area of reality it becomes consciously aware. It does this via embodiment — via the application in its own life and affairs of those higher ideals toward which it has aspired. The first step along the path of initiation has been taken. A point of crisis has been achieved at last, and the persona must make a major choice.

The choice will be concerned with the right — and the left-hand path, at this stage often defined as the forked path of decision. There will manifest in the path of the personality an opportunity to fulfill a long-wanted ambition or desire, but only at the expense of some principle or ideal the person has sought and found. A choice must be made. The first major test of initiation has been precipitated by both the Overshadowing Soul and the forces of evolution.

Many are not ready to go on, and they return to the path of experience for another cycle of incarnations. Some, a relatively small number in comparison with those who reach this point, seize the advantage offered in the crisis of opportunity, and pass through the first door of initiation where the real testing and training, the real bridge-building takes place.

Creative Thinking

Would that this aspect of the path could be made more clear, for it consists of the small, seemingly unimportant choices one must make many times daily: the thoughts one chooses to think; the feelings one chooses to radiate; the words one chooses with which to clothe and express a thought; and the many actions entered into moment by moment, hour by hour, day by day. A person's entire attitude toward living is altered here. Such people's attitudes, and hence their lives themselves undergo a tremendous change, and all because of their attention to what appears as the mundane.

All of this is accomplished because the human being has grasped the idea of translating the Wisdom of the Soul into that concrete science and knowledge which is applicable to their life and affairs. They begin to merge the abstract and concrete aspects of their mental body. They learn to think abstractly in concrete form, thus filling the dark void separating them from their overshadowing Soul with Light, the Light of understanding, of conscious Spiritual awareness.

How does one think abstractly in concrete form? By putting Principle into practical application. By relating Truth to experience, reality to actuality, and by following through with the thought precipitated into action.

What is the technique? It is so simple as to be overlooked. It consists in thinking truth before acting, in thinking principle before thought itself. It is that pause in Spiritual awareness that permits the translation of Wisdom into knowledge, of Truth into technique, to take place. It is the discipline of the mind to attend to the Wisdom of the Soul, rather than the impulses and automatic responses of the form nature.

Throughout these lessons, techniques of application have been given, but every student will find that these in themselves alone are not enough. All students are

472

their own path, their own teacher, and their own enemy. Even though there is always help available to them, all must find their own way. All must work out their own problems and their own salvation. Such is the *law*.

Therefore, when students are faced with a problem for which there is no written solution available, let them seek out via their own vertical alignment that Wisdom which has relationship to it, and then let them translate such Wisdom into a technique that they *can* use as a means of Spiritual Embodiment.

Example: I once knew a sincere student who found that pride was one of his major difficulties, amounting almost to a life problem. For many years he grappled with this aspect of his form nature, until finally, having grasped the concept of Spiritual equality regardless of outer position, he translated that idea into what was for him a workable technique.

He secured a job as janitor in a fashionable hotel where he had formerly lived periodically as a paying guest, and there amid the drudgery of scrub brushes and aching muscles he learned humility. After several years of such application, this student not only understood his concept of truth in theory, but he also knew it in practice; and so did everyone who came into contact with him, for he passed it on to others by the very fact of his presence.

Students must then go beyond the book. Theirs is the task of teaching themselves, of ordering their own life, so to speak. Thus do they purify their lower nature and approach the second door of initiation. Thus do they cross the dark void, becoming their own Light.

Creative Thinking

Notes

Lesson 37

Notes

Creative Thinking

LESSON 38

Devotion to An Ideal

An Ideal is a Thought-Form
that Carries an Idea of Perfection,
The Evolutionary Crisis of Humanity,
The Opposing Forces of Light and Darkness,
The Crisis of Decision,
The Proper Relationship
of The Soul to the Persona,
The Focused Ideal of Christ

LESSON 38

"The Christ Shall Reappear
When Humanity Recognizes
the Christ Principle Indwelling Everyone."

It is the nature of human consciousness to devote itself to an ideal, and to manifest both individually and collectively the outer picture of that ideal as experience. The evidence of this can be seen in the general tone, the life, and the affairs of every individual and group incarnate upon the planet. The ideal may be so-called good or bad. It may be beneficial and humanitarian, or it may be destructive and harmful in its effects upon others, but it is always present as a causal image to that which makes appearance. For instance, a thief is devoted to an ideal as surely as a philanthropist, and in either case the motivating impulse behind the ideal may or may not differ so greatly as would appear. Both may be striving for a place of importance in the world, dedicated to self, while each uses the only method of attainment each knows. One devotes efforts to stealing, the other to giving, and very often for much the same reason.

A child born into a society of thieves will most likely strive to be the greatest and most important among them as this individual matures into adulthood. The individual's ideal may change if their point of evolutionary development is above and beyond those of their immediate circle of brothers, but the ideal will constitute their idea of perfection. Thus, every human being, regardless of what they are manifesting, is but expressing their natural desire and need to be perfect. They are endeavoring to evolve beyond that which they are presently manifesting.

An ideal is a thought-form that conveys the idea of perfection according to the interpretation of the consciousness involved. Such a thought-form is an all-powerful
influence upon the minds and emotions of those who
embody it. We see manifesting in the world today the
influence of a thought-form of this kind as nations
strive to outdo one another socially, economically and
scientifically. Each wants to be first. Each wants to
dominate the actions of the others with its own ideology
or way of life. Each believes, deep within its own national consciousness, that if it can dominate, control
and rule the lives of others, it will arrive at and demonstrate its perfection. Each is devoted to an ideal with a
fanaticism so powerful that the world is kept in constant
turmoil during this major crisis in human evolution.

An evolutionary crisis is a cyclic interlude between the
past and the future within which the consciousness
involved is given an opportunity to choose the path its
growth shall take. It is a decisive pause between the
end of a particular phase of evolutionary development and
the beginning of a new one.

Today humanity stands within such a moment. We
have evolved into an egoic focus of self-awareness with
a well-developed and partly-integrated instrument of
creativity. During the past one hundred or so years, we
have conquered the material world, at least to a degree,
and we have achieved a much better mental and emotional control of our environment. Our mind is quick
and capable of comprehension. Our emotional nature
has become a powerful force for good or bad according to
our direction of it, and the etheric network within which
we live responds to our demands. Humanity is a unit of
self-consciousness in possession of the tools with which
to shape our own destiny. What shall that destiny be?

Two great opposing forces provide humanity with the conflict that characterizes our present crisis of opportunity. They are:

1. The Forces of Light — of the Oversoul of humanity, as that Soul seeks its Spiritual growth and development, and

2. The forces of materialism — of the separated self as each separated self seeks its own gain in the world of appearances.

Between these two, each individual and group of individuals must decide, and the choice each makes will determine the path of development for several or more incarnations. The choice of the majority will determine the path humanity shall take during the next twenty-five-hundred years. Will that path develop the Spiritual character of humanity or will it accentuate the form side of our nature? In what direction will we move our focus of self-consciousness? Toward domination of the form as a conscious Soul incarnate or toward imprisonment in the form as a separated ego? What is our idea of perfection? What will constitute our focused ideal?

This is not the first time in the history of humanity that we have stood at this particular place in evolution, nor is it the first time that we have been faced with this particular choice. At the height of the Atlantean civilization, humanity moved from such a cyclic interlude upon the path of the separated ego, choosing material gain against Spiritual growth, initiating the rise and fall of one civilization after another as we (humanity) constructed our life and affairs upon a false foundation. We not only hindered and delayed our own Divinely planned growth, but we chose a by-path which led to our fall from the high place which we had attained.

Today humanity is again put to the test. Have we learned

the lesson of our own selfishly created and painfully experienced failures? We shall know the answer to this question by the twenty-first century, for the decision will be made during the last of the twentieth.

Each individual contributes his or her own decision to that of humanity as a whole. Thus, each is called upon daily to choose between Spiritual growth and personal gain. The outer world of affairs reflects the inner choices made, and conflict appears as the note of the times.

Within the world, there are those who understand, if only in part, the real issues involved in the present conflict of energies and forces. They know that those issues are not always what they seem, that they have to do with opposition between Spirit or God's Will, and the nature of the form as that nature has been impressed upon substance by humanity in the course of evolution. They realize that no one person, group, or nation is totally right or wrong, but that the real conflict is the focus of both within each organized life. The outer balance of power must be maintained to permit the conflict manifesting within each organized life until that life reaches a solution one way or another and resolves its conflict. The outer balance of power merely preserves the battleground so that each human being, and each group or nation of human beings, is free within their own karmic limitations to wage their own fight and to make their own choice.

The outer struggle, in a world sense, with its apparent losses and gains simply reflects the inner problems of humanity during this crisis of opportunity.

It must be understood that much of that which stands as opposition to the planned progress of humanity in this day, was a part of the evolutionary growth and development of the times just past. In order to develop

482

human beings into a focus of self-consciousness, it was necessary to turn their attention to themselves as separated egos. Humanity had to think in terms of their own gain in order to build the tools with which to create forms out of intelligent substance. They had to be selfish, had to embody ambition and desire or they would never have evolved their awareness of self into the powerful focus of persona that it now is.

Do not overlook the importance of the persona in its proper relationship to the Soul. It is the means by which the Overshadowing Soul:

1. comes into contact with the three lower frequencies of vibrating matter within the Planetary body, etheric-physical, astral-emotional, and mental,

2. learns the characteristics and nature of those frequencies,

3. and finally, through domination of the forms created in the three frequencies of matter, lifts them into a higher rate of vibration, thus aiding the Planetary Logos in the working-out of His evolution.

It is via the persona that the Soul not only evolves, but, when that persona is itself refined, properly tuned, and dedicated, it is the instrument through which the Soul serves the Divine Plan.

We see the persona now at the height of its development as a separated ego. It has reached that place where it can, at long last, be of real use to the Soul. It can begin to fulfill the Purpose for which it was created. It can now come into its own function, but first, the Soul has one last major task in relationship to it. It must subjugate that ego-identified extension of itself in the persona to its own higher Will, and finally merge with it.

In reality, the persona is but an aggregate of energies and forces with which the incarnating consciousness has identified. It has been temporarily imbued with a will-desire nature in order to develop it as an adequate instrument. In other words, the incarnating consciousness has been permitted to impress upon the persona certain likes and dislikes, certain desires and ambitions. Now, however, since the persona is complete, and the Overshadowing Soul has learned all it needs to know of the nature of its substance, that will-desire nature is being abstracted from it, back into consciousness itself.

This is the real crisis in human evolution, the battle between the persona and the overshadowing Soul. It is as if the Reality and Its form of appearance were battling for control of the indwelling consciousness.

Thus, we see that that which was a part of the Divine Order of growth during the past has now become obsolete. It is no longer the higher way. Brotherhood, built upon goodwill, love and sacrifice or service has become the Divine Order of our times. These must take precedence over ambition for one's self and one's family, misguided sympathy, loyalty, and patriotism, etc., if humanity is to correct the mistakes of Atlantis. This is by no means easy in a world where the real issues are as clouded as they now are. Emotionalism must give way to mental comprehension of God's Plan for humanity, both individually and collectively, if we are to avert another disaster.

The ideals of the persona have to be exchanged for the ideals of the Soul. The latter can be summed up into one vision: the focused Ideal of The Christ.

This is an ideal which humanity does not have to create, for it has already been created within the Divine Mind, and it has been impressed upon substance as the goal toward which all evolution moves.

It has been stated many times in various lessons of this thought-form presentation of the Wisdom that consciousness is born of the interplay between Spirit and matter, or Will and intelligence. Let us now consider what that essential interplay is.

It is a threefold energy that we define, for lack of better terminology as the essence of God. It is the energy of Purpose, Quality, and Activity that together manifest all that is.

Out of Love, Spirit impregnates matter with Itself, (the Will of God, or in essence, the Christ potential) which produces in matter a form-making activity. That activity, from the very beginning, is directed toward the building of an ultimate vehicle of incarnation (the body of Christ). The Soul, which is born of this interplay, is in essence the indwelling principle of Christ. This principle indwelling both consciousness and the very substance of the bodies insures and guides the evolutionary development of humanity so that it must eventually reach its divine destiny. Humanity's free will enables us only to choose the way in which we shall evolve (whether through pain and loss, or through joy and understanding), but evolve we must, and eventually to manifest the appearance of Christ.

Jesus appeared within the world of affairs as a foreshadowing of the coming event in the consciousness of humanity. He portrayed not only what every human being is in reality, but the evolutionary path of initiation itself, the way in which humanity consciously becomes in appearance what it is in reality. He demonstrated, from the birth of a persona and its death to the reappearance (resurrection) of Christ, the Divine Plan for humanity during the coming age. The real meaning of His victory over death, which was actually the reappearance of Christ after the final sacrifice of the separated self, has been lost in concentration upon the form the event took in substance. This finale to the Christ Story is its major lesson in truth, the divine destiny of humankind.

We see then that the focused ideal of Christ is the realization in consciousness of the Christ Principle indwelling every human being. Once this is grasped and understood as a reality, the ordinary individual becomes a disciple dedicated to serve this plan for their brothers. They see this indwelling Principle in every instance, regardless of outer appearances and conditions, and through their concentration and meditation upon it, they aid its growth to its final Reappearance as a Master of the form nature.

As an assignment, please relate this concept, the overshadowing reality, to your own life and affairs; translating its Wisdom into concrete knowledge and science as a technique which you can apply in service to the Plan. Give the written technique to your teacher before going on to the next lesson.

Lesson 38

Notes

Creative Thinking

Notes

_____

_____

_____

_____

_____

_____

_____

_____

_____

_____

_____

_____

_____

_____

_____

_____

_____

_____

_____

Lesson 38

Notes

Creative Thinking

LESSON 39

The Seventh Law

Three Major Types of Disciplinary Training,
Soul-Imposed Disciplinary Training,
The Kind of Persona is Determined by The Soul,
Serving the One Life Through Spiritual Growth,
The System of Checks and Balances,
Establishing a Regular Morning Meditation,
Disciplining the Mind,
Evening Reflection

LESSON 39

"Through the initiation of a planned activity of growth,
humanity may cooperate with the Law of Evolution
to reach a desired goal of Spiritual development."

Our Planetary Logos holds a unique place in the cosmic
scheme of things, for He it is Who provides the training
ground for those lives who are out of harmony with the
cosmic order. Those who are willful and deliberate, take
an oppositional path; those who are laggards in any
particular evolution, and those who through serious
misinterpretation are responsible for major failures find
their way to this planet. These make up our humanity.
We are each and every one of us here to reconstruct our
own inner natures into a harmonious relationship with
and within the One Life. Even those who come from
outside this system to serve within it at great sacrifice,
do so out of karmic necessity — a karmic relationship
with our Logos.

In cooperation with Saturn and Sirius our Planetary
Logos balances a certain aspect of cosmic karma.

Thus, we glimpse something of Planetary Purpose and
our relationship to it. We also come to understand more
clearly the meaning underlying the experiences of pain
and loss that are so characteristic here, for all life on
the planet is actually a disciplinary training. That training
falls into three major categories:

1. That which is Logoically-imposed.

2. That which is Soul-imposed.

3. That which is self-imposed.

The fact that all life must serve with its own life is a part of the disciplinary training imposed by the Logos. Each kingdom in nature, and each life within each kingdom, is subjected to this law. From the mineral to the conscious Soul, every organized life becomes food, or drink, or house, i.e., sustenance, for that which is higher, and is in truth sacrificed via evolution that the higher might live and find its expression on earth.

The division of humanity into races, the visitations of disease upon the various kingdoms, the violent outbursts of nature resulting in disaster; these and many other manifestations are all a part of the disciplinary training imposed upon the life of the planet by the Logos Himself. That life is gradually cleansed and purified via the experience of living and working through these various conditions. It is tempered, so to speak, to stand the growth of the evolutionary process.

Growth without this kind of tempering would be a dangerous process, for knowledge must be wedded to wisdom if it is to serve the good of the One Life. It can be said that science without an idealistic, creative philosophy is a danger, not only to humanity, but, to all life within our sphere of influence. If it were not for the protection of certain cosmic Beings and of cosmic law, such could be a threat to evolution itself, for it is the heart, not the mind, which establishes and maintains humanity's relationship with God. While the head must rule the emotions and the body, so must the true heart of the being rule the head.

Right growth, then, is a balanced expansion of consciousness, and a balanced embodiment of that expansion. It must include both theory and fact working from the overshadowing truth to its specific relationship to the life in time and space. The principle is grasped and understood by the mentality as a concept. It must then be applied to the daily life and affairs before it can be accepted as actual. The ideal must take on a tangible experience.

Soul-imposed disciplinary training is of two kinds:

1. The imposition upon the persona and its environment of those qualities, characteristics, and conditions that are most conducive to the growth of the incarnating consciousness at any given time.

2. The application, by the Overshadowing Soul, of the law of karma to its personality in the three lower worlds.

The type of environment into which the incarnating consciousness is born is determined by the Overshadowing Soul according to the karmic necessities of the present life, the particular growth desired, and the point of evolutionary development already gained. It should be remembered that every incarnation of the lower consciousness is really a Soul-planned activity insofar as its growth and development, and eventually its service, are concerned. Hence, the Overshadowing Soul determines, according to its Plan, the conditions into which the incarnating consciousness must be born. There are no accidents of either birth or death.

The particular kind of persona itself is determined by the Overshadowing Soul. Its qualities and characteristics, its tendencies and talents, are all built into the persona by the Overshadowing Soul as a part of the disciplinary training to be imposed upon the incarnating consciousness.

For example, if the human being in the brain began to develop a feeling of superiority in response to the precipitation of a fortunate karma, even though presently controlled and unexpressed, in the next incarnation that feeling might very well be exaggerated by the Soul as a tendency of the persona toward a superiority complex. This time the person would express a separative concept of his or her own ego, but without the outer justification of good or fortunate karma as a basis for it. In one lifetime, a person might have been blessed with an attractive and pleasant personality that gave rise to a feeling of superiority over others. If this one's training was such that he or she did not openly express such separativeness, nonetheless it would take root in their subconscious, and if unchecked it would grow in strength, until in some lifetime it could manifest as a real block to further growth in the direction desired. To offset such a possibility, the Soul would very likely give the individual an unpleasant personality the next time around, at the same time exaggerating the sense of superiority into an unjustifiable vanity. Thus, the human being in the brain would unconsciously learn by experience the fallacy of such an attitude in relationship to others, as these were repelled from that person by that attitude. And, at a deeper level of the subconscious, this person would be learning a more subtle truth: that the outer appearance is not the reality, that things are not always what they seem, that one cannot base one's evaluation upon the form alone.

This is one of the common means by which the Overshadowing Soul deflects the beginning of an undesirable development into a more desirable one.

Any incarnation, or series of them, is planned by the Soul from its own perspective for one major purpose: that is, that through the Spiritual growth and development of the incarnating consciousness, the evolutionary plan of the One Life shall be served.

Another example may be given here which is a common

experience in the growth of many.

John Doe is born into a wealthy family and given every opportunity that the finest environment can give to develop his potentials into a real service to humanity. He not only is equipped with the tendencies and talents necessary to make a major contribution to the world in which he lives, but the way is made easy for him by outer circumstances.

This man, however, like so many of his brothers, has failed to learn how to make right use of that which he has. He does not seize advantage of the opportunity, but turns instead to pleasure. He fulfills the sensual desires of the instrument and permits his fortunate karma to slip away without having gained or given any Spiritual good from it.

In his next incarnation, he will be born into the reverse of the former situation. Without the material advantages of the past life, he will be equipped with the same talents, plus the desire to achieve or serve (according to his point of evolutionary development) which will be fanned into a flame by the focus of the Overshadowing Soul. Every tiny bit of growth, development, and success he makes will be against tremendous odds, as the Soul imposes the necessary disciplines upon this consciousness. Such will be his life or lives until he reaches the point of growth or service that was possible to him in the one incarnation of opportunity.

This condition is particularly common among many of the higher-developed persons of the world in this cycle. They come into incarnation with the gifts of various talents, and higher intelligence, yet the circumstances into which they are born and must live present obstacle after obstacle to the contribution they would make. Many disciples themselves are continually hampered in their service activities by these same circumstances and conditions. Their motivation, dedication and inner capacity to serve in given fields cannot be questioned, but past indifference, waste, and misuse rise up to defeat them now.

The answer to this problem is discipline: self-imposed disciplinary training until the lessons of the past have been balanced and accounted for.

Thus, we see that cycles of opportunity are determined by the overshadowing Soul according to the point of evolution of the incarnating consciousness and the disciplines necessary to further evolution along the right lines. A human being may have stored in reserve much fortunate karma that the Soul does not precipitate as opportunity until a certain point or level of development is reached. On the other hand, an opportunity may be precipitated before the human being in the brain is likely to make right use of it, in order to redirect this person's evolution from one path onto a more desirable one. In such an instance, the Soul knows that nothing will be gained from the opportunity except several incarnations of severe disciplinary training, nonetheless, an offside development — such as a growing hatred of those who have wealth, position or status as a result of several lives spent in poverty and oppression — may be deterred by such an experience. Acquiring and experiencing that which one covets tends to shift the emotional tone.

Thus, the overshadowing Soul uses a system of checks and balances in guiding the evolution of its lower self until that self is cognizant of the higher laws, and can begin to work with them. Sooner or later, the human being in the brain awakens to the Spiritual facts of life, this one's consciousness is gradually illumined with the Light of Truth, and the power of that Truth begins to make itself felt in this one's life and affairs. Such people begin to grasp the concept and law of self-initiated growth. From this moment, regardless of how slowly their outer life and affairs may appear to change, they live in a different realm. They are an altered consciousness, and for them nothing will ever again be quite the same. This could be said to be the moment when the great shift in polarity from persona-identification to Soul-identification is actually begun. Even though these human beings do not fully realize that they are a Soul, they have glimpsed into the higher consciousness, grasped the concept of self-initiated growth, and unconsciously identified with it. Thus, they have literally knocked on the door of initiation, turning their steps to a new and different path where experience is created consciously with a definite goal in mind.

This seventh law, which we have re-stated at the beginning of the lesson, sets a new rhythm into motion in the life and affairs of the human being who wields it. Initiation is the imposition of a new rhythm upon an old one. It is the altering of the form to convey a new expression of consciousness, in this instance the expression of a degree of Soul consciousness.

That degree, which is actually the particular initiation to which the human being is applying, and which indicates their point of evolutionary development, is determined by their cognition of Truth, its frequency, and the clarity with which they are able to formulate it into a goal of Spiritual growth and development.

The Truth to which human beings are aspiring is first of all the truth of their own being. It consists of the Overshadowing Spiritual realities that are the polar opposites of the discordant notes within their lower nature. They must come to know themselves, both that which is higher and that which is lower. It is not enough to seek the good, the true, and the beautiful. One must also cast the gaze down into the sphere of the subconscious and unconscious motivations to find that which stands in the way of the manifestation of the Soul's Plan. For every wrong evaluation and negative response within the realm of the persona, there is that overshadowing Truth in the realm of the Soul that constitutes the path of initiation or of return for the human being in the brain. These constitute their goal, their law and their path.

It can be seen then, that true aspirants seek within themselves into that which lies both above and below the threshold of their awareness, and that they formulate their goal of Spiritual growth and development out of what they find in the two halves of their sphere of consciousness. Where they discover resentment, they build loving response as a part of their goal; where they discover a will for personal gain, desire for sensation, etc., they build the will to good, aspiration to the plan, etc. Thus, they formulate their goal out of that truth which they find within the self.

After having formulated the goal, they set out to create that experience which will produce the inner growth necessary to its fulfillment. They cooperate with the law of evolution upon this planet, imposing upon the self those disciplines that set their life and affairs into a new rhythm.

First, they establish a regular period each day for a morning meditation within which they contemplate their goal, facet by facet, coming to understand the higher concepts with which they have fashioned it, more clearly. In this manner, they appropriate and bring into their instrument the energy of those concepts, so that during the day they will be enabled to embody these via their action.

Secondly they discipline their mind to think the thoughts they select for it; their emotions to make the responses they dictate; and the actions of their physical body to serve the needs of their Soul rather than of their persona.

Thirdly, they establish a regular period each day for an evening reflection within which they go over the events of the day, determining where they succeeded — and where they failed — to carry out the disciplinary program they have created. In this manner, they glean as much understanding of their own lower nature and of their path as is possible to them at any given time.

Such a rhythmic program of planned activity will result in those experiences necessary to produce the growth desired. Such growth will not take place overnight, but it will proceed naturally and steadily if these aspirants are persistent and honest in their application of it. This is a law that will work for any man or woman if he or she sincerely applies it, regardless of the present point of evolution, or of the outer circumstances involved.

Creative Thinking

Notes

Lesson 39

Notes

Creative Thinking

LESSON 40

The Conscious Soul Incarnate

The Human Soul;
The Magnetic Field of Awareness
Between Spirit and Matter;
Universal Truth;
Two Basic Needs of the Evolving Soul:
Creativity, to Serve Humanity;
There are no shortcuts;
Accepted Disciples are both
Inspired and Inspiring

LESSON 40

We have said previously that the Soul is consciousness, the magnetic field of awareness between Spirit and Matter. That consciousness is of Being in degree after degree, until the entire field between Spirit and Matter, which is capable of such awareness, knows itself to be. We begin as little more than animal at a very low degree of self-awareness. We are just able to identify, and that first identification is with form. As our awareness spreads inward and upward from Matter and the forms created out of it, toward Spirit, we shift our identification from one form to many and so become a species, a member of the human family. We define this degree of consciousness as that of the human soul. A person knows his or her self to be a human being, one of many.

The human soul is characteristically selfish, for its awareness is more of the self separated by its form from all other lives than of the One Life of which it is but an expression. It manifests this selfishness in many ways, all of which are normal and natural to it, and which constitute its evolutionary path of development. The human soul is naturally possessive, both of things and of people. It naturally desires its own good or gain and that of its close associates, above and beyond others of its kind, because its identification and hence its awareness, is of the separated self. This awareness of separation breeds all of the emotions, good or bad, that the human soul is capable of knowing and hence it manifests itself as the many conflicts which characterize the world of affairs thus far in the evolutionary process of the planet.

Consciousness evolves beyond this point of development,

however, into that degree which is awareness of Being itself. It becomes aware of itself as the consciousness (Soul) that lies within and behind the form in the subjective realm of reality. The term reality is used to define that area of cause that produces the appearance of form. The magnetic field of awareness that the consciousness or Soul actually inhabits between Spirit and Matter is causal to the appearance of things as they are. This area relates Spirit and Matter in such a way as to produce the two polarities in an appearance of form. When we speak of this field of awareness, we are referring to that magnetic field between Spirit and Matter within which awareness is possible. All truths, ideas, concepts, potential expressions, etc., are here, pre-existent to both form and consciousness as the two polarities of Spirit and Matter relate in varying degrees of frequency. As consciousness, which is born in Matter, moves into or evolves through this magnetic field of awareness, it gives Life and Soul to the subjective reality there, causing that reality of which it has become aware to take on appearance.

It can be seen from the above that evolution proceeds as the incarnating consciousness responds to the overshadowing reality, and to the outer reflection (its own experience in the world of form) of that reality it has already become. Students meditate because in so doing they are enabled to withdraw their consciousness inward and focus it upward, thus becoming cognizant of that which immediately overshadows them in the magnetic field of awareness between Spirit and Matter. They become that which they cognize as they embody it (give it form) and reflect it outwardly in time and space as experience. When students can learn to do this, and know what they are doing, they may solve any problem via meditation by resolving the manifesting condition or situation back into its essential reality. Of course, this is not to say that they will always appreciate the obvious solution, but it is there awaiting their cognition within the subjective realm of reality.

The Conscious Soul Incarnate within the brain is as different in nature from the human soul as humanity is different from the animal. This one's identification is with consciousness rather than with the form so that while this one is focused into and functions through a physical brain, this one is not identified with it. This one is aware of Being; this one's consciousness of identification is within the magnetic field of awareness behind the form to whatever degree of development this one's evolution permits, so in that degree this one is consciously causal to form; i.e., causal to this one's bodies and environment. Thus, this one, as consciousness, is aware of being causal to this one's own experience. This one embodies that overshadowing reality which this one wishes to experience outwardly in this one's life and affairs. If this one wishes to experience Love, this one embodies the essential reality of Love and reflects it into the substance of this one's world.

Because this one has become centered within the reality of Soul, this one does not identify as a separated being, but as Being itself. This one knows the self to be a focal point of consciousness within a much vaster consciousness of Being, and therefore, an expression of a One Life. Within the One Life this one is related to all of its parts, and cannot by this one's very nature act in a way which is counter to the one Purpose which governs and holds those parts together in a Divine relationship. This one simply cannot be selfish because this one's nature is selfless.

Human beings who are becoming Soul-conscious share the nature of the Spiritual Soul according to the degree of their awareness of it, so that divine nature is always evolving within them.

For many students the concept itself of Soul consciousness

is difficult because its growth is seemingly slow, and in many ways its presence is subtle and difficult to discern in its beginnings. Many students will say, "If we could only separate the Spiritual Soul from the human soul and say definitely, 'this is the one and this is the other'."

This can be done by one who has attained to Soul identification. Such a one knows the difference with a knowledge that is instantaneous and sure, but it is almost an impossibility to transfer that knowledge to one who is still centered within and identified with the form of appearance.

If there is present within the brain a conscious motivation to serve the betterment of humanity regardless of the effect upon the self, human beings are Soul conscious to this degree, even though they do not yet realize it. The human soul cannot truly desire to serve the good of the whole because it is identified as a separated being, and can be motivated only by that separated identification. Whatever the human soul does, it does for self.

There are many men and women in the world who have sacrificed and many more who will sacrifice, the apparent good of the person for the good of the total. You will note the term used indicates the whole of humanity, and not a part of it. Certainly most persons, given the right set of circumstances, will sacrifice self for wife, husband, son, daughter, etc., but we are speaking here of service to humanity as a whole.

This motivation is impulsed by the Overshadowing Spiritual Soul, and is the first indication of the evolving Soul consciousness within the persona. Some call it the Will to Good, others, the love of humanity, and still others define it as probationer Discipleship.

In addition to this motivation, every concept of universal truth toward which human beings can aspire is a part of the overshadowing reality of their higher being. A universal truth is that truth which applies equally to everyone, regardless of their race, creed, color or their station in life. For instance, the concept of loving one's brother applies to all humanity alike. The concept of turning one's cheek does not become obsolete when there is an apparently justifiable reason for violence. There are truths and laws behind these concepts that are a part of the consciousness of the Spiritual Soul, and until humanity attains to an understanding and an embodiment of them, we cannot know peace. Violence is a vicious circle that can only be brought to an end as humanity accepts the karma generated by past violence in an attitude of loving peace. Thus, peace becomes a cause, rather than an effect to be sought after. It is difficult for the human soul to even conceive of such an attitude.

When such a concept of truth is grasped, to the degree that it illumines the mind with its Light, causing a Spiritual re-evaluation of what persons think they know, to that degree are they in contact with their Overshadowing Spiritual Soul. When that concept of truth is the foundational basis of human beings' response to their experience, to that degree have they embodied and so become the Spiritual Soul. When individuals are capable of, and naturally respond to every situation, person, or group of persons with the love that seeks no return, they are the Conscious Soul Incarnate.

All students should pause cyclically to discover wherein their consciousness has shifted from the confining limitations of their personality to the reality of the Spiritual Soul. Each one is endeavoring, via meditation and intelligent activity, to identify as Soul. Because such identification does produce an evolution of Soul consciousness, it would aid the process itself if students could learn to look for and recognize that degree of Soul which they are as an incarnate focus of Being, that ever evolving and expanding degree of Soul which the human being in the brain has become.

Whatsoever degree of right motivation you possess, and whatsoever truth or truths you have actually embodied, to that degree you are a Conscious Soul Incarnate.

The evolving Soul consciousness within the more or less integrated persona has two basic needs which, when fulfilled, aid its evolution and stabilize the expression of its present point of development. These are:

1. The need for creativity.

2. The need to serve humanity.

The Spiritual Soul is essentially creative. As it comes into incarnation, it needs to enter into creative activity in order to further its own Spiritual growth, just as the young child needs to enter into physical activity in order to further its physical growth.

Because the Spiritual Soul is naturally identified with the One Life, it evolves more quickly and easily as it serves that aspect of the One Life into which it is focused. It needs, as a human being needs food and drink, to serve humanity.

These two needs can be integrated into one and fulfilled by one activity, namely creative service, which is actually the path of discipleship.

We define creativity as that activity which produces an adequate vehicle of Truth, or purity of expression. Regardless of the type of vehicle produced, whether it be a book, a painting, a symphony, an electrical machine, a home, or a word, if it adequately conveys a Truth, it is pure in its expression, and thus, it is a creative masterpiece.

512

Lesson 40

Student endeavoring to become Soul conscious via meditation and intelligent activity use these two methods to create those vehicles of Truth which will, in their purity of expression, serve the growth and development of human consciousness. Thus, they give their Overshadowing Spiritual Soul an opportunity to incarnate, and at the same time, they stabilize that degree of Soul that has already come into the brain and with which they are in process of merging.

Obviously, the first vehicles with which they are concerned are their own bodies and their environment. Their bodies and their persona are recreated in the image of their ideal (their vision and understanding of their Soul) and their environment is recreated as a temple of that ideal; thus rendering visible to their associates the influence of the Spiritual Soul, or the truth of it. They recreate these forms into the instruments of the divine plan or growth for humanity, and in this way they enter into that creative service which is the path of discipleship.

They learn to do this via discipline. In order to change the appearance of things they have to discipline their instrument to convey the reality they know. They recreate their thoughts, their feelings, their words, and their deeds into pure expressions of their own Overshadowing Spiritual Soul until they become that in actuality.

There is no great shortcut in the evolutionary process, no way in which this disciplinary training can be avoided by sincere students intent upon reaching their Spiritual goal. They are learning to be of creative service in the world of affairs. If they think they have gone beyond this necessity, and fail in their attempted endeavors to serve their brothers, they had best attend to the beginnings of the path. Disciples can serve only in the capacity and to the degree of their embodiment. Regardless of their degree of mental cognition of Truth, or their facility with its words, they will be faced with this necessity again and again in the appearance of things, until their own instrumentality is a reflection of that Truth, and a conductor of its energies (influence) in the outer life and affairs. Only then will the appearances be in harmony with the overshadowing Plan, for the only bridge from subjectivity to objectivity which that Plan can take is the disciple's own instrument of contact with both the overshadowing reality and the physical plane of appearances.

When students have perfected their instrument of creativity so that it obeys their will at any given time, their creative service can then be inspirational, i.e., it is both inspired from above and inspiring to those states of consciousness who have not yet achieved to their degree of Wisdom. Thus, the probationer disciple becomes an accepted disciple, a true servant of the Divine Plan within the body of humanity.

Lesson 40

Notes

Creative Thinking

Notes

_____

_____

_____

_____

_____

_____

_____

_____

_____

_____

_____

_____

_____

_____

_____

Lesson 40

Notes

Creative Thinking

How To Study
Creative Thinking

Creative Thinking is a course in self-initiated spiritual growth and development. It is designed to facilitate step-by-step cleansing of the persona instrument and initiate Soul Awareness, in preparation for conscious service to the One Life. Each lesson in this course is a step in a transformative process. This process includes:

I.

A. Studying the Material: The information included in the course is presented in a cyclic fashion. Each lesson builds a foundation for understanding and prepares the way for the next lesson. This progression from one lesson to the next creates an harmonic rhythm which aids the transformation process.

In order to establish and maintain this rhythm, we suggest that all students of the course do the following:

1. Begin with the Introductory Lesson and study each lesson in turn. Skipping around or starting in the middle will break the rhythm and cause confusion.

2. Spend at least one week (seven days) studying each lesson. Begin a new lesson on the same day of a week. You may devote more than one week to each lesson, but if you do, spend the same number of weeks with each lesson.

3. While studying the course, concentrate your attention on the course. Avoid practicing internal exercises from other disciplines, as they may not combine well with the exercises in *Creative Thinking*.

Creative Thinking

We do not mean to imply that this course is in any way superior to any other course or discipline. In order to maintain the internal rhythm of this course, you must stay in the course. Once you have completed C.T. (*Creative Thinking*), we encourage you to include other schools and disciplines in your study and practice.

4. Complete the assignments. The structure of the course is similar to that of a textbook and includes frequent assignments. These assignments can be divided into three types:

   a. Subjective: These include internal activities such as the meditations.

   b. Objective: These include external activities such as writing a paper.

   c. Subjective and Objective: These combine internal and external activities in a single assignment (such as keeping a meditation log).

In each case, the assignment is there for a specific purpose, to help you expand your awareness or embody a new concept. Completing the assignments is part of the rhythm of the course.

B. Practicing the Meditation Techniques: The internal disciplines included in *Creative Thinking* are presented in a natural progression from basic to advanced. The meditations are the heart of the course; the information in the lessons is designed to aid your practice and comprehension of the meditations.

1. Practice each of the meditation techniques exactly as described.

2. Keep a meditation log: A daily written record helps you move the abstract realizations gained

520

in meditation into your outer life and affairs. Each entry should include the day and date, the meditation technique, and any noticeable results. Include all realizations and internal experiences which occur during the meditation, and any related insights and experiences which occur during the day or in your dreams.

3. Learn the meditation forms. Be patient with the process. Over time the results will become apparent. We encourage you to practice these techniques as an on-going process for your inner growth.

C. Embodying What You Learn: The *Creative Thinking* course is designed to help you find your place, and take up your work, in the One Life. It does this through:

1. The Course of Instruction: This instruction consists of 40 lessons and lasts approximately ten months. During this period you concentrate on learning the ideas, practicing the techniques, and making The Wisdom a part of your daily life and affairs. Studying the lessons and practicing the techniques begin the process of self-transformation. You complete that process as you apply your new understanding.

2. The Embodiment Cycle: The months of instruction are followed by a matching period of application. *Creative Thinking* course is completed by moving what you learn from the instruction beyond your immediate environment. This application or embodiment of The Wisdom includes:

   a. Subjective activity: Most of your service will be subjective, and may include many of the techniques you learned in *Creative Thinking* and its sister courses. If you continue to practice The Wisdom after completing the instruction, you will create an opportunity to help transform your environment.

b. Objective service: Your subjective practice may result in opportunities for providing objective service to family, friends, co-workers or environment.

II.

Because students often approach a new course with preconceptions based on previous experiences, keeping an open mind and an open heart will allow your intuition to integrate those experiences with the new material presented in the course.

There are a variety of methods of studying *Creative Thinking*. A positive approach is one which helps the student initiate his or her own growth and development. One method which is most supportive of self-initiation is Individual Self-directed Study.

Initiating your own spiritual growth and development means choosing a path of study, practice, and application which is right for you.

The primary value of individual, self-directed study lies in:

1. A stronger focus of will: Every time you decide to study a lesson, practice a technique, or do an assignment, you are exercising your will. As with any other kind of exercise, in order to receive the benefit you must do the work. No one can do it for you.

2. That process is described in this recommendation from *The Path of Initiation, Vol. II, lesson 4*:

Appendix A

"Many students reading this lesson will wonder how to do this work of lifting the polarization without direct contact with a teacher. I shall answer that question in several ways.

"Firstly, let us understand that all [those] aspiring to the Soul are in direct contact with a teacher, namely their own Soul; and by continued aspiration, they will soon come to recognize the contact.

"Secondly, aspirants are enabled, through their right aspiration, to contact higher levels of awareness, and from these levels draw down those concepts of Truth which provide a sure foundation for their later understanding.

"Thirdly, aspirants learn to recognize experience as a great teacher, and through their efforts to live the Truth which they have grasped, they develop in the school of experience a consciousness rich in understanding. They do this deliberately, in full awareness of the activity, and their everyday life becomes a thing of beauty, regardless of appearances."

    3. Self-initiated service: As you subjectively respond to the needs of your environment, you expand your awareness of your place and function in the One Life. This in turn leads to conscious service to that Life as you take your place in It.

III.

If you are considering teaching *Creative Thinking*, we earnestly suggest that you first experience the course. Experiencing the course will help you:

A. Become aware of the difficulties attached to teaching. These include:

    1. The sage on a stage: The idea of being a spiritual

teacher can be very attractive. Often the idea is so attractive that seekers attempt to create the outer form without first achieving the inner content. This difficulty can be avoided by:

a. Studying the course materials: You cannot teach what you do not know. Before you can facilitate the course, you must first experience it for yourself.

b. Practicing what you learn: You cannot teach what you cannot perform. Before you can teach someone else the techniques, you must practice and perform them yourself. Example is the best form of teaching.

2. Being a "successful" teacher: This difficulty is based on the idea that an effective teacher has a classroom full of students. An effective teacher doesn't have to have a lot of students. Teaching is not a popularity contest. Such a focus turns the teacher's attention on the student and away from the Wisdom. Neither does teaching have to occur in a conventional classroom.

Creative Thinking is neither a treatise on The Ageless Wisdom nor a meditation manual. Only through right aspiration to the Soul and successful completion of all the materials and exercises will one truly know *Creative Thinking* and be ready to assist others in preparing for service to the One Life.

Further Information

For further information on *Creative Thinking*, and related courses and materials, see:

www.wisdomimpressions.com

or write to:

Wisdom Impressions
P.O. Box 6457
Whittier, CA 90609

INDEX TO CREATIVE THINKING

Index

Child's faith, murdered, 30
Childbirth—
  death in, 65
  pain of, 63
Children—
  of God, 66
  reminded of sinful nature, 65
  taught to be good, 30
  teach goodness, 66
  world's, 262
Choice, right and left, 471
Christ—
  adulthood as, 252
  adulthood in, 98
  appearance, manifest the, 485
  apply teachings, 195
  become one with, 469
  body of, 485
  brothers in, 192, 265
  Child—
    of God, born in cave of heart, 112
    Soul, 31
    story of, 29
  disciple of, 195
  disciples of, 205
  focal point of, 252
  grow in expression of, 241
  inner, matures, 20
  Life—
    consciousness, part of, 206
    identified within, 374
    part of, 21
  Light, blue-white, 331
  Light and Love of, 42
  Love, expression of, 238
  mind of, 440
  one with and in, 66
  opened up heart to, 125
  path of, ill through inhibition, 157
  Presence of, 263
  Principle, 426—
    indwelling, 486
  Reappearance of, 251
  resurrection, 485
  sacrifice of separated identity, 125
  Savior of humanity, 20
  seek to invoke, 288
  silver light of, 195
  teaching of, 275

  the consciousness, 31
  the ideal, 331
  this is, 192
  visualized light of, 331
Christian children, 65
Christmas—
  carols, 4
  real meaning of, 30
Circulatory motion, 320
Civilization—
  contribute to, 307
  new, 319
  rise and fall, 481
Cleansing, inner, 114
Collective consciousness—
  ideas and beliefs of, 170
  of family, 355
Color and quality, 75
Color or tone, 366
Commercialism, 3
Communism, found entry into
  humanity, 274
Community, field of service, 307
Concentrate—
  first learn to, 444
  training mind to, 442
Concentration, focusing attention, 442
Concentration, Meditation, and
  Contemplation, 441
Concrete science and knowledge, 334—
  translating Wisdom into, 472
Conscious—
  as separation, 40
  awareness, separative shell of, 249
  initiation, of a predetermined
    goal, 53
  work, 6
Conscious Soul Incarnate, 511—
  become a, 351, 374
  evolved into, 317
  individual becomes the, 278
  within brain, 509
Conscious thinking "I"—
  brain awareness, 55
  goes to sleep, 77
Consciously—
  aware, via embodiment, 471
  creative, to become, 100
  initiated growth, process of, 171

Creative Thinking

in order to act, 353
Consciousness—
  awareness of being, 374
  birth of, 39
  born, 485
  born in matter, 508
  breath of life, 17
  divine, 374
  focus of in cave of heart, 113
  focused intent, 292
  formulating thought, 215
  golden light of, 195
  growth and development, 266, 287
  growth of, 229
  held prisoner within emotional
    nature, 137
  human, control substance, 227
  humanity a unit of, 133
  identifies with Spirit, 41
  imprisoned, 27, 317
  imprisoning within form, 253
  incarnates, 227
  individual state of, 155
  integration in time and place, 303
  lost in reflection, 350
  moving in, 262
  national, 109
  nature of, 290
  of Being, 20, 507
  of personality, integrate, 254
  of self, 40
  of the Spirit, 40
  polarized in mind, 137
  produced, within form, 74
  purpose is the growth of, 301
  relationship with other units, 318
  Son of God, 27
  spiritual age of, 267
  state of, 52—
    conforms to ego image, 67
  takes on limitations of form, 40
  thread, 373—
    awareness latent, 470
    begins to vibrate, 471
    comes into use, 471
    continuity, 470
    expands, 373
    via tiny, 470
  three aspects, function in any, 413

  timeless, 361
  true vehicle, 353
  units of, 318
  which resides in mind, 137
  will and intelligence, 379
  will upon mind, 218
  within a form, 227
  within the form, 508
Contemplate—
  before one can truly, 444
  being God's child, 27
Contemplation, abstract into concrete, 444
Correct our thinking, in order to, 27
Cosmic—
  beings, 494
  karma, 493
  law, 494
  love, 399—
    seven divine expressions, 411
  order, out of harmony with, 493
  principle, related to humanity, 388
Cosmos, out of tune with, 15
Create—
  choose to, 239
  with mind, 99
Creative—
  consciously, 208—
    to become, 100
  control, over life and affairs, 218
  imagination, 334, 416
  law, works on all levels, 229
  polarity, will and intelligence, 227
  potential, degree of, 218—
    masse discovery of, 53
  process, 205—
    every experience the result of, 228
    key to, 228
    three major laws, 217, 241
  service, 512
  unconsciously, 99
Creativity, realm of pure, 440
Criminal behavior, cause of, 67
Crisis—
  of opportunity, the great, 362
  this time of great, 134
Cross of flesh, 192
Cycle—
  first major, 302—

530

Index

Index

cedure, 167
Emotionally polarized, 100—
  awareness negative to emotional
  response, 137
Emotions—
  all of, 507
  automatic responses, 55
  frequency of, 203
  identified with, 77
  lives from within, 135
  permitted expression, 156
  possessing, 133
  repressed, 102
  ruled by, 100
  taught to inhibit, 156
  we create, 145
Empathy, 333
Enemy, love our, 403
Energies, wield from mind, 207
Energy—
  a potential, 379
  bodies, reception, perception,
  and distribution of forces, 136
  follows thought, 239—
    laws behind, 215
    why, 215
  is Divine, 403
  must be appropriated, 402
  no difference in, 147
  of Purpose, 485
  responds to focused will, 402
  subtle streams, 349
Energy, force, and substance, 348—
  combination, 402
  frequencies of, 362
  interplay, 350
Enlightened, gradually become, 194
Environment—
  astral force, 366
  control the, 138
  emotional and mental, 167
  negative to, 137
  one third emotional, 361
  real, 362
  relationship between you and, 137
  temple of ideal, 513
Environmental force, tonal quality, 366
Equation, of Spirit, matter, consciousness, 228

Etheric—
  body, of an individual, 354
  centers, system of, 354
  channels, 350
  forms, 349
  lives, attract the, 363
  network, major, 354
  objectification, 353
  perception, experiments, 353
  plane, 348—
    perceive, 352
  substance, energy or force of action, 352
  true vehicle of consciousness, 353
Evening reflection, 501
Evil—
  inhibiting, 155
  nothing ever totally, 288
Evolution—
  checks and balances, 498
  laggards, 493
  point of, 498
Evolutionary—
  crisis, 457—
    a cyclic interlude, 480
  development—
    individual height, 469
    low point, 413
    of humanity, 253
  process, 227—
    drag against, 367
Experience, create, 500
Externalization, kingdom in process of, 251
Extra sensory perception, study, 347

F

Faith—
  restoration of, 29
  secure in, 29
False security, 274
Family—
  ego image, 65
  karmic responsibilities, 306
Fate, master of our, 367
Father—
  as God, 28
  closer contact with, 102

533

Index

535

prejudices of own, 169
Groups—
of people, adjustments for, 262
think and feel similarly, 167
Growth—
consciously initiated, 121
graduation from a phase, 301
initiate now, 125
initiate own, 205
unconscious, 53
Guilt—
false, 66
harm, 156
original, 65

H

Habits, influence of consciousness, 321
Happiness—
a feeling, 148
illusory, 148
Harmonic response, 455
Harmony, 433—
inherent within love, 455
integral part of Love, 456
out of conflict, creative act, 430
Head—
direct love into, 112
energies carried up into, 101
establish residence in, 415
focused in, 321
mental polarization, 102
polarization, 102
residence in, 322
residence in the, 322
rule emotions and body, 494
think in, 99
Health, precipitating energies of, 220
Heart—
and head, combined, 101
as feel with, 99
energies of, 101
polarized in idealistic aspect, 101
relationship with God, 494
rules, 100
true, rule the head, 494
Heart center, direct attention to, 111
Heaven, experience of, 77
Hell, experience of, 77

Higher consciousness, 278—
awareness of, 290
Higher kingdoms, guide human
evolution, 263
His—
Intelligence, gave you birth, 27
Will, conceived you, 27
Hitler, a person like, 207
Hobby, 417
Holy place of the Most High, The, 102
Holy Spirit—
re-enters the physical plane, 77
remains or withdraws, 77
withdrawn from physical, 76
Holy Trinity—
second aspect, 426
second person, 229
third aspect, 363
Three Persons in One, Will,
Mind, Consciousness, 31
Human—
being—
creative faculty, 411
influenced by others, 367
Spirit, matter, consciousness,
227
beings—
newly awakened, 266
separately identified, integration, 98
shared purpose, 43
telepathic, 440
consciousness—
growth and development, 513
imprisoned by form nature, 290
nature of, 479
family—
same Spirit, 39
one motivating cause, 124
form, potential life cycle, 302
kingdom, related with higher
kingdoms, 263
psychology, basis of, 428
rights, 109
soul, 510—
degree of consciousness, 507
possessive, 507
selfish, 507
thought and emotion, world of, 167

Index

seed-thought, 64
sense of, 17
separated, sacrifice, 125
Ideology, prey to, 274
Illumination, clear light of, 231
Image, miniature, of yourself, 112
Imagination, experiencing in, 113
Imagine—
  field of force, 364
  higher frequency, 364
Imitation—
  child learns through, 156
  unconscious, 167
Impact, what kind, 365
Impression, on world, 56
Incarnate consciousness, void in
  awareness, 469
Incarnating consciousness—
  abstracted from form, 302
  type of environment, 495
Incarnation—
  do not come into alone, 250
  next, patterns carried into, 206
  planned by Soul, 496
  purpose, 496—
    align with, 304
  soul-planned activity, 495
Incarnations, future, prepare for, 310
Independence, from others, 123
Individual—
  astral prison, 367
  becomes positive, 367
  related with Planetary Life, 263
  reorient their life, 264
  world of affairs, 99
Individualization—
  recapitulation, 303
  self-conscious "I", 303
Individuals—
  need to improve, 147
  particular quality, 366
Inertia, 319
Infant, sensitive in its consciousness, 64
Inhibited force, 330
Initiate, transmutation technique, 456
Initiation, process of, 455
Initiatory effort, 306
Inner—

attitude, and our future, 134
emotional life, vast subjective
  aspect, 55
lives, change, 56
meaning of My Life, The, 122
thought-life, subjective aspect of
  life, 54
Insects, repel, 366
Insecurity, hidden, 250
Inspiration, faculty of, 231
Instrument—
  all aspects of, 364
  control of, 193
  mind, emotions, and body, 125
  of creativity, 480—
    perfected, 514
  patterns of action, 206
  permit to relax, 307
  three aspects, 273
Instrumentality, a reflection of
  truth, 514
Integration—
  in order to achieve, 276
  of human beings, 98
  of substantial forces, 273
Intelligence, intent into, 229
Intelligent Activity—
  inherited by the Son, 333
  plane of, 363
  third point of triangle, 333
Intelligent substance, responds to
  will of God, 287
Intent—
  focus, 238
  focused, 218
  motivating, 229
  to Be, 379
Interlude, pause between cycles, 304
International conflict, impact of
  science in, 134
Intuitive faculty, 388

J

Jehovah, formed man out of dust, 17
Jesus—
  appeared, 485
  died on cross, 65
  gentle, 28

Index

Creative Thinking

golden energy of, 111
if I have, 135
in the mind, produces right understanding, 431
into head, 112
is a divine energy, 426
is magnetic, 431
must come from within, 98
nature one of, 66
not an emotion, 403
partner to hate, 428
polar opposite, 428
pure reason, 101
quality of, 267
radiating, 112
real, an energy of God, 135
repels, 432
second aspect, 426
seven potential expressions, 403
techniques of, drilling in, 241
the teaching of, 429
true meaning of, 466
which brings reason, 135
which passes understanding, 125
which results in brotherhood, 73
Loving understanding, responding
with, 416
Lower concrete mind, polarized in, 469

M

Magic—
black, definition, 206
definition, 205
the creative process, 205
white, definition, 205
working with cause, 205
Magician, three laws, 216
Magnetic—
field, of creativity, 242
light, field of, 374
radiation, nature of consciousness, 290
Magnetically attractive, 291
Man—
definition, 249
image and likeness, 216
Manifest peace, within environment, 43

Manifestation, power of, 63, 101, 365
Mansions, many, 19
Mass—
consciousness, 3
mind —
and heart, 98
a thought-form in, 28
violence, 331
Masses, common reeducation, 275
Master, of the form, 486
Masters, 252
Mastery, 457
Matter—
expresses as pure intelligence, 289
lowest frequency, 351
nature of, 40
negative pole, 289
Matter Aspect, 289—
intelligent substance, 51
mind of God, 229
seems divided, 39
Meditate—
inward and upward, 508
receptive to ideas, 374
Meditation—
established at regular period, 113
focusing attention in the mind, 443
identify as Soul, 511
morning, 500
solve any problem, 508
vehicles of Truth, 513
you have just completed, 112
Mental—
activity, three-fold, 415
body, 290—
cycle of growth, 303
decline, 308
humanity building, 391
development, path of, 227
energy—
formulation into thoughts, 373
nature of, 375
environment, 7—
consists of, 375
matter, nature of, 379
plane, 348—
causative to physical, 204
closer to reality, 215
door of entry, 391

540

Index

polarization, 414—
  aids to, 417
  beginning of, 206
  evolving, 133
  final step, 191
  positive to emotions, 138
  shift into, 114
  substance, 75—
    activate, 470
    conceive plans in, 76
  world, we live in, 361
Mentally polarized—
  attempting to become, 121
  create conditions, 204
  through conscious effort, 205
Military defense, 276
Mind—
  attentive to Soul, 310
  attracted into heart, 100
  cognizes the meaning, 136
  continue journey into, 125
  discipline, 500
  groups that teach humanity is, 133
  growth and development of a, 304
  highest plane of persona, 388
  home in world of, 193
  identifies with, 77
  infused with Light of Christ, 337
  intelligent substance, 228
  laws, 203—
    study, 205
  laws of, energy follows thought, 215
  learning to live from, 203
  living within, 133
  magnetic field of, 442
  man who lives in, 414
  nature of, 133
  negative to, 137
  overshadowed by consciousness, 374
  perceiving with, 441
  polarized in, 137
  power of, 15
  quiescent, 242
  read with, 418
  receptive to will, 373
  setting laws into motion, 113
  shifting into, 100
  solution within, 261
  thought-forms in, 388
  trained, 441
  unconsciously create with, 99
  where reason found, 100
  will solve emotional problems, 114
  world of, 110—
    goodly distance from emotions, 112
Minds—
  dedicated to humanity, 262
  move up into, 110
Mineral Kingdom, 251
Mineral, vegetable, animal, and human kingdoms, 51
Misplaced sympathy, 275
Mistakes, right to make, 98
Moment, live in the, 352
Monadic consciousness, 470
Moral and *ethical* principle
  greater attention, 304
Morning exercise, 112
Mother, Intelligent Activity, 333
Mother Aspect, 51
  influence, 52
  womb of matter, 39
Mother's, suffering, 64
Mountain—
  long journey up, 121
  reached top of, 191
Movies, 378
Music, 378

N

National, forms, 167
Natural followers, 275
Nature of—
  a life in form, 287
  the form, to separately identify, 40
Need—
  for creativity, 512
  of our times, attuned to, 110
  to serve humanity, 512
Negative—
  forces, transmuted, 330, 331
  Pole of Manifestation, astral plane, 363
New age—
  education, 305
  of growth, 305

541

New moon, 113—
next, 113
Normal responses, 454
Not-self, the, 456

O

Occult—
appropriation, rudiments, 402
bridge building, process of, 467
journey, 470
One Life, 192—
activity of, 287
all forms interrelated, 288
awakening to, 262
connotations of, 263
contemplate as a Soul, 254
Divine Central Directing Will, 414
Divine Purpose within, 262
economy, 287
economy of, 317, 319
every one part of, 262
evolves, 264
focused into the many, 319
fulfillment of being, 250
heart of, 194
humanity within, 373
includes all humanity, 230
indwells all forms, 250
inherited from, 241
intuitively aware of, 261
major arteries, 354
plan served, 496
positive contribution to, 323
reconstruct relationship, 493
respond to, 252-53
service to, 124
to know is to serve, 264
One to seven years, cycle of
growth, 303
Opposition, 482
Order, cannot manifest because, 350
Outer—
condition—
discontent, 123
fear, pain, unhappiness, 124
peace, love, creative work, 124
reflect Divine Intent, 126
experience, adds to emotional

form, 55
world, thought-life blueprint of, 203
Overshadowing—
Soul—
above form nature, 374
extends a thread, 373
home of the, 373
how to control substance, 351
incarnates in full consciousness, 374
invoke attention downward, 194
learned all it needs, 484
on its own plane, 373
Plan, harmony with, 514
sounds new note, 466, 470
withdrawn, 354
Spiritual Soul—
contact with, 511
incarnation of, 375
opportunity to incarnate, 513

P

Pain—
to escape, 123
unconsciously create, 100
Pairs of opposites—
always manifest, 205
resolved, 467
Parapsychology, contribution, 347
Parent, hermaphroditic, 361
Past—
continuity with, 305
lessons of the, 498
Path—
as we choose, 133
of development, choice, 481
of discipleship, 512
creative service, 513
of initiation, 500—
beginnings, 470
first step, 471
of least resistance, of consciousness, 138
of liberation, 468
of Light, discover your own, 280
set feet upon, 206
Pathway, silver and gold, 192
Pattern, left free to act, 156

Index

aiding, 483
place, 493
purpose, 493
ring-pass-not, defined, 252
Planned—
activities, 469
activity—
formulate, 417
producing, 301
Plans, conceive in mental substance, 76
Plant and Animal Kingdoms, as entities, 349
Plant Kingdom, creating impression on, 264
Pleasure, to achieve greatest, 122
Polar opposites, 467—
at-oned, 471
marriage of, 469
observation of, 446
Polarization—
determine your own, 102
reveals relations with bodies, 136
shifting from emotional, 100
within mind, 135
Political leaders, 378
Position and power, right use, 440
Positive pole—
focus of emotion, 100
of magnetic attraction, 100
of manifestation, 229
Poverty, dangers, 274
Power—
for good, transformed into, 335
of attraction, inner drive, 76
of darkness, within us, 6
of the many, 97
released from emotional body, 136
to Be, an individual's intent, 387
Prejudice, 170—
impossible to live in, 135
Present conflict, real issues, 482
Prison of flesh, 191
Probationer Discipleship, 510
Problem, both sides of, 261
Product, perfection of, 76
Psyche, inner person, 52
Psychiatry—
great strides, 133

relieving pressure, 100
Psychic phenomena, 347
Psychology—
great strides, 133
methods of releasing, 100
Public opinion, power, 97
Pure Being, 374
Purification, inner, 114
Purify, own lower nature, 473
Purpose—
beyond personal self, 230
constant radiation of, 138
for living, 121
greatest pleasure, 122
illusory, changing, 126
motivating intent, 40
of humanity, 41
of life, 231
one, of human life, 126
personal, contradiction to law of life, 124
revealed, 264
service to one life, 124
to escape pain, 123

R

Race—
annihilation, fear of, 377
mind—
receive thoughts from, 390
thought-form, 167—
weaken, 30
ego-image, 63
Racial—
forms, 167
patterns, acceptance, 169
Radiate, through mental, emotional, and physical, 291
Rain-cloud of knowable things, 374
Razor's edge, 192
React, according to patterns, 147
Reaction—
meet with love, 149
of force, 364
Reactions, what kind, 365
Real environment, mental, emotional, and etheric, 380
Reality, lost to, 350

Index

Reappearance, 6
Reason—
  emotion does not know, 135
  that love which brings, 135
Reasoning process, reveals plan of
  action, 136
Rebirth, in mental substance, 379
Recapitulate, birth to maturity, 155
Recapitulating, development of
  will, 303
Recapitulation, 303—
  bring up children, 156
  of evolution, 155
  through book learning, 304
Reception, of forces, 136
Reincarnation—
  concept presented, 74
  cyclic period for, 77
  Spiritual Soul contemplating, 293
  three-fifths believe in, 73
Relate, with love, 319
Relationship—
  of brotherhood, 265
  patterns of, 363
  problems of, 27
  proper, 228
  realization of, 261
Relationships—
  consciousness to consciousness, 264
  intuitively recognize, 265
  purpose of, 266
Religion—
  image of self, 65
  negative in teaching of it, 65
  this is their heart, 73
Religious—
  concepts, basic, 73
  freedom, 109
Residence, in world of thought, 380
Respiratory system, 354
Response—
  inhibited, 156
  mechanism, train, 148
  must find outlet, 156
  re-evaluate, 417
  type, strength, and quality, 149
Responses—
  built-in, 54
  control over, 135

Resurrection, the, what is it, 18
Rhythm, new, 499—
  disciplines, 500
Rhythmic program, 501
Right—
  action—
    initiation of, 321
    in life and affairs, 334
    aspiration, meditation, applica-
      tion, 294
    and left-hand path, 469
    behavior, teaching child, 156
    human relations, a need and a
      problem, 265
    motivation, 512
    relationship—
      achieved when, 292
      for all concerned, 239
      knowledge of, 39
      manifestation, 42
      within own vehicle, 273
    understanding, 333—
      is born, 433
Rightful place, take our, 362
Ring-pass-not, defined, 252

S

Saints, 252
Santa Claus, taught to believe in, 28
Satan, remindful of, 66
Saturn, 493
Science—
  of occult appropriation, 402
  vibratory barrier, 347
Scientific progress, 376
Seasons, part of form nature, 294
Seed-thought, ideal used as a, 335
Seed-thoughts for twelve months, 338
Seekers, discover Will of God, 230
Self—
  as the center, 249
  body, the, 250
  conscious, a person is, 253
  conscious 'I', Soul in form, 290
  consciousness, stage of, 470
  definition, 249
  imposed disciplinary action, 330
  imposed disciplinary training, 498

545

Index

focal point of consciousness, 31
fourth dimensional, 290
function in realm of, 310
golden age of the, 7
growth and development, aid, 380
holds a definite Purpose, 293
human—
  adulthood as Christ, 230
  brought into being, 228
  child of God, 229
  ideates Cosmic Principle, 388
  identification, 510—
    purpose, goal, and outer con-
    dition, 124
identifies with body, 74
identify as, 322
imposed disciplinary training, 495
impulsed from, 321
initiates new motion, 322
intuitive faculty of, 252
is consciousness, 17
lost to its identity, 351
magnetic field, 507
magnetic influence, 320
magnetically attractive, 289
mask, 321
mediator, 320
natural plane of, 361
of humanity, 193
plan—
  consciously aware of, 305
  lies within form, 293
  of growth, 301
plans from the end to, 301
positive to persona, 470
precipitates Wisdom, 374
purpose—
  consciously aware of, 305
  for incarnation, 264
  realization of, 305
realize that you are a, 254
relationship to individual, 277
resurrection of, 192
serving evolution of, 319
wisdom of, 193
Souls—
  all men and women are, 447
  family of, 52
  identified as, 401

in process of evolution, 361
we are, 17
Sphere of—
  consciousness, two halves, 500
  spiritual light, 373
Spiral pattern, 320
Spirit—
  and Matter
    field between, 507
    magnetic field between, 508
    two polarities of one energy, 289
  and Substance, interaction be-
    tween, 74
  enters into matter, 229
  expresses as Divine Will, 289
  impregnates matter, 485
  nature of, 40
  of Christ, right relationship, 239
  of Love, 63
  of Planetary Life, 51
  of Truth, 63
  one, in many bodies, 39
  positive pole, 289
  will is, 228
  within humanity, 63
Spiritual—
  age, age of the Soul, 264
  alchemy, a science, 331
  force, triangle of, 334
  goal of achievement, 332
  growth, work out, 319
  hunger, 63
  identity—
    ignorance of, 63
    in Christ, 5
    in One Life, 290
  kingdom of Conscious Souls, 251
  knowledge, vaster field of, 455
  leader, 378
  maturity, grow into, 99
  opportunity, 445
  relationship, reflected out-
    wardly, 265
  relationships—
    field of, 249, 261, 264
    recognition, 446
  therapy, 114
  truths, embody, 292
  will, interpretation, 388

Index

Index

circumstance, 101, 204, 361—
   so-called, 367
Violence, as a way of life, 146
Vision, clear, 193
Vital – life bodies, 349
Void—
   in awareness, 466—
   on mental levels, 469
   Soul must cross, 469
   of the abstract mind, yet to be
      crossed, 470

W

War—
   era free from, 274
   fears and threats of, 172
Wars, two great, 376
Wealth, to attain great, 122
Wed the spiritual to the material, 5
What is Truth, 6
White Magic—
   definition, 205
   practicing techniques of, 241
White Magician—
   a disciple becomes by, 241
   become, 403
Will—
   and Intelligence—
      creative polarity, 227
      polar forces of creativity, 241
   and mind, manipulation of, 373
   and thought, differentiation, 387
   a self-centered, 303
   align with Will of God, 230
   an extension of Spirit, 230
   attracts horizontal, 389
   contemplate, 230
   definition, 387
   development of, 230
   divine purpose, 411
   focused as intent, 415
   God's, 98
   invocative of God's will, 98
   is an initiator, 390
   is creative, 390
   is directive, creative, magnetic, 231
   is essentially creative, 411
   is magnetic, 389

magnetic quality, 239
measure of, 203
motivating Spirit, 387
of God, seekers discover, 230
of the Soul, responsive to, 454
personal, extension of Spirit, 230
to Be, 379, 388
   attracts, 431
   impregnated Pure Intelli-
      gence, 253
   in Mind of God, 216
   universal, 329
to Good, 332, 510
   power of, 98
to Love, a law and an energy,
   411
Will of God—
   expressed via laws, 287
   impressed upon substance, 252
   substance responds to, 287
   supersedes wills of humanity, 288
   three major laws, 287
Wisdom—
   aspiration to, 277
   entered path of, 228
   formulating into concepts, 309
   new realms of, 455
   no interest in, 470
   of the soul, 194
   precipitate, 467
   pure reason of Love, 101
   seek, 374
   students of the, 133
   thread of, 228
   transference of, 375
   universal, 73
   we attain, 20
Wisdom of the Soul, 3, 5
   align problems with the, 279
   directly overhead, 374
   in life and affairs, 305
   into appearance, 6
   invoked via, 294
   part of human consciousness, 302
Wisdom teaching, stresses humanity a Son of God, 133
Wisdom, The, student of, 465
Wish-life, 329—
   position and power, 121

551